MORE

AMAZING

Mets

TRIVIA

Also by Ken Samelson

The Baseball Maniac's Almanac (by Bert Randolph Sugar, revised)

Incredible Baseball Stories (ed.)

The Miracle Has Landed (with Matthew Silverman, eds.)

Echoes of Georgia Football (ed.)

Echoes of Texas Football (ed.)

Amazing Mets Trivia (with Ross Adell)

The Macmillan Baseball Quiz Book (with Scott Flatow)

The Great All-Time Baseball Record Book (by Joseph L. Reichler, revised)

Also by David Russell

Fabulous to Futile in Flushing

Rod Gaspar: Miracle Met (with Rod Gaspar)

Tom Gamboa: My Life in Baseball (with Tom Gamboa)

MORE
AMAZING
Mets
TRIVIA

Ken Samelson      David Russell

LP

LYONS
PRESS

Essex, Connecticut

An imprint of Globe Pequot, the trade division of
The Globe Pequot Publishing Group, Inc.
64 South Main St.
Essex, CT 06426
www.GlobePequot.com

Distributed by NATIONAL BOOK NETWORK

British Library Cataloguing in Publication Information available

Library of Congress Cataloging-in-Publication Data

Names: Samelson, Ken, author. | Russell, David, 1992– author.
Title: More amazing Mets trivia / Ken Samelson and David Russell.
Description: Essex, Connecticut : Lyons Press : Distributed by National Book
    Network, [2025]
Identifiers: LCCN 2024042667 (print) | LCCN 2024042668 (ebook) | ISBN
    9781493072255 (paperback) | ISBN 9781493072262 (epub)
Subjects: LCSH: New York Mets (Baseball team)—Miscellanea.
Classification: LCC GV875.N45 S36 2025 (print) | LCC GV875.N45 (ebook) |
    DDC 796.357/64097471—dc23/eng/20241224
LC record available at https://lccn.loc.gov/2024042667
LC ebook record available at https://lccn.loc.gov/2024042668

CONTENTS

INTRODUCTION

Following the Mets' 2000 World Series appearance, I was approached by Matt Fulks of Addax, a sports book publisher based in Kansas City, to write a New York Mets trivia book. I teamed up with my good friend, Mets history maven Ross Adell, and after a long delay when Addax was acquired by Taylor Trade Publishing, an imprint of the Globe Pequot Publishing Group, *Amazing Mets Trivia* hit the shelves in November 2003. "Amazingly," the book is still in print, although now quite out of date. Naturally, the fine people at Globe Pequot felt it was about time for a new edition. Sadly, Ross passed away in 2006, so I turned to David Russell, another good friend, who had authored a wonderful book, *Fabulous to Futile in Flushing: A Year-by-Year History of the Mets*. In David, I found someone who, despite his relative youth, has an impressive grasp of the Mets' colorful history, which is demonstrated throughout this book.

—Ken Samelson

*   *   *

The first Mets game my dad went to with his father was against the Giants at Shea Stadium in 1966. The first time my dad took me to Shea was in 1997, and the Mets were also playing the Giants. It was not only their home opener but also a doubleheader. I don't remember those games—the first one I do recall attending was a September 1998 win against the Braves. In that game, Tony Phillips, only briefly a Met, hit a go-ahead home run in the bottom of the eighth inning—one of only 50 homers he hit in 18 major league seasons.

The 1999 season was the first in which I really followed the Mets daily. I watched as many games as I could and read about each game in the paper the next day. It was good timing on my part as it marked the team's first playoff appearance in 11 years, a far cry from the 95-loss Mets team my dad was introduced to 33 years earlier. It was a dramatic season featuring what *Sports Illustrated* speculated could be the "best infield ever" (John Olerud, Edgardo Alfonzo, Rey Ordonez, and Robin Ventura), the best leadoff hitter ever (Rickey Henderson), the best offensive catcher in history (Mike Piazza), and a plethora of comeback victories.

It still appeared the Mets might miss the playoffs but a couple of Brewers wins against the Reds opened the door and the Mets went all the way to the NLCS after defeating the Reds in a one-game playoff—and I even got to attend my first postseason game as John Olerud was the hero in Game 4 against Atlanta with the go-ahead hit off Mets nemesis John Rocker. Though the Mets lost the series, they came back in 2000 with another highly entertaining team, more dramatic victories, and this time they went to the World Series before falling to the Yankees in the first Subway Series in 44 years.

Not only did I enjoy watching the teams and players of my youth but I quickly became interested in the history of the game. I read as much as I could about baseball—stats, stories, game results.

A few years later, my dad bought me a copy of *Amazing Mets Trivia*, written by Ross Adell and Ken Samelson. I devoured the information in that book, reading it over and over again. I have been in attendance for some memorable Mets moments over the years—the game where David Wright collected his first hit, the first Mets win at Citi Field in 2009, and Pete Alonso setting the rookie record with his 53rd home run of 2019. I knew plenty of Mets trivia, but what I didn't know was that I would actually become friends with Ken, thanks in part to the late Joe Masi, a great college basketball announcer I had worked with who happened to be Ken's best friend.

Over the years, my writing career advanced, and I even got to cover the 2015 World Series at Citi Field. My first book, *Tom Gamboa: My Life in Baseball*, was written with the longtime coach who I got to know while I covered the Brooklyn Cyclones teams he managed. Tom is a natural storyteller, skilled at telling both baseball anecdotes and jokes. And he had so many stories from his career which included time coaching at the major league level with the Cubs and Royals. A few years later, I worked on *Rod Gaspar: Miracle Met*, with the 1969 World Series champion outfielder. I couldn't believe I was writing a book with a player from one of the most celebrated teams in sports history. A mutual friend had put us in touch and the timing was right—the book was released during the summer of the 50th anniversary of the team's first championship. Then came *Fabulous to Futile in Flushing: A Year-by-Year History of the Mets*. It was a labor of love, the longest research project I've ever done. And I learned so much about some of the team's more obscure seasons—the ones that don't show up on *Mets Classics* on SNY.

I was thrilled when Ken asked me to work on this book with him both as his friend and as a Mets fan. I like to think I was a natural fit considering we send each other tidbits of trivia daily anyway as well as comparing Immaculate Grid results. So much has happened in the last 20 years (except winning a World Series):

David Wright's entire big-league career, for example.

Shea Stadium was torn down and Citi Field was built up.

The son of a Mets pitcher led a team to three Super Bowl titles.

While the results on the field might be mixed, the Mets are rarely dull and are backed by one of the most passionate fan bases in the sport. We hope you will enjoy this book—whether you are a Mets superfan or a newer fan who wants to learn more about the history of the team.

—David Russell

LEAGUE LEADERS

1. Which Met led the league in losses in 1962?
a. Jay Hook   b. Al Jackson   c. Roger Craig   d. Clem Labine

2. This Met led the league in losses in 1965 and 1967. Who is he?
a. Al Jackson   b. Jack Fisher   c. Galen Cisco   d. Gary Kroll

3. How many games did Tom Seaver win in 1969 to lead the National League?
a. 19   b. 21   c. 24   d. 25

4. Who led the league in shutouts in 1974?
a. Tom Seaver   b. Jerry Koosman   c. Jon Matlack   d. George Stone

5. Who was the first Mets batter to lead the league in home runs?
a. Frank Thomas   b. Dave Kingman   c. Darryl Strawberry
d. Howard Johnson

6. Which Met led the league in ERA in 1978?
a. Craig Swan   b. Jerry Koosman   c. Pat Zachry   d. Skip Lockwood

7. Who allowed the most earned runs in the league in 1978?
a. Jerry Koosman   b. Nino Espinosa   c. Kevin Kobel
d. Mike Bruhert

8. This Met led the league in losses and walks in 1983. Who is he?
a. Tom Seaver   b. Mike Torrez   c. Craig Swan   d. Ed Lynch

9. Who is the only Met to lead the NL in runs scored in a season?
a. Mookie Wilson   b. Howard Johnson   c. Keith Hernandez
d. Gary Carter

10. Which pitcher led the league in saves in 1990?
a. Jesse Orosco   b. Randy Myers   c. John Franco   d. Roger McDowell

11. Which Met led the league in doubles in 1990?
a. Gregg Jefferies   b. Darryl Strawberry   c. Howard Johnson
d. Kevin McReynolds

12. In 1990 and 1991, this Mets pitcher led the league in strikeouts. Who is he?
a. Dwight Gooden   b. David Cone   c. Sid Fernandez   d. Ron Darling

13. Which Met led the NL in RBIs in 1991?
a. Howard Johnson   b. Dave Magadan   c. Vince Coleman
d. Kevin McReynolds

14. Which Met tied for the NL lead with five shutouts in 1992 despite not pitching a full season with the team?
a. Ron Darling   b. David Cone   c. Frank Viola   d. Sid Fernandez

15. Which Mets batter led the league in hit by pitches in 1994?
a. Todd Hundley   b. David Segui   c. José Vizcaino
d. Fernando Viña

16. Who led the league in hits in 1996?
a. Lance Johnson   b. Bernard Gilkey   c. Todd Hundley
d. Edgardo Alfonzo

17. Which Mets pitcher led the league in both home runs allowed and batters hit in 2002?
a. Shawn Estes   b. Mike Bacsik   c. Jeff D'Amico   d. Pedro Astacio

18. Which Met led the league in hits in 2008?
a. David Wright   b. José Reyes   c. Carlos Beltrán   d. Carlos Delgado

19. This Mets pitcher led the league in appearances three seasons in a row. Who is he?
a. Pedro Feliciano   b. Aaron Heilman   c. Joe Smith   d. Billy Wagner

20. Which Met led the league in shutouts in 2012?
a. Johan Santana   b. R. A. Dickey   c. Matt Harvey   d. Dillon Gee

21. Which Met led the league in singles in 2019?
a. Brandon Nimmo   b. Dom Smith   c. Michael Conforto
d. Amed Rosario

22. Through 2024, how many times has Pete Alonso led the NL in home runs?
a. 0   b. 1   c. 2   d. 3

23. Who led the league in hit by pitches in 2022?
a. Mark Canha   b. Pete Alonso   c. Jeff McNeil   d. Starling Marte

24. Which Met tied for the league lead with 12 sacrifices in 2022?
a. Brandon Nimmo   b. Jacob deGrom   c. Tomás Nido
d. Jeff McNeil

25. Who is the only Mets pitcher to lead the league in wild pitches?
a. Mike Pelfrey   b. R. A. Dickey   c. Rick Ankiel   d. Kodai Senga

ANSWERS

1. c. Roger Craig
The right-hander lost a league-high 24 games for the beleaguered first-year expansion team, accounting for 20 percent of the Mets' 120 losses. He was 49–38 in seven seasons with the Dodgers and was a hero of their 1959 title team but was coming off a 6.15 ERA 1961 season. Craig lost seven games in July, including one out of the bullpen. He would also lead the league in losses with 22 more in 1963, including 18 straight decisions as his record went from 2–2 to

2–20. On the bright side, Craig would move on to help the Cardinals win the 1964 World Series.

2. b. Jack Fisher

"Fat Jack" lost 24 games in 1965 and 18 more in 1967 to lead the National League. In 1965, Fisher was 7–11 in late July before losing 13 of his final 14 decisions to finish 8–24. But Fisher is best remembered by baseball fans for his time with the Orioles. In 1960, Ted Williams homered off Fisher in the final at-bat of his career. And in 1961, Roger Maris hit his 60th home run of the season off Fisher. The righty would be the first Mets pitcher to start a game at Shea Stadium, a 4–3 loss to the Pirates on April 17, 1964.

3. d. 25

After winning 16 games in each of his first two seasons, "The Franchise" picked up 25 of the Mets' 100 victories in 1969. Seaver actually got off to a 1–2 start before winning five decisions in a row. After a loss at Houston, he won eight straight decisions. A loss in early August to the Reds dropped him to 15–7 but in his final 11

RUCKER ARCHIVE

Tom Seaver

starts he would go 10-0, a major factor in the Mets overtaking the Cubs for the NL East title. Seaver was awarded the Cy Young Award and was runner-up to Willie McCovey in the MVP voting.

4. c. Jon Matlack
Pitching in the shadow of Seaver and Koosman, Matlack led the NL with seven shutouts. The highlight of his 1974 campaign came on June 29 against the Cardinals when he tossed a one-hit shutout in a 4-0 win. Opposing pitcher John Curtis's third-inning single was the only hit. He also blanked the eventual pennant-winning Dodgers in a 3-0 win at Shea on August 13. Matlack was selected to his first All-Star team but would finish the season 13-15 despite a 2.41 ERA, due to dismal run support. In 1976, Matlack's six shutouts would tie him for the league lead with San Francisco's John Montefusco.

5. b. Dave Kingman
In his second tour of duty with the Mets, Kingman led the NL with 37 homers in 1982. The slugger accomplished the feat despite batting .204 with a league-high 156 strikeouts. The entire Mets team finished with 97 homers. Kong got off to a hot start with eight home runs in April, including a two-homer game against the Expos. He homered six times from July 9-17. Though he went homerless in his final two weeks, it was enough to edge out Dale Murphy's 36. Cy Young winner Steve Carlton finished the season with a .218 batting average, 14 points higher than Kingman's.

6. a. Craig Swan
While Ron Guidry got most of the attention for his 1.74 ERA in the Bronx, across town Swan led the NL with a 2.43 ERA. The right-hander was a rare bright spot for the 1978 Mets and following a 1-5 record at the All-Star break, went 8-1 in the second half of the season. Montreal's Steve Rogers finished with a 2.47 ERA but didn't pitch in September due to injuries. In Swan's last start of the season, he gave up one earned run in seven innings in a 3-1 win over the Cardinals, lowering his ERA from 2.47 to 2.43.

7. b. Nino Espinosa

The right-hander allowed a league-high 107 earned runs and finished with an 11–15 record. He was 5–2 with a 3.33 ERA at the end of May but struggled mightily in the final four months of the season, going 6–13 the rest of the way, giving up 20 earned runs during one four-loss stretch. Espinosa allowed a season-high eight earned runs in a September loss to the Phillies. Espinosa would move on to the Phillies and start 12 games for the 1980 World Champs. Espinosa died in 1987 of a heart attack at the age of 34.

8. b. Mike Torrez

In his 17th big league season, Torrez went 10–17 for the Mets and also walked a league-high 113 batters. A postseason hero with the 1977 Yankees and a Red Sox goat in 1978, Torrez struggled with control during the season, including a 10-walk performance against the Reds. The good news for the Mets was Torrez pitched 222⅓ innings while the young starters in the minors, including Ron Darling and Dwight Gooden, were getting ready to come up. Torrez's best stretch came in late July when he pitched 10 innings against the Braves and followed it up with 11 shutout innings against the Pirates.

9. b. Howard Johnson

HoJo scored 104 runs in 1989, tying him with Ryne Sandberg and Will Clark for the league lead. Johnson got off to a good start with two runs on Opening Day and four in his first four games. He scored a season-high 25 runs in June, including three-run games against the Pirates and Cubs. Johnson scored four runs in the final three games, including two on the last day of the season to tie Clark. Sandberg scored one run in the Cubs' final game. Johnson, who hit 36 homers and stole 41 bases, finished fifth in the MVP voting.

10. c. John Franco

In his first season with the Mets, Franco led the league with 33 saves. A three-time All-Star with the Reds, Franco was acquired for another southpaw closer, Randy Myers. The Brooklyn native closed out wins in his first seven opportunities and would save 17 straight from July to September. Franco would again lead the league in 1994, notching 30 saves in the strike-shortened season and finishing seventh in the Cy Young voting. Franco, who became a setup man late in his career, would retire with 424 saves, still the most by a left-hander and the second-highest overall total behind Lee Smith at the time of his retirement.

11. a. Gregg Jefferies

Jefferies doubled 40 times, edging out Pittsburgh's Bobby Bonilla, who finished with 39. In May, he delivered a season-high nine doubles. The second baseman had four multi-double games during the season, including two on June 12 at Wrigley Field in a 19–8 drubbing of the Cubs. Jefferies was only the second Met with a 40-double season; Howard Johnson had done it the year before. He was much better at Shea in 1990, batting .318 at home and .246 on the road. Jefferies was traded to the Royals after the 1991 season and would make the All-Star team as a Cardinal in 1993 and 1994.

12. b. David Cone

Cone fanned 233 batters in 1990, good for the NL high. The Mets had four of the top five marks in the league with Dwight Gooden, Frank Viola, and Sid Fernandez in the group and with Los Angeles' Ramon Martinez finishing third. For an encore, Cone struck out 241 batters in 1991, the only pitcher in the NL to reach the 200 mark. He struck out 13 in wins against the Padres and Reds but saved his best strikeout game for last. On the final day of the season, Cone struck out 19 Phillies in a 7–0 win at Veterans Stadium to tie the National League record.

13. a. Howard Johnson

Johnson's 117 RBIs led the National League, as did his 38 home runs. From the start of September through the end of the season, Johnson hit 10 homers and drove in 31 runs. He edged out Barry Bonds and Will Clark, who both finished with 116 RBIs. Johnson's RBI single off Philadelphia's Bruce Ruffin on the last day of the season gave him sole ownership of the title. From August 31 to September 24, Johnson had 10 multi-RBI games, including five games with three RBIs. Despite the Mets' losing season, Johnson finished fifth in the MVP voting for the second time in three years.

14. b. David Cone
Before trading Cone to the Blue Jays in late August, the Mets got all they could out of the right-hander, with five shutouts among his 13 victories. He threw four shutouts in a six-start span from late April to late May, including a 146-pitch gem against the Padres. His masterpiece was a 1–0 win over the Giants on July 17, when he fanned 13 and threw 166 pitches. Not worried about his arm, Toronto traded for Cone and watched as the hired gun helped them to their first World Series title, even throwing six innings of one-run ball in the Series clincher in Atlanta.

15. d. Fernando Viña
In his only year in a Mets uniform, the utilityman was hit by pitches a league-high 12 times in the strike-shortened season. June was Viña's most painful month, as he was plunked four times. Remarkably he was hit a dozen times in only 150 plate appearances in 1994. Jeff Kent was among the league leaders, being hit 10 times in 452 plate appearances. It was a brushback year for the team, with Viña, Kent, and Ryan Thompson all among the league leaders. Viña would lead the NL in hit by pitches again in 2000 with the Cardinals, getting drilled 28 times.

16. a. Lance Johnson
The newly acquired leadoff hitter led the league with 227 hits, as well as plate appearances, at-bats, and triples. Johnson, who led the AL in hits in 1995 with the White Sox, collected at least 30 hits in each month in 1996. He also notched three hits in the All-Star Game, a 6–0 NL win. In the final month of the season, Johnson batted .405 with 45 hits, outpacing Rockies slugger Ellis Burks, who finished with 211 hits. Johnson also stole a career-high 50 bases and received some MVP votes despite the Mets' disappointing season.

17. d. Pedro Astacio

The right-hander allowed 32 home runs and hit 16 batters, both league highs. He was 11–4 with an ERA under three in early August but finished 1–7 with his ERA increasing by nearly two full runs. Lowlights included giving up four homers to the Braves at Turner Field and then getting ejected for drilling Gary Sheffield; and plunking three Phillies in a loss at Shea. It was not Astacio's first time leading the NL in both categories. In 1998, as a member of the Rockies, he allowed 39 home runs while hitting 17 batters. He also led the league in homers allowed in 1999, surrendering 38 more.

18. b. José Reyes

Reyes led the NL with 204 hits, while his teammate on the left side of the infield, David Wright, finished second with 189. After collecting at least 190 hits three straight seasons, Reyes became the second Met in history with a 200-hit season. His best months came in June and August when he had 41 hits apiece. The star shortstop also led the league in plate appearances, at-bats, and triples. It is the last time to date a Met led the NL in hits. Reyes led the league with a .337 batting average in 2011 but finished eighth in hits.

19. a. Pedro Feliciano

The lefty was often called upon by Willie Randolph and then Jerry Manuel, making 86, 88, and a whopping 92 appearances from 2008 to 2010. Even with the 2010 squad long out of contention, Feliciano made 23 appearances in the final month of the season. The only pitchers with more than 92 appearances in a season are Salomon Torres (94, 2006 Pirates), Kent Tekulve (94, 1979 Pirates), and Mike Marshall (106, 1974 Dodgers). The Yankees signed Feliciano in 2011, but he never pitched for them due to injuries.

20. b. R. A. Dickey

Dickey came into the season with two career shutouts and tossed three in his unlikely Cy Young season. On June 2, the day after Johan Santana's no-hitter, Dickey provided an encore by tossing a seven-hit shutout in a 5–0 win over the Cardinals. On June 18, he pitched a one-hit shutout in a 5–0 win over the Orioles. And on August 31 he beat the Marlins in Miami 3–0. Dickey also led the NL in starts, complete games, innings pitched, and strikeouts. He would throw only one more shutout over the last five years of his career, with the Blue Jays in 2013.

21. d. Amed Rosario

The young shortstop had a league-high 125 singles. Rosario finished with 177 hits, the fifth-most in the NL. After ups and downs in 2017 and 2018, Rosario batted .287 in 2019. He batted .319 after the All-Star break and was a key factor as the Mets went from 10 games under .500 at the break to 10 over at the end of the season. Strangely, he was much better away from Citi Field, batting .323 on the road and .248 at home. But after a disappointing 2020 season, Rosario was traded to Cleveland in the deal that brought Francisco Lindor to Queens.

22. b. 1

In 2019, Alonso set both the team record and the major league rookie record for homers, going deep 53 times. He didn't waste much time, hitting nine homers in the first month of the season and 10 more in May. He hit his 42nd home run on August 27 to set the club record, passing Todd Hundley and Carlos Beltrán. Alonso would hit 11 homers in the final month of the season, with his 53rd and final dinger passing Aaron Judge's rookie record set in 2017. Alonso was the first Met to win Rookie of the Year since Jacob deGrom earned it in 2014.

23. a. Mark Canha

Canha was hit a league-high 27 times as a member of the Oakland A's in 2021 and outdid himself in 2022, getting plunked 28 times, surpassing Brandon Nimmo's previous team record of 22. The outfielder was hit a whopping 11 times in the final four weeks of the season. He set the record in style, getting hit twice in one game against the Brewers. It was a team effort—the Mets set a major league record with 112 hit batsmen. Nimmo, Starling Marte, Pete Alonso, Jeff McNeil, and Francisco Lindor were all hit at least 10 times.

24. c. Tomás Nido

The Mets' light-hitting catcher had 12 sacrifices on the season, tied with Arizona's Geraldo Perdomo for the league lead, though Nido did it in nearly 200 fewer plate appearances. Nido had one sacrifice in his first five seasons but new manager Buck Showalter had him bunt throughout the season. Despite his low batting average, he proved an adept bat-handler when the Mets played small ball, including a squeeze play against the Braves and bunts in two straight plate appearances against the Yankees.

25. d. Kodai Senga

The rookie right-hander led the NL with 14 wild pitches in an otherwise excellent season. The starter from Japan went 12–7 with a 2.98 ERA in 2023, made the All-Star team, and was runner-up for Rookie of the Year. He was also seventh in Cy Young voting. His specialty ghost fork pitch helped him fan 202 batters but occasionally got away from his catchers. His 14 wild pitches were the most by a Mets pitcher since Jason Isringhausen threw 14 in 1996. David Cone unleashed 14 in 1989 and 17 in 1991. Jack Hamilton let go a team record 18 in 1966.

1960s

1. Ed Kranepool played the most games for the Mets in the 1960s. Who played the second most games?
a. Ron Hunt   b. Jim Hickman   c. Cleon Jones   d. Ron Swoboda

2. Which pitcher lost the most games for the Mets during the 1960s?
a. Al Jackson   b. Roger Craig   c. Jack Fisher   d. Galen Cisco

3. Which former major leaguer was *not* a member of manager Casey Stengel's coaching staff in 1962?
a. Whitey Lockman   b. Cookie Lavagetto   c. Red Ruffing
d. Rogers Hornsby

4. The 1962 Mets had a losing record against every opponent except one. They split 18 games against which rival during that first season in which they lost 120 games?
a. Houston Colt .45s   b. Philadelphia Phillies   c. Milwaukee Braves
d. Chicago Cubs

5. The Mets had a player in its farm system from 1962 to 1964 with a very similar name to a player on their 1969 World Championship team. Who was this minor leaguer?
a. Al Wise   b. Cleo James   c. Ron Gasper   d. Rob Taylor

6. Who was the first Met to collect five hits in a game?
a. Richie Ashburn   b. Dick Smith   c. Charley Neal   d. Bobby Klaus

7. In 1963, who became the first Mets pitcher to smack a grand slam?
a. Carl Willey   b. Roger Craig   c. Tracy Stallard   d. Al Jackson

8. Which future Met closed out the Giants' 23-inning victory over the Mets in the second game of a Memorial Day doubleheader in 1964?
a. Ron Herbel   b. Bob Shaw   c. Bob Hendley   d. Ray Sadecki

9. Which Met broke up Reds pitcher Jim Maloney's no-hit bid with an 11th-inning home run in 1965?
a. Jim Hickman   b. Ron Swoboda   c. Johnny Lewis   d. Charley Smith

10. After Tom Seaver's contract was nullified by the commissioner of baseball in 1966, the Mets were awarded his rights via a lottery involving two other teams, the Cleveland Indians and which National League rival?
a. Chicago Cubs   b. Philadelphia Phillies   c. Los Angeles Dodgers   d. Pittsburgh Pirates

11. Who was the losing pitcher for the Mets in their 24-inning game against the Houston Astros in 1968?
a. Cal Koonce   b. Bill Short   c. Bill Connors   d. Les Rohr

12. The Mets lost this minor league player to the San Diego Padres in the expansion draft after the 1968 season and he would return to the organization more than a decade later. Name him.
a. Jerry Morales   b. Gil Flores   c. Dyar Miller   d. Dave Roberts

13. Tommie Agee hit a home run into the upper deck at Shea Stadium in a 1969 game, the only player ever to do so. Against which team did he hit that tape-measure shot?
a. Chicago Cubs   b. San Diego Padres   c. Philadelphia Phillies   d. Montreal Expos

14. Cleon Jones batted .340 in 1969 and finished third in the batting race. Which player won the title with a .348 average?
a. Pete Rose   b. Roberto Clemente   c. Billy Williams   d. Joe Torre

15. Which West Division club was the only opponent to take the season series from the Mets in the miracle summer of 1969?
a. Los Angeles Dodgers   b. Houston Astros   c. Atlanta Braves
d. Cincinnati Reds

16. Which Met had the team's longest hitting streak (18 games) during the 1960s?
a. Cleon Jones   b. Ron Hunt   c. Frank Thomas   d. Tommy Davis

17. Nolan Ryan gave up a home run to which future Met in his major league debut in 1966?
a. Art Shamsky   b. Rusty Staub   c. Donn Clendenon   d. Joe Torre

18. What was catcher "Choo Choo" Coleman's real first name?
a. Charles   b. Clarence   c. Carl   d. Craig

19. What year did the Mets first avoid finishing in last place?
a. 1966   b. 1967   c. 1968   d. 1969

20. Who was the first Mets player to get a hit at Shea Stadium?
a. Jim Hickman   b. Ron Hunt   c. Tim Harkness   d. George Altman

21. Which player batted .348 in 90 games for the Mets in 1967?
a. Larry Stahl   b. Tommie Reynolds   c. Bob Johnson   d. Al Luplow

22. After the Mets lost their inaugural game to Larry Jackson of the St. Louis Cardinals in 1962, their next three losses all came at the hands of future Mets pitchers. Which hurler was not a member of that trio of winning pitchers?
a. Tom Sturdivant   b. Vinegar Bend Mizell   c. Bob Friend
d. Warren Spahn

23. In what year did the Mets post their lowest-ever batting average (.219)?
a. 1962   b. 1963   c. 1967   d. 1968

24. The Cardinals defeated the Mets on the last day of the 1964 season at St. Louis to clinch the National League pennant. Which Mets batter made the final out of that game?
a. Ed Kranepool   b. Bobby Klaus   c. Hawk Taylor   d. George Altman

25. In 1969, the Mets turned the tables on the Cardinals and clinched the National League East title against them at Shea Stadium. Who was the final Cardinals batter that evening?
a. Lou Brock   b. Joe Torre   c. Tim McCarver   d. Julian Javier

ANSWERS

1. b. Jim Hickman
An original Met, Jim Hickman played in 624 games for the Amazins from 1962 to 1966, second to Ed Kranepool's 887 appearances during the 1960s. Selected by the Mets from the St. Louis Cardinals in the expansion draft, the versatile right-handed batter played all three outfield positions, primarily center, as well as first base and third base. He has the distinction of being the first Met to hit for the cycle (August 7, 1963) and to hit three home runs in a game (September 3, 1965), both feats coming at the expense of the Cardinals. After an injury-plagued 1966 season, Hickman was traded to the Los Angeles Dodgers in a deal for two-time batting champion Tommy Davis.

2. a. Al Jackson
Like Hickman an original Met, left-hander "Little Al" Jackson went 43–80 in two stints with the club (1962–1965 and 1968–1969). His 80 losses were seven more than Jack Fisher suffered in a Mets uniform. Despite losing 20 games twice, Jackson was one of the Mets' most dependable starters, tossing 10 shutouts, including a one-hitter. Dealt to the St. Louis Cardinals after the 1965 season for All-Star third baseman Ken Boyer, Jackson had two fairly good seasons in St. Louis before returning to the Mets for the 1968 season. He appeared in nine games for the 1969 World Champions before he was sold to the Cincinnati Reds that June. Jackson

later spent several seasons as a coach in the Mets organization, including two seasons in the majors (1999 and 2000) under manager Bobby Valentine.

3. a. Whitey Lockman

Casey Stengel's first Mets coaching staff consisted of two Hall of Famers (Rogers Hornsby and Yankees great Red Ruffing), a Brooklyn Dodgers World Series hero (Cookie Lavagetto), as well as former major league manager Solly Hemus and Red Kress, a longtime major league infielder and coach. On a sad note, Kress and Hornsby both passed away shortly after that season ended. Whitey Lockman, who appeared in two World Series for the New York Giants in the 1950s, was the third-base coach for the now San Francisco Giants in 1962. He later managed the Chicago Cubs (1972–1974).

4. d. Chicago Cubs

The 1962 Chicago Cubs, managed by a rotating "College of Coaches" (El Tappe, Lou Klein, and Charlie Metro) instead of one manager, went 59–103, finished 42½ games out of first place and six games behind the expansion Houston Colt .45s, yet easily escaped the NL basement due to the Mets' 120-loss ineptitude. New York could at least take solace in the fact they were able to split the season series with the ninth-place Cubs, going 5–4 at Wrigley Field and 4–5 at the Polo Grounds. By contrast, Casey's Amazins went 2–16 against both the Los Angeles Dodgers and Pittsburgh Pirates.

5. c. Ron Gasper

Not to be confused with Miracle Met Rod Gaspar, who made several key contributions as the team's fourth outfielder in 1969, Ron Gasper was a career minor leaguer who played in the Mets farm system from 1962 to 1964. The catcher-third baseman played for the Mets' Santa Barbara affiliate in the Class C California League in 1962, where one of his teammates was future Gold Glove outfielder Paul Blair, who the Mets let get away, and would play for the Baltimore Orioles against them in the 1969 World Series. Gasper then spent his last two professional seasons with Salinas of the California League, now in Class A. He was joined there by Bud

Harrelson, who would eventually man shortstop for the Mets in two World Series and appear in two All-Star Games.

6. b. Dick Smith
Rookie first baseman Dick Smith went 5-for-6 and scored three runs in a 19-1 victory over the Chicago Cubs at Wrigley Field on May 25, 1964. He led off the game with a single off Cubs starter Bob Buhl and scored the first of four first-inning runs. After he was retired by Wayne Schurr on a drive to right field in the second inning, Smith added singles off Sterling Slaughter in the fourth and fifth, the latter making it 9-0. Smith followed with an RBI double in the seventh off Glen Hobbie for an 11-1 lead and then scored the Mets' 13th run on a balk by Jack Spring. In the ninth, Smith tripled off Don Elston to start a six-run uprising.

7. a. Carl Willey
The Mets trailed the Houston Colt .45s, 2-1, in the bottom of the second inning of the first game of a doubleheader at the Polo Grounds on July 15, 1963, but had the bases loaded with one out when Mets starter Carl Willey swung at a pitch thrown by Houston right-hander Ken Johnson and drove it over the right-field wall. It was the first home run of any kind hit by a Mets pitcher and keyed a 14-5 rout for Willey's seventh victory of a 9-14 season.

8. c. Bob Hendley
The Mets have played numerous marathon games in their history but the most memorable may be the one they played against the San Francisco Giants on May 31, 1964. After the Mets overcame an early five-run deficit to tie the game, 6-6, extra innings featured everything from Willie Mays playing shortstop to the Mets turning a triple play to Gaylord Perry throwing his famed spitball in a big spot for the first time. Finally, in the top of the 23rd inning, Jim Davenport tripled and Del Crandall, batting for Perry, drove him home with the tiebreaking run. Jesus Alou singled home an insurance tally and the Giants turned the game over to Bob Hendley to protect the 8-6 lead, which he did by retiring the Mets in order.

Hendley would join the Mets in a trade with the Chicago Cubs during the 1967 season, going 3–3 in 15 games (13 starts).

9. c. Johnny Lewis

On June 15, 1965, Cincinnati Reds All-Star right-hander Jim Maloney held the Mets hitless for 10 innings at Crosley Field before right fielder Johnny Lewis, who had struck out in his three previous at-bats, homered to center field on a 2-1 pitch leading off the 11th inning. Maloney allowed another hit later in the inning, a single by Roy McMillan. The Mets went on to win, 1–0, with Frank Lary (eight innings) and Larry Bearnarth (three) combining on the shutout. Maloney had allowed only two baserunners through the first 10 frames. He went on to pitch a 10-inning no-hitter against the Chicago Cubs a month later at Wrigley Field.

10. b. Philadelphia Phillies

April 3, 1966, was a momentous day in the history of the Mets as they were awarded the rights to sign USC pitcher Tom Seaver in a special lottery ordered by Commissioner William Eckert. The Atlanta Braves had selected Seaver in the January 1966 supplemental draft and signed him to a contract a month later. However, the Trojans had played two exhibition games by the time he signed, so Eckert voided the deal. The NCAA ruled Seaver ineligible to play college baseball due to signing a professional contract, and his father threatened a lawsuit. The commissioner said any team willing to match the $40,000 contract Seaver had signed with Atlanta could enter a drawing to sign him. The Mets, Cleveland Indians, and Philadelphia Phillies were the three interested teams and the Mets were the lucky team to have their entry pulled out of a hat.

11. d. Les Rohr

Four years after the 23-inning marathon with the Giants, the Mets suffered a 24-inning loss to Houston at the Astrodome. The Astros scored the only run of the game off lefty Les Rohr when Mets shortstop Al Weis let a potential inning-ending double play ball hit by future Met Bob Aspromonte go through his legs to score Norm Miller from third base and end the game after six hours and six minutes. The Mets' 3 and 4 hitters, Tommie Agee and Ron Swoboda, who entered the game batting .313 and .385 respectively, both went 0-for-10, dropping their averages to .192 and .217. As for Rohr, who the Mets selected with their first pick in the very first major league amateur draft in 1965, that game was one of only six appearances he made in his big-league career from 1967 to 1969.

12. a. Jerry Morales
The Mets lost six players in the October 1968 National League expansion draft—pitchers Don Shaw, Ernie McAnally, and John Glass to the Montreal Expos and pitcher Dick Selma and outfielders Larry Stahl and Jerry Morales to the San Diego Padres. Morales, a native of Puerto Rico, reached the majors with San Diego for 19 games at the end of the 1969 season and played there until joining the Chicago Cubs in 1974. The journeyman outfielder then moved on to the St. Louis Cardinals and Detroit Tigers; from there he was traded to the Mets after the 1979 season (along with third baseman Phil Mankowski) for third baseman Richie Hebner. Morales was the Mets' Opening Day center fielder in 1980 and batted .254 in 94 games in his only season in New York before signing back with the Cubs as a free agent.

13. d. Montreal Expos
Tommie Agee hit two home runs against righty Larry Jaster of the expansion Montreal Expos on April 10, 1969, and the first one was the only ball to ever reach the upper deck of the grandstand at Shea Stadium. The second-inning solo shot gave the Mets a 3–1 lead and went an estimated 480 feet before bouncing back onto the field and landing in front of the left-field fence. Teammate Ed Charles claimed the ball was hit as far as one Mickey Mantle hit six years earlier high off the Yankee Stadium facade against his Kansas City Athletics. Agee belted another off Jaster in the seventh as the Mets went on to win, 4–2. In 1994, a marker commemorating Agee's blast was added in Section 48 near the spot where the ball landed.

14. a. Pete Rose

Pete Rose of the Cincinnati Reds won his second consecutive batting title in 1969 with a .348 average, beating out fellow All-Star outfielders Roberto Clemente of the Pittsburgh Pirates (.345) and Jones (.340). Jones got off to a hot start in 1969, batting .410 in April, and had the league's top batting average as late as September 24, the night the Mets clinched their first NL East title. Rose went 4-for-5 in his next game to take the lead, .347 to .343. Still, Jones finished with what is still the second-highest batting average in Mets history, surpassed only by John Olerud's .354 in 1998. Rose went on to win a third batting title in 1973, the year he got into a celebrated fight with Mets shortstop Bud Harrelson in Game 3 of the NL Championship Series at Shea Stadium.

15. b. Houston Astros

The Mets dropped 10 of 12 contests to the Astros during their 1969 championship campaign, including all six contests at the Astrodome. The Mets experienced two of their lowest points of the 1969 season at the hands of Houston. On July 30, they dropped both ends of a doubleheader by lopsided scores of 16–3 and 11–5, improbably giving up 11 runs in the ninth inning of the opener and 10 runs in the third inning of the nightcap. The Astros completed a series sweep the next day and would sweep the Mets again at the Astrodome two weeks later, dropping the Mets to third place and 10 games out of first place before the Amazins recovered to win the National League East by eight games.

16. c. Frank Thomas

A month into the Mets' first season of 1962, left fielder Frank Thomas hit in 18 consecutive games from the first game of a doubleheader on May 12 at the Polo Grounds against the Milwaukee Braves to the first game of a doubleheader on May 30 against the Los Angeles Dodgers, also at the Polo Grounds. During his streak, he had eight multi-hit games, including two three-hit contests. Thomas went 28-for-74 (.378) with five home runs and 16 RBIs. It remained the team's longest-hitting streak until Tommie Agee hit in 20 straight from April 16 to May 9, 1970.

17. d. Joe Torre

Nolan Ryan made his first major league appearance in a relief role in the Mets' 8–3 loss to the Atlanta Braves at Shea Stadium on September 11, 1966. He entered the game to begin the top of the sixth inning with the Mets trailing, 6–1. Ryan set the Braves down in order, picking up the first two of his major league record 5,714 strikeouts, against winning pitcher Pat Jarvis and future Hall of Famer Eddie Mathews. After retiring another future Cooperstown enshrinee, Hank Aaron, on a ground ball to start the seventh, Ryan surrendered a home run to Braves cleanup hitter Joe Torre. It was the 35th of Torre's career-high 36 home runs that season. He would later play for the Mets from 1975 to 1977 and manage the team from 1977 to 1981, briefly serving as a player-manager.

18. b. Clarence

Clarence Coleman was given his nickname of "Choo Choo" by childhood friends in Orlando, Florida, because he was fast and liked to run around. He played parts of two seasons for the Philadelphia Phillies before the Mets selected him in the October 1961 expansion draft. During spring training in 1962, the left-handed hitting catcher hit the first home run in team history in an exhibition game against the St. Louis Cardinals. Choo Choo did not make the team but was eventually called up in July and batted .250 in 55 games. He spent the entire 1963 season with the Mets, getting into 106 games (91 of them behind the plate, more than any other catcher on the roster), but he batted just .178 with three home runs and nine RBIs. He spent the 1964 and 1965 seasons in the minors but returned to the Mets for a brief stint in 1966.

19. a. 1966

After losing 120, 111, 109, and 112 games, respectively, during their first four seasons, the Mets went 66–95 in 1966 under Wes Westrum in his first season in the dugout. They finished in ninth place for the first time, 7½ games clear of the 59–103 10th-place Chicago Cubs. What's more, the Mets never spent one day in last place and after winning two of their first three games, even had a winning record for the first time. Former Brooklyn Dodgers and New York Giants manager Leo Durocher had taken over the Cubs after an eighth-place finish in 1965 and famously said, "I am not the manager of an eighth-place team," and proved it by finishing two spots lower.

20. c. Tim Harkness
First baseman Tim Harkness grounded out to shortstop as the first Met to step into the batter's box in the first game played at Shea Stadium on April 17, 1964, but pulled a single to right field in his next at-bat against Pirates righty Bob Friend two innings later for the Mets' first hit. The Pirates went on to spoil the Shea opener, 4–3, breaking a 3–3 tie on Hall of Famer Bill Mazeroski's RBI single in the top of the ninth off Ed Bauta. Harkness played a season-and-a-half with the Mets before being traded to the Cincinnati Reds for second baseman Bobby Klaus in July 1964.

21. c. Bob Johnson
The Mets purchased utilityman Bob Johnson early in the 1967 season from the Baltimore Orioles and he spent time at all four infield positions. He also appeared at least once in all nine positions in the batting order. Johnson excelled as a pinch-hitter, leading the National League with 12 pinch hits in 31 at-bats for a .387 average. Johnson was traded after the 1967 season to the Cincinnati Reds for Art Shamsky, who would help the Mets win it all two years later. That 1969 World Series championship Mets team included a different Bob Johnson, a late-season callup who pitched in two games before being included in an ill-fated deal along with future All-Star Amos Otis to the Kansas City Royals for third baseman Joe Foy after the season.

22. d. Warren Spahn
After losing the first game in team history at St. Louis, the Mets opened their home schedule at the Polo Grounds the weekend of April 13–15 and were swept by the Pittsburgh Pirates by scores of 4–3 (Tom Sturdivant over Sherman "Roadblock" Jones), 6–2 (Vinegar Bend Mizell over Al Jackson), and 7–2 (Bob Friend over

Roger Craig). The Mets picked up Sturdivant in May 1964 after he was released by the Kansas City A's, but he only lasted a month before being let go. The Mets acquired Mizell less than a month after he beat them, but he was released that August. Friend was purchased from the Yankees in June 1966 and released after the season. As for the correct answer, Warren Spahn, like the other pitchers, had a short tenure with the Mets. The future Hall of Famer joined the Mets in 1965 and went 4–12 before being released that July.

23. b. 1963
The second edition of the Mets set the team record for lowest batting average, which was actually 21 points lower than their first season. One factor might have been due to a change in the definition of the strike zone that year from the top of the shoulder to the knees (it would change again in 1969 from the armpits to the top of the knees). The league batting average dropped from .261 to .245 in 1963, with the Mets bringing up the rear at .219. They were shut out 30 times, still a team record.

24. a. Ed Kranepool
The St. Louis Cardinals needed a victory over the Mets and a loss by the Cincinnati Reds to the Philadelphia Phillies on the final day of the 1964 season to clinch their first National League pennant since 1946. The Mets beat the Cardinals in the first two games of the weekend series in St. Louis, but the Cards stormed to an 11–5 win that ended when reliever Barney Schultz retired Ed Kranepool on a foul popup to catcher Tim McCarver. With the Reds having lost to the Phillies, the Cardinals celebrated, a scene that would be repeated when they would go on to beat the Yankees on the same field to win the World Series.

25. b. Joe Torre
A crowd of close to 55,000 showed up at Shea Stadium on the evening of September 24, 1969, for the Mets' last home game of the season against the St. Louis Cardinals to see if the Mets could

clinch their first-ever championship by finishing first in the National League East. They wasted no time as Donn Clendenon slammed a three-run homer off Steve Carlton and Ed Charles added a two-run shot for a quick 5–0 lead in the first inning. Clendenon homered again in the fifth, and rookie starter Gary Gentry held the Cardinals scoreless into the ninth. He gave up two singles before striking out Vada Pinson and getting future Mets player and manager Joe Torre to hit a ground ball to shortstop Bud Harrelson, who started a game-ending double play as fans swarmed the field.

1970s

1. Who collected the most hits for the Mets during the 1970s?

a. Ed Kranepool   b. Rusty Staub   c. Felix Millan   d. Bud Harrelson

2. Who drove in the winning run in extra innings in the team's very first Opening Day victory in 1970?

a. Donn Clendenon   b. Ron Swoboda   c. Art Shamsky   d. Joe Foy

3. Which Met had both the most home runs and RBIs during the 1970s?

a. John Milner   b. Dave Kingman   c. Ed Kranepool   d. Rusty Staub

4. Against which team did Tom Seaver hit his first major league home run in 1970?

a. Pittsburgh Pirates   b. Chicago Cubs   c. San Diego Padres
d. Montreal Expos

5. Which bench player hit two home runs, including a walk-off, on his birthday in 1972?

a. Dave Marshall   b. Jim Beauchamp   c. Bill Sudakis   d. Dave Schneck

6. Which Pittsburgh Pirates baserunner was thrown out at the plate in the 13th inning of a crucial September 1973 victory that moved the Mets to within a half-game of first place?

a. Dave Cash   b. Richie Hebner   c. Richie Zisk   d. Bob Robertson

7. Which St. Louis Cardinal scored from first on a wild pickoff throw to beat the Mets in the 25th inning on September 11, 1974, in the longest game in Shea Stadium history?
a. Ted Sizemore   b. Bake McBride   c. Reggie Smith   d. Lou Brock

8. Which 1970s Mets second baseman set a then–major league record by playing 85 consecutive errorless games?
a. Ken Boswell   b. Al Weis   c. Felix Millan   d. Doug Flynn

9. In 1976, Jerry Koosman won 20 games and finished second in voting for the Cy Young Award to
a. Don Sutton   b. Steve Carlton   c. J. R. Richard   d. Randy Jones

10. Who was the first Met to drive in 100 runs in a season?
a. Dave Kingman   b. Donn Clendenon   c. Willie Montañez
d. Rusty Staub

11. What year did the Mets participate in an 18-game postseason tour of Japan?
a. 1970   b. 1972   c. 1974   d. 1976

12. Who was the Mets' opponent when their game was suspended due to the 1977 New York City blackout?
a. Chicago Cubs   b. Atlanta Braves   c. Pittsburgh Pirates
d. San Diego Padres

13. The Mets cut this 1979 spring training invitee, a veteran pitcher with World Series credentials, in favor of younger and less expensive options:
a. Pat Dobson   b. Nelson Briles   c. Ken Holtzman   d. Jack Billingham

14. Which future Hall of Famer registered his 3,000th career hit against the Mets?
a. Willie Mays   b. Roberto Clemente   c. Hank Aaron   d. Lou Brock

15. Who was the Mets' Opening Day third baseman in 1977?

a. Lenny Randle   b. Mike Phillips   c. Dave Kingman   d. Roy Staiger

16. Who led the Mets' 1973 pennant-winning team in stolen bases with a total of only six?

a. Bud Harrelson   b. Ted Martinez   c. Wayne Garrett   d. Don Hahn

17. What was Dave Kingman's highest batting average in a season while playing for the Mets?

a. .231   b. .238   c. .244 d. .253

18. What was the only year the Mets lost an Opening Day game in the 1970s?

a. 1974   b. 1975   c. 1978   d. 1979

19. Which 1970s Mets pitcher went 0-for-41 as a batter in his major league career?

a. Randy Tate   b. Jackson Todd   c. Mike Bruhert   d. Hank Webb

20. Who was the only member of the 1962 team other than Ed Kranepool to appear in a game for the Mets in the 1970s?

a. Jim Hickman   b. Bob Miller   c. Al Jackson   d. Chris Cannizzaro

21. Which pitcher led the majors in ERA in 1974 after leaving the Mets?

a. Gary Gentry   b. Nolan Ryan   c. Jim McAndrew   d. Buzz Capra

22. In 1973, which opposing team defeated Tom Seaver and the Mets 2–0 in the shortest nine-inning game (1 hour, 36 minutes) in team history?

a. Montreal Expos   b. Philadelphia Phillies   c. Atlanta Braves
d. Houston Astros

23. How many home runs did Willie Mays hit in his two seasons with the Mets in 1972 and 1973?

a. 14   b. 16   c. 18   d. 20

24. Which Mets pitcher defeated Steve Carlton by driving in the only run of a 1977 game at Philadelphia?
a. Jerry Koosman   b. Craig Swan   c. Pat Zachry   d. Nino Espinosa

25. Which 1970s Met was not previously a member of the Seattle Pilots?
a. Jack Aker   b. Dave Marshall   c. Jim Gosger   d. Skip Lockwood

ANSWERS

1. c. Felix Millan

The Mets' best trade of the 1970s brought them second baseman Felix Millan, whose 743 hits from 1973 to 1977 was the most of any Mets player during the decade. He was acquired from the Atlanta Braves with pitcher George Stone for pitchers Gary Gentry and Danny Frisella after the 1972 season. The deal paid immediate dividends when Millan (185 hits) and Stone (12–3, 2.80 ERA) helped the Mets win the National League pennant. Millan was annually one of the toughest players in baseball to strike out, and he solidified the Mets infield.

2. a. Donn Clendenon

The Mets had dropped their first eight Opening Day games when they began defense of their 1969 World Championship at Pittsburgh's Forbes Field on April 7, 1970. The Mets scored twice off Steve Blass in the first inning, but the Pirates tied it with single runs in the first two innings off Tom Seaver. After the Mets regained the lead in the third on Joe Foy's sacrifice fly, the home team evened the score in the sixth on Roberto Clemente's second run-scoring hit. Seaver left the game after eight innings, while Blass pitched ten innings. The Mets put on the first two runners against reliever Chuck Hartenstein in the 11th. After a bunt and intentional walk loaded the bases, Joe Gibbon came on to face pinch-hitter Donn Clendenon, who singled home two runs to give the Mets a 5–3 victory.

3. a. John Milner

First baseman and outfielder John Milner led all Mets batters during the 1970s with 94 home runs and 338 RBIs. A 14th-round selection in the June 1968 amateur draft from South Fulton High School in East Point, Georgia, the powerful left-handed hitter came up to the Mets for nine games at the end of the 1971 season. He then put together a strong campaign in 1972, leading the team with 17 home runs and finishing third in voting for NL Rookie of the Year, won by teammate Jon Matlack. It was the first of three straight seasons and four times overall through 1977, his last season in New York, that he was the team's leading home run hitter.

4. d. Montreal Expos

July 9, 1970, was the one-year anniversary of Tom Seaver's near-perfect game against the Chicago Cubs and Tom Terrific was on the mound that night against the Montreal Expos at Shea Stadium. He had yet to hit a home run in his major league career, but finally got a chance to round the bases when he drove a pitch from Expos starter Rich Nye into the visitors' bullpen in left field leading off the fourth inning, giving the Mets a 6-0 lead. Ron Swoboda had hit a grand slam an inning earlier. Seaver pitched a complete-game three-hitter in the Mets' 7-1 victory. He hit five more home runs for the Mets, including three during the 1972 season.

5. b. Jim Beauchamp

It was quite a 33rd birthday for Jim Beauchamp on August 21, 1972. Starting at first base, he broke a 1-1 tie with a solo home run off Houston Astros lefty Jerry Reuss in the seventh inning. The Astros tied the game back up in the eighth, and the game looked headed for extra innings until Beauchamp came through with a two-run shot in the bottom of the ninth off righty Jim Ray to give the Mets a 4-2 victory. The birthday celebration continued the next night when he went 3-for-4 with a home run and four RBIs as the Mets beat the Astros again by the same score.

6. c. Richie Zisk

The Mets trailed the first place Pittsburgh Pirates by 1½ games when the two teams battled at Shea Stadium. In the top of the 13th of a see-saw game with the score tied 3–3, Dave Augustine faced Ray Sadecki with two outs and Richie Zisk on first base. He slammed a drive to deep left field that struck the top of the bullpen fence and bounded to Cleon Jones, who relayed the ball to Wayne Garrett. The shortstop's throw home was in time for catcher Ron Hodges to tag out Zisk to end the inning. The Mets won the game in the bottom of the inning when Hodges singled to left field against Dave Giusti, scoring John Milner from second base, cutting the Pirates' division lead to a half-game. The Mets would beat the Pirates again the next night to move into first place, where they would remain for the remainder of the season.

7. b. Bake McBride

The longest game in Mets history by innings took place at Shea Stadium on September 11, 1974, against the St. Louis Cardinals. The Mets had led, 3–1, with two outs in the ninth when Ken Reitz hit a two-run homer off Jerry Koosman to send the game into extra frames. Neither team could push across a run for the next 15 innings. Bake McBride led off the 25th with a single and with Reitz batting, Hank Webb, the Mets' sixth pitcher of the night, attempted to pick off McBride but threw the ball past first baseman John Milner into foul territory. McBride kept running past second and third as Milner retrieved the ball and threw home. Catcher Ron Hodges couldn't handle the throw and was charged with an error as the Cardinals took the lead and held on to beat the Mets, 4–3, in a game that lasted more than seven hours and ended after three o'clock in the morning.

8. a. Ken Boswell

Known more for his bat than his glove until he set the errorless games record, Ken Boswell made just two errors in 101 games as the Mets second baseman in 1970. His 85-game errorless streak ranged from April 29 until he mishandled Al Oliver's ground ball in the fourth inning of a loss to the Pirates on September 27 that eliminated the Mets from the division race. Boswell broke the record of 78 games set by Ken Hubbs of the Chicago Cubs eight years earlier. Rich Dauer of the Baltimore Orioles broke Boswell's major league mark with an 86-game streak in 1978, and Boswell held on to the National League record until Manny Trillo of the Philadelphia Phillies went 89 consecutive games without an error in 1982.

9. d. Randy Jones

After finishing second to Tom Seaver in voting for the 1975 NL Cy Young Award, San Diego Padres lefty Randy Jones bested Jerry Koosman for the 1976 honors, taking 15 of the 26 first-place votes to 7 for Kooz. The Mets' top three starters all received votes with Jon Matlack coming in sixth and Seaver eighth. Jones, who went 16–3 in the first half and started the All-Star Game, finished with a 22–15 record. His league-leading wins total was one more than Koosman and he also led in complete games (25) and innings pitched (315⅓). It was Jones's last winning season, and he pitched the final two seasons of his career with the Mets in 1981 and 1982.

10. d. Rusty Staub

No Mets player had put together a 100-RBI season until 1975 when Rusty Staub drove in 105 runs. Donn Clendenon had come closest to the mark with 97 RBIs five seasons earlier. One of the most popular players in team history, Staub had two tours of duties with the Mets. The slugging right fielder was acquired from the Montreal Expos on the eve of the 1972 season for Ken Singleton, Tim Foli, and Mike Jorgensen and helped the Mets win the National League pennant the following season and batted .423 in the World Series. He was then shipped to the Detroit Tigers for lefty Mickey Lolich immediately following his 105-RBI season. Staub returned to the Mets in 1981 and served as one of the best pinch-hitters in baseball until retiring after the 1985 season.

11. c. 1974

Following a dismal 71–91 season in defense of their 1973 NL pennant, the Mets embarked on an 18-game goodwill tour of Japan from October 26 to November 20, 1974. Facing various teams including the Yomiuri Giants and a team of Japanese All-Stars, the Mets went 9–7–2. Those games marked the Mets debut of Joe Torre, who had been acquired from the St. Louis Cardinals on October 13 for pitchers Ray Sadecki and Tommy Moore. The third baseman hit five home runs and was named the most valuable player of the exhibition series. Ed Kranepool hit seven home runs and Hank Aaron used one of Krane's bats to beat Sadaharu Oh in a home run derby before one of the games, which was televised in the United States.

12. a. Chicago Cubs

Shortly after 9:30 p.m. on July 13, 1977, a blackout hit New York City as Mets third baseman Lenny Randle was batting against Chicago Cubs righty Ray Burris with one out and the bases empty in the bottom of the sixth inning at Shea Stadium with Chicago leading, 2–1. An emergency generator provided some light in the stadium's corridors as the teams began to wait out a delay. Two Mets, Joel Youngblood and Craig Swan, drove their cars onto the field and turned on headlights as the team held a phantom infield practice. After a little more than an hour, the game was suspended and was finished in September with the Cubs winning, 5–2.

13. b. Nelson Briles

The Mets decided to carry five rookies on their 1979 Opening Day roster, and one of the final players cut from the squad was Nelson Briles, a 14-year veteran who had pitched in three World Series for the St. Louis Cardinals (1967, 1968) and Pittsburgh Pirates (1971 when he pitched a two-hit shutout against the Baltimore Orioles in Game 3). Briles was let go over the objections of manager Joe Torre, his former teammate in St. Louis, and never pitched in the majors again. One of the rookie pitchers who made the team was Mike Scott, who would pitch four seasons in New York before becoming a star with the Houston Astros and tormenting the Mets during the 1986 National League playoffs.

14. b. Roberto Clemente

On September 30, 1972, Pirates star right fielder Roberto Clemente hit a fourth-inning double against Mets rookie lefty Jon

Matlack at Pittsburgh's Three Rivers Stadium to become the 11th player in baseball history with 3,000 hits. It was the last regular season hit of Clemente's career as he died tragically in a plane crash the following New Year's Eve on his way to deliver aid to victims of an earthquake in Nicaragua. The Baseball Hall of Fame changed its rule about a five-year waiting period and Clemente was posthumously enshrined in 1973. The native of Puerto Rico became the first Latino player honored.

15. d. Roy Staiger

When the Mets took the field to begin the 1977 season in Chicago, Roy Staiger became their sixth different Opening Day third baseman since 1970 after Joe Foy, Bob Aspromonte, Jim Fregosi (twice), Wayne Garrett (twice), and Joe Torre. The Mets had selected Staiger in the first round of the January 1970 secondary draft and called him up to the majors in August 1975 while he was spending his third season in Triple-A. He took over as the team's starting third baseman after Garrett was traded to the Montreal Expos during the 1976 season, but lost the job to Lenny Randle after Joe Torre took over as manager early in the 1977 season. Staiger, who batted just .226 and hit four home runs in parts of three seasons with the Mets, was traded to the Yankees that December for infielder Sergio Ferrer.

16. c. Wayne Garrett

The pennant-winning Mets attempted the fewest stolen bases in the majors in 1973 with Wayne Garrett's six leading the team, followed by Bud Harrelson with five and Ted Martinez with three. Felix Millan and Don Hahn had two apiece while nine different players, including Tom Seaver, stole one base. The team did not steal a base in either its victory over the Cincinnati Reds in the NLCS or its loss to the Oakland A's in the World Series.

17. b. .238

Dave "Kong" or "Sky King" Kingman joined the Mets in 1975 and set a new team home run record that season with 36. He was leading the league in home runs in 1976 when he tore ligaments in his left thumb diving for a fly ball in late July. He missed more than a month and still finished with 37, just one behind league leader Mike Schmidt. His .238 average would be his highest as a Met. After being dealt to the San Diego Padres as part of the "Midnight Massacre" that included Tom Seaver being traded to the Cincinnati Reds in June 1977, he moved on to the Chicago Cubs, where he led the NL with 48 home runs in 1979. He rejoined the Mets in 1981 and led the league with 37 long balls the next season. He was released after the 1983 season and ended his Mets career with a .219 average and 154 home runs in six seasons.

18. a. 1974

The Mets' defense of their 1973 National League championship got off to a bad start when Philadelphia's Mike Schmidt hit a two-run homer off Tug McGraw in the bottom of the ninth to hand the Mets a disheartening 5–4 loss in the season opener at Veterans Stadium on April 6, 1974. Tom Seaver couldn't hold a 3–1 lead in the sixth, allowing the Phillies to tie the game before the Mets regained the lead in the seventh thanks to an error by Phillies catcher Bob Boone. It was the Mets' only Opening Day loss between 1970 and 1983.

19. a. Randy Tate

Pitching behind the "big three" of Tom Seaver, Jon Matlack, and Jerry Koosman in the Mets rotation, 22-year-old rookie right-hander Randy Tate went just 5–13 in 1975, his only season in the majors. He also failed to get a hit in 47 plate appearances including one walk and five sacrifice bunts. His most memorable pitching performance came at Shea Stadium on August 4 against the Montreal Expos when he struck out 10 batters in the first five innings (he finished with 13) and carried a no-hitter into the eighth before giving up a one-out single to pinch-hitter Jim Lyttle. Later in the inning, former Met Mike Jorgensen clubbed a three-run homer to hand Tate a 4–3 loss.

20. b. Bob Miller

One of two pitchers with the same name on the 1962 Mets, Bob "Righty" Miller lost his first 12 decisions that year before beating the Chicago Cubs at Wrigley Field with a complete game in the penultimate contest of the Mets' first season. He was traded to the Los Angeles Dodgers after the season for infielder Larry Burright and first baseman Tim Harkness. He returned to the Mets during the 1973 stretch drive and made one appearance. Miller finished his 17-season, 10-team career with the Mets the following year, appearing in 58 games out of the bullpen and notching two wins and two saves.

21. d. Buzz Capra

Righty Buzz Capra joined the Mets as a September callup in 1971 and served as a reliever and spot starter until he was sold to the Atlanta Braves during spring training in 1974. He started the season in relief, saving the game in which Hank Aaron broke Babe Ruth's home run record. He eventually moved into the starting rotation and made the All-Star team, finishing the season with a 16–8 record, including nine consecutive victories, and a 2.28 ERA, the best in the majors that year. He injured his arm early the following season and never returned to form.

22. c. Atlanta Braves

Tom Seaver only allowed three hits in seven innings at Atlanta-Fulton County Stadium on April 27, 1973, but two of them were consecutive home runs by Hank Aaron and Darrell Evans in the fourth inning for the only runs of the quickest nine-inning game in Mets history. Pat Dobson, who joined the Braves in an offseason trade and was one of the Baltimore Orioles' four 20-game winners two seasons earlier, also allowed just three hits in a complete-game victory. The Mets put the tying run on base in the ninth inning when Felix Millan singled with one out and went to second on a wild pitch, but Dobson struck out Willie Mays and retired Rusty Staub on a grounder to first base to end the game.

23. a. 14

The Mets brought 41-year-old Willie Mays back home to New York, where he played for the Giants before they moved to San Francisco, early in the 1972 season. In his first game with the Mets, against the Giants at Shea Stadium on Mother's Day, he hit a tiebreaking home run in the fifth inning of a 5–4 victory. He also homered in his first game back at Candlestick Park against the Giants that July. Mays finished the season with a total of eight home runs in 69 games and then hit six in 66 games in 1973, finishing his illustrious career with 660, behind only Babe Ruth and Hank Aaron on the all-time home run list at the time.

24. d. Nino Espinosa
The Mets didn't have many highlights during a terrible 1977 season in which they traded Tom Seaver and finished last, but Nino Espinosa gave them one on September 14 at Veterans Stadium. The righty shut down the eventual NL East champions with a three-hitter and drove in the game's only run to best Steve Carlton, who would go on to win his second of four Cy Young awards that year. Espinosa's two-out single in the fourth inning drove home Luis Rosado to give the Mets a 1–0 lead and he made the lead stand up, finishing the game by retiring Larry Bowa, Mike Schmidt, and Greg Luzinski in order. Espinosa posted double-figure win totals that year and next, then was traded to the Phillies in 1979 for third baseman Richie Hebner.

25. b. Dave Marshall
The Seattle Pilots joined the American League as an expansion team in 1969 before moving to Milwaukee and becoming the Brewers in 1970. The team featured two players who previously played for the Mets (Tommy Davis and Greg Goossen) and four who would later join them (Jack Aker, Jim Gosger, Skip Lockwood, and Mike Marshall). Outfielder Dave Marshall, who didn't play for the Pilots, was a member of the San Francisco Giants in 1969 and played for the Mets from 1970 to 1972. He was traded to the Mets in a deal involving Gosger, who had joined the Mets late in the 1969 season as the player to be named later in an earlier deal that sent Goossen to Seattle.

1980s

1. Which Mets player appeared in the most games during the 1980s?
a. Mookie Wilson   b. Howard Johnson   c. Keith Hernandez
d. Darryl Strawberry

2. Besides Tom Seaver, which Met played for the team in the 1960s, 1970s, and 1980s?
a. Bud Harrelson   b. Mike Jorgensen   c. Ed Kranepool
d. Ron Hodges

3. Only two Mets hit as many as 100 home runs during the 1980s. Darryl Strawberry slammed 215. Who was the other slugger to reach the century mark?
a. Gary Carter   b. Howard Johnson   c. George Foster
d. Keith Hernandez

4. Which Met stole 21 bases in 21 attempts in 1988?
a. Lenny Dykstra   b. Mookie Wilson   c. Howard Johnson
d. Kevin McReynolds

5. Who threw the most innings for the Mets in the 1980s?
a. Ed Lynch   b. Sid Fernandez   c. Ron Darling   d. Dwight Gooden

6. Which Met's 10 home runs in just 79 games in 1980 was good enough for second on the team behind Lee Mazzilli's 16?
a. Claudell Washington   b. Jerry Morales   c. Joel Youngblood
d. Mike Jorgensen

7. How many games did Tom Seaver win in his return to the Mets in 1983?

a. 7   b. 9   c. 11   d. 13

8. Which opposing pitcher had a perfect 4–0 record against the Mets during their 1986 World Championship season?

a. Mike Krukow   b. Kevin Gross   c. Zane Smith
d. Fernando Valenzuela

9. Which team did David Cone defeat for his 20th victory of the 1988 season?

a. St. Louis Cardinals   b. Montreal Expos   c. Chicago Cubs
d. Philadelphia Phillies

10. Which Met set a team record with three triples in a game in 1980?

a. Lee Mazzilli   b. Steve Henderson   c. Frank Taveras   d. Doug Flynn

11. How many games did the Mets play during the strike-shortened 1981 season?

a. 102   b. 105   c. 108   d. 111

12. Which future Met was the first overall pick in the amateur draft in 1982, the year the Mets chose Dwight Gooden with the fifth pick?

a. Frank Viola   b. Kevin McReynolds   c. Shawon Dunston
d. Daryl Boston

13. Which Met hit a record five home runs in a two-game span in 1985?

a. Darryl Strawberry   b. Keith Hernandez   c. Gary Carter
d. George Foster

14. Which Mets pitcher won his first ten decisions in 1987?

a. Rick Aguilera   b. Terry Leach   c. Sid Fernandez
d. Roger McDowell

15. Who recorded the save in the Mets' 1989 Opening Day victory?

a. Don Aase   b. Randy Myers   c. Rick Aguilera   d. Roger McDowell

16. Which Mets pitcher gave up Hall of Famer Mike Schmidt's 300th home run in 1981?

a. Randy Jones   b. Pete Falcone   c. Mike Scott   d. Neil Allen

17. Who hit a game-winning three-run home run in the 13th inning to win Darryl Strawberry's major league debut in 1983?

a. Hubie Brooks   b. Dave Kingman   c. Danny Heep   d. George Foster

18. Who was the Opening Day starting pitcher for the Mets in 1984?

a. Dwight Gooden   b. Craig Swan   c. Bruce Berenyi   d. Mike Torrez

19. Which player did not play for the Mets in 1986?

a. Clint Hurdle   b. Tim Corcoran   c. Barry Lyons   d. John Mitchell

20. Against which team did the Mets clinch the National League East title in 1988?

a. St. Louis Cardinals   b. Philadelphia Phillies   c. Chicago Cubs
d. Montreal Expos

21. Where did 1980s Mets third baseman Hubie Brooks play college baseball?

a. Arizona State   b. USC   c. Wichita State   d. Miami

22. Which player was not a first-round draft choice of the Mets?

a. John Gibbons   b. Terry Blocker   c. Dave Magadan
d. Chris Donnels

23. Which Mets pitcher hit two home runs in a game in 1983?

a. Tom Seaver   b. Walt Terrell   c. Ed Lynch   d. Craig Swan

24. Which Met hit for the cycle in a wild 19-inning victory against the Braves in Atlanta in 1985?

a. Gary Carter   b. Howard Johnson   c. Lenny Dykstra
d. Keith Hernandez

25. Which Met hit a pinch-hit grand slam in extra innings to beat the Phillies in 1986?
a. Danny Heep   b. Ray Knight   c. Tim Teufel   d. Kevin Mitchell

ANSWERS

1. a. Mookie Wilson
The popular outfielder appeared in 1,116 games in a Mets uniform, just ahead of Darryl Strawberry's 1,109. A second-round pick in the 1977 amateur draft, Wilson joined the Mets late in the 1980 season. A key member of the 1986 World Championship team whose key at-bat in Game 6 of the World Series kept the team's postseason alive, he ranks in the franchise's top ten in several offensive categories, including stolen bases and triples (second) and at-bats, runs scored, and hits (sixth). Wilson was traded to the Toronto Blue Jays in July 1989 and finished his major league career with them in 1991.

2. b. Mike Jorgensen
Local Queens product Mike Jorgensen had two tours of duty with the Mets (1968, 1970–1971, and 1980–1983). The first baseman was a September callup in 1968, was back in the minors in 1969, then made the team in 1970. He was traded to the Montreal Expos shortly before the start of the 1972 season, then rejoined the Mets after the 1979 season from the Texas Rangers as a player to be named later in an earlier trade involving Willie Montañez. Jorgensen saw more playing time his second time around at first base, the outfield, and as a pinch-hitter before he was sold to the Atlanta Braves the same day the Mets acquired Keith Hernandez from the St. Louis Cardinals.

3. b. Howard Johnson
Two-time All-Star third baseman Howard Johnson hit 117 of his 192 Mets home runs during the 1980s. Acquired from the Detroit Tigers for pitcher Walt Terrell after the 1984 season, he helped the Mets win the 1986 World Series and then really came into his own

in 1987 when he hit 36 home runs and stole 32 bases for his first of three 30-30 seasons. He was the National League's starting third baseman in the 1989 All-Star Game and also appeared in the 1991 contest, the year he led in the league in both home runs (38) and RBIs (117). Injuries got the best of him the next two seasons and he finished his career playing one year each for the Colorado Rockies and Chicago Cubs.

4. d. Kevin McReynolds
A little over a month after winning the 1986 World Series, the Mets traded five players, including a former first overall draft pick (Shawn Abner) and a future Most Valuable Player (Kevin Mitchell) to the San Diego Padres for the services of left fielder Kevin McReynolds. The laid-back Arkansan finished third behind Kirk Gibson and Darryl Strawberry in MVP voting in 1988, the season he was successful in all 21 of his stolen base attempts, helping the Mets win the NL East. McReynolds ended up stealing 33 consecutive bases without being thrown out from June 7, 1987, through April 9, 1989.

5. c. Ron Darling
A mainstay of the Mets pitching staff in the 1980s, Ron Darling worked 1,391⅔ innings during the decade. A former first-round pick of the Texas Rangers, he was acquired along with fellow righty Walt Terrell before the 1982 season for Lee Mazzilli. Darling made it to the majors the following September, then moved into the rotation in 1984. He was an All-Star the following season, and in 1986, started the first, fourth, and seventh games of the World Series. Two years later, he pitched a complete game against the Philadelphia Phillies to clinch the division but went on to lose Game 7 of the NLCS to Orel Hershiser and the Los Angeles Dodgers. Darling was traded to the Montreal Expos in 1991 and finished his career with the Oakland A's in 1995.

6. a. Claudell Washington
The Mets hit only 61 home runs as a team during the 1980 season, exactly as many as Roger Maris of the Yankees hit by himself in 1961.

Lee Mazzilli and Claudell Washington were the only two players to reach double figures. Three regulars—catcher Alex Treviño, second baseman Doug Flynn, and shortstop Frank Taveras—did not hit a home run that year. Washington, a left-handed-hitting right fielder, was a midseason acquisition from the Chicago White Sox in Frank Cashen's first trade as general manager of the Mets. Two weeks after joining the team, Washington hit three home runs in a game at Dodger Stadium. After the season, the right fielder signed as a free agent with the Atlanta Braves.

7. b. 9
After being exiled to Cincinnati in 1977, Tom Seaver returned to the Mets after the 1982 season. He would go 9–14 in 1983, a year the Mets finished in last place with 94 losses. He made a triumphant return on Opening Day, pitching six scoreless innings but getting a no decision against the Philadelphia Phillies in a game the Mets would win 2–0. He only won consecutive starts once in his return but did pitch two shutouts. He was shockingly left off the Mets roster of protected players after the season and was selected by the Chicago White Sox in a compensation draft for losing free agent pitcher Dennis Lamp.

8. a. Mike Krukow
In 1986, San Francisco Giants right-hander Mike Krukow won 20 games and made the All-Star team, both for the only time in his 14 years in the majors. He won all four of his starts against the Mets, who would go on to win 108 games and the World Series that season. His success against the Mets in 1986 wasn't a one-year thing, either—he finished his career with a 22–7 lifetime record against the Mets as a member of the Chicago Cubs and Giants between 1976 and 1989. Krukow is now a popular broadcaster for the Giants, working with one-time teammate Duane Kuiper.

9. a. St. Louis Cardinals
Although David Cone didn't join the Mets rotation in 1988 until the beginning of May, he put together a spectacular season with 20 wins (against just three losses) and 213 strikeouts. The right-

hander's .870 winning percentage was the best in the majors, and he finished third in Cy Young voting behind the Dodgers' Orel Hershiser (who had a season for the ages including finishing the year with 59 consecutive scoreless innings) and Danny Jackson, who won 23 games for the Cincinnati Reds. Cone's 20th win came in his last start on the final weekend of the season. Facing the St. Louis Cardinals at Shea Stadium on September 30, Cone pitched a complete game while striking out seven in a 4–2 win.

10. d. Doug Flynn

Doug Flynn, one of the four players the Mets received when they traded Tom Seaver to the Cincinnati Reds in 1977, tied a major league record when he hit three triples on August 5, 1980, against the Montreal Expos at Olympic Stadium. Batting eighth in the order, the second baseman tripled twice against Bill Gullickson and once against Elias Sosa. All three triples came leading off innings. Flynn had one more at-bat with two runners on base in the ninth inning but Sosa got him to ground into a double play to end the game won by the Expos, 11–5.

11. b. 105

The 1981 season was shortened after players went out on strike for 50 days on June 12. When they returned on August 10, the season was divided into halves with the winners of each half meeting in the very first Division Series. Teams ended up playing anywhere from 102 games to 110 games, with the Mets playing 105, including two ties (one in each half of the split season). They went 17–34 before the strike to finish in fifth place in the National League East but played better in the second half and were in contention late into September before finishing fourth with a record of 24–28, giving them an overall 1981 record of 41–62.

12. c. Shawon Dunston

Strong-armed shortstop Shawon Dunston from Brooklyn's Thomas Jefferson High School was taken by the Chicago Cubs with the first overall pick in the 1982 amateur draft. He made it to the majors in 1985, and played the first 12 seasons of his 18-year career in Chicago, making two All-Star teams along the way. He bounced around the majors after that, landing with the Mets at the 1999 trading deadline to help with a playoff push. He batted .344 in 44 games and filled in at all three outfield positions as well as one game at third base. Dunston drew a leadoff walk and scored the tying run in the 15th inning of Game 5 of that year's NLCS against Atlanta just before Robin Ventura's game-winning "grand slam single."

13. c. Gary Carter

The Mets' acquisition of Hall of Fame catcher Gary Carter after the 1984 season was one of the major components on the road to their 1986 World Championship. During his first season in New York, Carter hit a career-high 32 home runs, five of them coming in a two-game stretch against the San Diego Padres to tie a major league record. On September 3 at San Diego, he slammed home runs in his first three at-bats, two off Padres starter Dave Dravecky and the third off Luis DeLeon, driving in six runs in an 8–3 victory. The next night, he homered against former Met Roy Lee Jackson in the second inning and hit another against reliever Ed Wojna five innings later as the Mets won again, 9–2.

14. b. Terry Leach

The Mets were hit hard by injuries to their pitching staff in 1987—and had to compensate for Dwight Gooden's two-month suspension at the start of the season—so Terry Leach became a real godsend, posting an 11–1 record. Leach had first broken in with the Mets in 1981 and also pitched for them in 1982 before spending time in the minors with the Chicago Cubs and Atlanta Braves organizations. He was back with the Mets by 1985 but spent most of the 1986 season in the minors. In 1987, he won his first three decisions in relief before moving into the rotation at the beginning of June. Leach then won his next seven decisions, a string broken when he lost to the Cubs at Wrigley Field, 7–3, on August 15.

15. a. Don Aase

On April 3, 1989, the Mets appeared headed for an easy Opening Day victory, leading the St. Louis Cardinals 7–3 in the eighth inning behind Dwight Gooden. But the first two batters reached before Pedro Guerrero's single brought home a run and the tying run to the plate. Manager Davey Johnson then called upon offseason acquisition Don Aase. The former Baltimore Orioles righty, an All-Star three seasons earlier, retired the next three batters. Howard Johnson added some insurance in the bottom of the inning with a home run, and Aase closed out the 8–4 victory with a scoreless ninth inning.

16. c. Mike Scott
On August 14, 1981, in the Mets' first game back at Shea Stadium following the players' strike, slugging third baseman Mike Schmidt of the Philadelphia Phillies hit the 300th home run of his Hall of Fame career. Facing righty Mike Scott in the third inning with one on and one out, Schmidt gave Philadelphia a 4–1 lead with his milestone home run, and Philadelphia went on to win the game, 8–4. After going 14–27 with a 4.64 ERA in three seasons with the Mets, Scott turned his career around after being traded to the Houston Astros before the 1983 season. He learned a split-finger fastball from original Met Roger Craig and would win the Cy Young Award in 1986, the year he dominated two playoff outings while Mets players claimed he was throwing scuffed baseballs.

17. d. George Foster
George Foster's game-winning shot against his former team capped an improbable victory in Darryl Strawberry's first major league game on May 6, 1983. Reds ace Mario Soto was holding a 3–1 lead in the ninth and had just struck out Strawberry for the second time when Dave Kingman hit a dramatic game-tying home run with two men out to send the game into extra innings. The Reds regained the lead in the top of the 10th, but Hubie Brooks slammed a two-out home run off Tom Hume to keep the Mets alive. Strawberry started the winning rally in the 13th with a two-out walk against Bill Scherrer and stole second. Following a walk to Mike Jorgensen, the Reds called on Frank Pastore and Foster drove his first pitch over the fence in left-center field to win the game, 7–4.

18. d. Mike Torrez

New Mets manager Davey Johnson went with veteran right-hander Mike Torrez to pitch the season opener at Cincinnati on April 2, 1984. Torrez had been acquired from the Boston Red Sox before the previous season, going 10–17 and leading the league in both losses and walks. Things didn't get much better in 1984 as the 36-year-old dropped the opener, 8–1, giving up six runs in an inning and a third. It was the Mets' first Opening Day loss after nine straight victories and only their second one since 1970. The Mets released Torrez in June with a 1–5 record and an ERA of 5.02.

19. a. Clint Hurdle

Utilityman Clint Hurdle played for the Mets in 1983, 1985, and 1987 and spent the 1986 season with the St. Louis Cardinals, meaning he saw the Cardinals go to the postseason in 1985 and 1987 when he was with the Mets and the Mets go to the postseason in 1986 when he was with the Cardinals. In 1988, the Mets hired him as a minor league manager, and he skippered teams at all three levels before joining the Colorado Rockies organization, eventually being promoted to manager in 2002. He was let go in 2009—two years after leading the Rockies to the World Series—and took over the Pittsburgh Pirates two years later. Hurdle was named NL Manager of the Year in 2013.

20. b. Philadelphia Phillies

On September 22, 1988, the Mets had a magic number of one to clinch the National League East, and a victory over the Philadelphia Phillies would give them their second division title in three seasons. It was the last game of a homestand and a crowd of over 45,000 at Shea Stadium was hoping to see them celebrate before the team would go on the road. The Mets broke a 1–1 tie in the sixth when lefty Don Carman threw a wild pitch to score Darryl Strawberry. Kevin McReynolds's RBI single made it 3–1 an inning later. Ron Darling made the lead hold up, and when he struck out Lance Parrish on a check swing to end the game, the division title belonged to the Mets.

21. a. Arizona State

The Mets drafted Hubie Brooks with the third overall pick of the 1978 amateur draft following a stellar career at Arizona State University, where he won a College World Series in 1977 against a South Carolina squad that included Mookie Wilson. Brooks was a shortstop at ASU but was moved to third base in the minors. He joined the Mets as a September callup in 1980, and became the team's regular third baseman the following year, batting .307 and finishing third in Rookie of the Year voting. After the Mets acquired Ray Knight late in the 1984 season, Brooks was moved to shortstop but was traded after the season to the Montreal Expos in a blockbuster deal for Gary Carter. After a one-year stint with the Los Angeles Dodgers, Brooks returned to the Mets in 1991 for one season before moving on to the California Angels and then the Kansas City Royals, where he wound down his playing days in 1994.

22. c. Dave Magadan

First baseman Dave Magadan was a second-round pick in 1983 from the University of Alabama. After batting better than .300 at each of his minor league stops, he joined the Mets in September 1986 and had three hits and two RBIs in the Mets' division-clinching victory against the Cubs while filling in for Keith Hernandez. His best season in New York was 1990 when he finished third in the NL batting race with a .328 average. Never a power hitter, he set career highs that season with six home runs and 72 RBIs. Magadan left the Mets as a free agent after the 1992 season and played until 2001, bouncing around the majors with the Florida Marlins, Seattle Mariners, Houston Astros, Chicago Cubs, Oakland A's, and San Diego Padres.

23. b. Walt Terrell

A right-handed pitcher but a left-handed batter, rookie Walt Terrell connected for a pair of two-run homers off future Hall of Famer Ferguson Jenkins while pitching the Mets to a 4–1 victory over the Chicago Cubs at Wrigley Field on August 6, 1983. Terrell's first home run gave the Mets a 2–0 lead in the third inning and doubled their advantage an inning later with his second. He held the Cubs scoreless until the eighth inning when Ryne Sandberg hit a sacrifice fly. Terrell was relieved later in the inning by Carlos Diaz, who got the final five outs. Terrell would hit a three-run home run against the San Diego Padres later that month.

24. d. Keith Hernandez

Keith Hernandez went 4-for-10 as the Mets outlasted the Braves in a rain-delayed six-hour game affair at Atlanta's Fulton County Stadium that began shortly after 9 p.m. on July 4, 1985, and, abetted by weather delays, didn't end until just before 4 a.m. the next morning. Hernandez collected his four hits off four different Braves pitchers. He doubled in the first inning off starter Rick Mahler, hit a two-run triple and later scored against Jeff Dedmon in the fourth, homered in the eighth against Steve Shields, and completed the cycle with a 12th-inning single against Terry Forster. The Mets blew a late three-run lead before tying the game in the ninth and survived blowing two extra-inning leads, the second on reliever Rick Camp's two-out home run in the 18th.

25. c. Tim Teufel

One of the most memorable regular season games of the Mets' 1986 World Championship season was their 8–4 victory over the Philadelphia Phillies at Shea Stadium on June 10. In a seesaw contest in which Gary Carter homered in the eighth inning off ace reliever Steve Bedrosian to send the game toward extra innings, Tim Teufel, batting for fellow second baseman Wally Backman with the bases full in the 11th, drove a pitch from Tom Hume over the left field fence to give the Mets a dramatic win that started a seven-game winning streak. It was one of only four home runs Teufel would hit in 1986, two of them coming as a pinch-hitter. He would tie his career high with 14 a season later.

1990s

1. Which pitcher led the Mets in wins in the 1990s?
a. Dwight Gooden   b. Sid Fernandez   c. Bobby Jones   d. Al Leiter

2. Who started a critical early September 1990 game instead of Ron Darling?
a. Bob Ojeda   b. Julio Valera   c. Wally Whitehurst
d. Anthony Young

3. Who managed the Mets for only seven games?
a. Mike Cubbage   b. Mel Stottlemyre   c. Bill Robinson
d. Ray Knight

4. Which pitcher appeared in 69 games in 1991 without recording a win or a save?
a. John Franco   b. Alejandro Peña   c. Tim Burke   d. Jeff Innis

5. Who hit two home runs against the Cardinals on Opening Day 1992?
a. Howard Johnson   b. Bobby Bonilla   c. Eddie Murray
d. Kevin Elster

6. Which former Penn State running back played for the Mets in 1992?
a. Blair Thomas   b. Sam Gash   c. Richie Anderson   d. D. J. Dozier

7. Which Mets pitcher threw a shutout at Dodger Stadium in 1994 for his first major league victory?

a. Jason Jacome   b. Mike Remlinger   c. Juan Castillo   d. Eric Hillman

8. Who gave up a 13th-inning walk-off home run on Opening Day 1995 at Coors Field?

a. John Franco   b. Doug Henry   c. Mike Remlinger
d. Josias Manzanillo

9. How many pitches did Bill Pulsipher throw in his major league debut?

a. 4   b. 56   c. 100   d. 131

10. What future Mets outfielder was the first batter Jason Isringhausen faced in his major league debut?

a. Brian McRae   b. Roger Cedeño   c. Jermaine Allensworth
d. Darryl Hamilton

11. Name the three players, in order, who set Mets club records for doubles, triples, and home runs in 1996.

a. Rico Brogna, Butch Huskey, Jeff Kent
b. Bernard Gilkey, Lance Johnson, Todd Hundley
c. Chris Jones, José Vizcaino, Carl Everett
d. Alex Ochoa, Edgardo Alfonzo, Todd Hundley

12. Which Met did Carlos Baerga switch numbers with in 1997?

a. Manny Alexander   b. John Olerud   c. Dennis Cook
d. Edgardo Alfonzo

13. Who was the Mets' Opening Day starting pitcher in 1997?

a. Dave Mlicki   b. Mark Clark   c. Pete Harnisch   d. Bobby Jones

14. Who pitched a shutout in the Mets' first interleague game at Yankee Stadium?

a. Brian Bohanon   b. Steve Trachsel   c. Kenny Rogers
d. Dave Mlicki

15. Who hit the first regular season home run by a Mets player at Yankee Stadium?
a. Bernard Gilkey   b. Todd Hundley   c. John Olerud
d. Butch Huskey

16. Who was the Mets' Opening Day catcher in 1998?
a. Todd Hundley   b. Tim Spehr   c. Mike Piazza   d. Todd Pratt

17. Which Met drove in the only run of the game in their 14-inning Opening Day victory over the Philadelphia Phillies in 1998?
a. Jim Tatum   b. Rich Becker   c. Alberto Castillo   d. Luis Lopez

18. In the 1990s, which Met was traded to the Los Angeles Dodgers and then back to the Mets a month later?
a. Greg McMichael   b. Todd Zeile   c. Allen Watson   d. Brett Butler

19. Who delivered the walk-off sacrifice fly for the Mets' first regular season win against the Yankees at Shea Stadium?
a. Mike Piazza   b. Rey Ordoñez   c. Kurt Abbott   d. Luis Lopez

20. Roger Cedeño and Rickey Henderson combined for 103 of the Mets 150 stolen bases in 1999. Who was third on the team?
a. Edgardo Alfonzo   b. Rey Ordoñez   c. Brian McRae
d. Mike Piazza

21. This relief pitcher delivered the game-winning hit in the 13th inning of a Mets win at Wrigley Field on August 1, 1999. Name him.
a. Turk Wendell   b. Pat Mahomes   c. Dennis Cook   d. Rigo Beltrán

22. Which Met finished highest in the 1999 Most Valuable Player voting?
a. Mike Piazza   b. Edgardo Alfonzo.   c. Robin Ventura
d. Armando Benitez

23. Who led Mets batters in intentional walks in 1999?
a. Mike Piazza   b. Robin Ventura   c. John Olerud   d. Rey Ordoñez

24. Who was the only Mets pitcher to steal a base during the 1999 season?
a. Al Leiter   b. Orel Hershiser   c. John Franco   d. Rick Reed

25. Which pitchers gave up Mark McGwire's 50th home runs of 1998 and 1999 at Shea Stadium?
a. Willie Blair and Jeff Tam
b. Dennis Cook and Turk Wendell
c. John Franco and Armando Benitez
d. Greg McMichael and Kenny Rogers

ANSWERS

1. c. Bobby Jones
Jones went 63–50 during the 1990s. The right-hander went to Fresno High School, the same California school as Tom Seaver. Jones made his debut in August 1993 with a win over the Phillies at Veterans Stadium and finished eighth in the 1994 Rookie of the Year voting. Jones was a three-time Opening Day starter for the Mets and made the 1997 NL All-Star team, striking out Ken Griffey Jr. and Mark McGwire in the Midsummer Classic. Though not a particularly adept hitter, Jones homered off Marlins ace Liván Hernandez in the 1999 home opener at Shea Stadium.

2. b. Julio Valera
Trailing the Pirates by 2½ games in the NL East standings after being swept in a doubleheader in Pittsburgh the previous night, the Mets went with Julio Valera in his second career start instead of the veteran Darling, who had mostly struggled in his August outings. The Pirates tagged Valera for five runs (four earned) on eight hits in two-plus innings on September 6, a 7–1 Mets loss. Valera would only make one more start in 1991 and appear twice out of the bullpen in 1992 before being traded to the Angels. The Mets would finish the season four games behind the Pirates and would not have another winning season until 1997.

3. a. Mike Cubbage

After Bud Harrelson was fired with a week to go in the disappointing 1991 season, third-base coach Mike Cubbage was elevated to manager. Cubbage ended his eight-year playing career with the 1981 Mets, often serving as a pinch-hitter (his final swing in the majors produced a pinch-homer). Cubbage then became a manager in the Mets minor league system, working up the ranks from Single-A Lynchburg to Double-A Jackson and then Triple-A Tidewater. As Mets manager, Cubbage finished 3–4 including a 7–0 win on the final day of the season when David Cone struck out 19 Phillies. Cubbage later served as a coach with the Astros and Red Sox.

4. d. Jeff Innis

Innis, a righty reliever, went 0–2 with a 2.66 ERA in 1991, a year he was called upon to pitch 69 times, ninth-most in the NL. He suffered losses in his second and 65th outings of the season. Often tasked with keeping a deficit close, the offense could never rally after Innis left a game. Innis spent his entire seven-season career with the Mets from 1987 to 1993. All but one of his 288 appearances were out of the bullpen. After not recording a win in 69 games in 1991, he was the winning pitcher on Opening Day in 1992.

5. b. Bobby Bonilla

The Bronx-born Bonilla made a good first impression with the Mets after signing a five-year, $29 million contract to leave the Pirates. In the fourth inning of the 1992 opener, Bonilla homered off José DeLeon to give the Mets a 1–0 lead. With the game tied in the 10th inning, Bonilla crushed a two-run homer off Lee Smith to put New York ahead, 4–2. John Franco pitched a 1-2-3 bottom of the 10th to close out the win. Bonilla would hit 19 home runs in the 1992 campaign. He would hit 95 of his 287 career home runs in a Mets uniform.

6. d. D. J. Dozier

William Henry "D. J." Dozier was selected by the Tigers in the 18th round of the 1983 amateur draft but chose to go to Penn State and play football. He was the running back on the 1986 Nittany Lions' National Championship team and scored the go-ahead touchdown in the fourth quarter of the title game against the Miami Hurricanes in the Fiesta Bowl. He was selected by the Vikings in the first round of the NFL draft and played with Minnesota for four seasons and the Detroit Lions for one. An outfielder who was twice ranked as a Top 100 prospect by *Baseball America*, Dozier hit .191 in 25 games for the Mets in 1992 before being sent to the Padres after his only major league season in a deal for All-Star shortstop Tony Fernandez.

7. a. Jason Jacome

The southpaw tossed a six-hit shutout in Los Angeles in a 3-0 win on July 7. The Mets scored three runs in the fourth off Tom Candiotti, including a solo home run from Todd Hundley. Jacome induced Eric Karros into a 6-4-3 double play to end the game. Jacome threw 112 pitches in his second career start after losing his debut five nights earlier in San Diego. It was the first of four straight wins for Jacome. He would struggle as a starter in 1995 and later pitch out of the bullpen for Kansas City and Cleveland.

8. c. Mike Remlinger

Trying to hold on to a 9–8 lead in the 14th inning, the lefty surrendered a three-run home run to Dante Bichette. It was the first regular-season game for the Mets since a players' strike ended the 1994 season the previous August. It was also the first game in the history of Coors Field after the Rockies had played their first two seasons at Mile High Stadium. Rico Brogna hit the first homer at Coors Field and Todd Hundley crushed a grand slam. The Mets were one out from victory in the ninth when Larry Walker delivered an RBI double off John Franco.

9. d. 131

In a 7–3 loss to the Astros on June 17, 1995, manager Dallas Green left Pulsipher in to throw 131 pitches in seven innings. The rookie gave up five runs in the first inning before settling down. He gave up a run in the fifth and was leading off the bottom of the inning, but instead of being lifted for a pinch-hitter, Green left him in. In 1995, Pulsipher threw at least 90 pitches in each of his 17 starts and hit triple-digits in pitches 11 times. He threw at least 110 pitches in each of his first four starts. Pulsipher missed the entire 1996 season after undergoing Tommy John surgery.

10. a. Brian McRae

McRae was the Cubs' center fielder and leadoff hitter when Isringhausen made his debut at Wrigley Field on July 17, 1995. He went 0-for-3 against Izzy, who gave up two runs on two hits over seven innings. The Mets scored five times in the ninth for a 7–2 win. In August 1997, McRae was traded to the Mets with Mel Rojas and Turk Wendell for Lance Johnson, Mark Clark, and Manny Alexander. Both Isringhausen and McRae were traded by the Mets during the 1999 season. Izzy would return to Queens to post seven saves in 2011.

11. b. Bernard Gilkey, Lance Johnson, Todd Hundley

Gilkey delivered 44 doubles, Johnson legged out 21 triples, and Hundley homered 41 times. The Mets still finished 71–91 behind a subpar pitching staff. In one August game, Gilkey connected for three straight doubles off future Met Shawn Estes. Johnson, in his first season with the Mets, led the league in triples, hits, at-bats, and plate appearances. He also stole 50 bases and batted .333 in an All-Star campaign. Hundley set the record for most single-season home runs as a catcher, though his mark would be surpassed by Atlanta's Javy Lopez in 2003. Hundley's team home run record would be tied by Carlos Beltrán in 2006.

12. a. Manny Alexander

Baerga wore number 6 in 1996, the season the former All-Star and Silver Slugger–winning second baseman came to New York from Cleveland in exchange for Jeff Kent (the number 9 he wore as an Indian was already taken by Todd Hundley). When utilityman Alexander was acquired the following spring, the newest Met was given number 8, a digit he had reason to resist. Alexander had sat on the Orioles bench for a couple of years, ostensibly backing up iron man Cal Ripken Jr., who made number 8 iconic in Baltimore while playing in a record 2,632 consecutive games, a streak still *very* current during Alexander's tenure. Ripken didn't need much backing up, and Alexander didn't require a reminder of his previous situation—"Eight is bad luck," the infielder declared upon his arrival in Port St. Lucie. He was therefore more than happy to swap numbers with Baerga. Alexander appeared in only 54 games with the Mets before being sent to the Cubs in August 1997. Baerga turned out to be one of the last Mets to don number 8, with only Desi Relaford and coaches Cookie Rojas and Matt Galante later wearing it before it was unofficially removed from circulation once Gary Carter was elected to the Hall of Fame in 2003.

13. c. Pete Harnisch

The veteran righty, who had gone 8–12 the previous season, gave up three runs in five-plus innings in San Diego on Opening Day and wouldn't appear with the Mets again until August. A 1991 All-Star with the Astros, Harnisch took a leave of absence while battling depression. After struggling upon his return, he was briefly moved to the bullpen but was released after trading harsh words with manager Bobby Valentine, which came to a head with a confrontation in a hotel lobby. Harnisch would spend his final four seasons with the Reds, winning 14 games in 1998 and 16 in 1999, finishing his 14-year career with 111 victories.

14. d. Dave Mlicki

The journeyman pitcher was 24–30 with the Mets, but pitched himself into team lore with his nine-hit shutout in the Bronx on June 16, 1997. Spotted a three-run lead, the right-hander worked in and out of trouble against the defending World Series champions. Mlicki finished off the 6–0 win by striking out Derek Jeter looking. The Mets and Yankees had met numerous exhibition games over the previous 35 years, but this was the first meaningful intra-city game since the 1950s. Mlicki finished his career 66–80 with five teams. His only other shutout would come at Coors Field in 1998 as a member of the Dodgers.

15. a. Bernard Gilkey

Though the Mets won the Subway Series opener, the first Mets home run didn't come until the next night when Gilkey hit a two-run dinger to left off David Wells. The third-inning homer cut the lead to 4–3 but it was as close as the Mets would get in the 6–3 loss after the Yankees knocked out Armando Reynoso in the second inning. Mariano Rivera notched the first of his 20 career saves against the Mets. Gilkey, who hit 30 home runs in 1996, would finish the 1997 season with 18. The left fielder also had a cameo in the 1997 blockbuster *Men in Black*.

16. b. Tim Spehr

With Todd Hundley battling an injury, Bobby Valentine penciled the well-traveled Spehr into the Opening Day lineup in 1998. Spehr, who made his major league debut in 1991 with the Royals, also played with the Expos, Royals again, and the Braves before coming to Queens. He batted .137 in 21 games before being injured himself in an early May game against Arizona. Spehr broke a bone in his left wrist while tagging ex-Met Kelly Stinnett. A few weeks later, the Mets acquired Mike Piazza. Spehr wouldn't play in another game with the Mets, but he would go to the Kansas City Royals for a third tour of duty.

17. c. Alberto Castillo

The light-hitting catcher was used as a pinch-hitter with the bases loaded and two outs in a scoreless game. On a 3-2 pitch, Castillo singled to right field off Ricky Bottalico, bringing an end to the four-hour and 35-minute game. A reliable defensive catcher, Castillo played for eight teams in his 12-season career, batting .220. He only hit two home runs as a Met, but one was off Pedro Martinez at Fenway Park in a 9–2 win later in the 1998 season. He also returned to Shea and homered as a Cardinal off Jeff Tam in August 1999.

18. a. Greg McMichael

In June 1998, the Mets sent McMichael and Dave Mlicki to Los Angeles for starter Hideo Nomo. Then, needing a reliever five weeks later, they reacquired McMichael, with Brian Bohanon heading to the West Coast. "I should ask for a raise for mental stability," McMichael said. He went 4–1 after being reacquired. The one loss was to the Dodgers, and Mlicki was the winning pitcher. In 1999, the Mets sent McMichael to California again, trading him to Oakland in the deal that brought Kenny Rogers to Queens. He ended his career with the Braves in 2000, his second go-round in Atlanta.

19. d. Luis Lopez
Lopez's sac fly brought home Carlos Baerga for a 2–1 win over the Yankees on June 28, 1998. With runners on the corners, Lopez sent a Ramiro Mendoza pitch to right field. Paul O'Neill caught the ball and, with his back to the play, threw it to the infield. Derek Jeter took it and threw to first trying to double up Brian McRae before Baerga could score the winning run. There was some confusion between the umps as to the timing of the Yankees' attempted double play before Baerga crossed home, but after a spirited discussion, the Mets had a win.

20. a. Edgardo Alfonzo
In 1999, Roger Cedeño stole 66 bases to set a club record and 40-year-old Rickey Henderson swiped 37 bags. Alfonzo was third on the team with nine, followed by Rey Ordoñez with eight and Benny Agbayani with six. Shawon Dunston was sixth with four steals despite only playing with the Mets for two months. Slow-footed John Olerud set a career-high with three stolen bases. The season before, the Mets only swiped 62 bases, with 20 coming from Brian McRae. And without Cedeño, the entire 2000 Mets team stole a total of 66 bases.

21. b. Pat Mahomes
With two on and two out in the 13th of a 4-4 game, Mahomes hit an 0-2 pitch from Scott Sanders to short left field to drive in Roger Cedeño. Two days earlier, he also had an RBI double off Steve Trachsel. With two outs in the bottom of the 13th, Sanders doubled off Mahomes, but the righty finished things off with a strikeout of

Jeff Reed. Mahomes improved to 5–0 and would finish the year 8–0. He also batted .313 on the season. His son Patrick II has won two National Football League Most Valuable Players as quarterback for the Kansas City Chiefs.

22. c. Robin Ventura
Ventura finished sixth, Piazza seventh, and Alfonzo eighth in the MVP voting. In his first season with the Mets, Ventura hit .301 with 32 home runs and 120 RBIs. He also flashed the leather at the hot corner, winning a Gold Glove award. Piazza hit .303 with 40 home runs and a team-record 124 RBIs, earning a Silver Slugger. Alfonzo hit .304 with 27 home runs and 108 RBIs, also winning a Silver Slugger and playing a great second base as part of the acclaimed "Best Infield Ever." Mets nemesis Chipper Jones was named MVP for the 1999 season.

23. d. Rey Ordoñez
Yes, the light-hitting shortstop was intentionally walked 12 times to lead the Mets. Piazza was intentionally walked 11 times. Ordoñez's walks were a byproduct of him batting in front of the pitcher. Ordoñez drove in a career-high 60 runs in 1999. As he did in each of his first four seasons, he hit one home run, with each blast coming in September. The 1999 blast was a grand slam. In 2001, Ordoñez would be intentionally passed 17 times, though he finished behind Piazza's 19 for the team lead. In Ordoñez's nine-season career, 64 of his 191 walks were of the intentional variety.

24. b. Orel Hershiser
The 40-year-old "Bulldog" swiped third base against the Expos on July 22. Even better for Hershiser, it was the night he won his 200th career game with a 7–4 decision in Montreal. It was the first stolen base by a Mets pitcher since Dwight Gooden in April 1991, also against the Expos. Hershiser, who batted .145 on the season, collected two hits off Dustin Hermanson. His steal came against lefty Steve Kline in the seventh inning just after Kline entered the game. It was one of eight bases Hershiser swiped in his 18-season career.

25. a. Willie Blair and Jeff Tam

On August 20, 1998, McGwire hit number 50 off Blair in the seventh inning of a 2–0 Cardinals victory in the first game of a doubleheader. Almost a year to the day later, August 22, 1999, McGwire hit number 50 off Tam, several innings after hitting number 49 off the Shea scoreboard versus Octavio Dotel in the Mets' 8–7 win, also in the first game of a doubleheader. Blair was 1–1 in 11 appearances (two starts) for New York in 1998. Tam was decision-less in nine appearances out of the bullpen in 1999. McGwire also hit his 400th career home run at Shea off Rick Reed on May 8, 1998. Blair went 60–86 with a 5.04 ERA in his 12-season career. Tam was 7–14 with a 3.91 ERA in six major league seasons.

2000s

1. Which Met hit a game-winning grand slam against the Cubs in Japan in 2000?
a. Jay Payton   b. Benny Agbayani   c. Jon Nunnally   d. Todd Pratt

2. Which Met played six positions for the team in 2000?
a. Melvin Mora   b. Joe McEwing   c. Todd Zeile   d. Matt Franco

3. Which member of "Generation K" returned to make two starts in 2000?
a. Paul Wilson   b. Jason Isringhausen   c. Bill Pulsipher
d. Bobby Jones

4. Who became the first Met with a 40-save season?
a. John Franco   b. Billy Wagner   c. Armando Benitez   d. Francisco Rodriguez

5. Who was the Mets' starting pitcher in the first game in New York after 9/11?
a. Bruce Chen   b. Kevin Appier   c. Glendon Rusch   d. Steve Trachsel

6. Which Met set the major league career pinch-hit record late in the 2001 season?
a. Lenny Harris   b. Rickey Henderson   c. Matt Franco
d. Darryl Hamilton

7. In 2002, who became the first Mets pitcher in six years to win his first two career starts?
a. Jeremy Griffith   b. Jae Weong Seo   c. Mike Bacsik
d. Aaron Heilman

8. Which 2004 Mets pitcher started a game in Atlanta the day after pitching in relief?
a. Dan Wheeler   b. Ricky Bottalico   c. Aaron Heilman
d. Matt Ginter

9. Which Met had walk-off hits in consecutive games against the Tigers in 2004?
a. Kaz Matsui   b. Ty Wigginton   c. Mike Cameron   d. Jeff Duncan

10. Which Met hit for the cycle in Montreal in 2004?
a. José Reyes   b. Craig Brazell   c. Victor Diaz   d. Eric Valent

11. In 2004, which Met homered in a team-record five straight games?
a. Cliff Floyd   b. Richard Hidalgo   c. Todd Zeile   d. Mike Piazza

12. Which Met tied a game against the Angels with a ninth-inning inside-the-park home run in 2005?
a. Marlon Anderson   b. José Reyes   c. Miguel Cairo   d. Anderson Hernandez

13. Which Mets reliever doubled off Randy Johnson and then scored from second on a bunt in 2005?
a. Heath Bell   b. Danny Graves   c. Felix Heredia   d. Dae-Sung Koo

14. Who was the Mets' Opening Day catcher in 2006?
a. Paul Lo Duca   b. Ramon Castro   c. Kelly Stinnett   d. Mike DiFelice

15. Which Mets pitcher got the decision in the 2006 NL East clincher?
a. Pedro Martinez   b. Tom Glavine   c. John Maine
d. Steve Trachsel

16. Which 2006 Met tied Todd Hundley's team record with 41 home runs in a season?
a. Carlos Beltrán   b. Carlos Delgado   c. David Wright
d. Mike Piazza

17. In 2007, who became the first Mets pitcher to win six of his first seven starts with the team?
a. Mike Pelfrey   b. Jorge Sosa   c. John Maine   d. Dave Williams

18. Which Met set the team record with 78 stolen bases in a season in 2007?
a. José Reyes   b. Carlos Beltrán   c. Lance Johnson   d. David Wright

19. In 2008, which Met set a franchise record with a 30-game hit streak?
a. David Wright   b. Moises Alou   c. José Reyes   d. Julio Franco

20. Which Met drove in a team record nine runs in one game against the Yankees in 2008?
a. Jeromy Burnitz   b. Carlos Delgado   c. Julio Franco
d. Xavier Nady

21. Which Met led the National League in games started and walks issued in the same year?
a. Kevin Appier   b. Oliver Perez   c. Mike Pelfrey   d. Steve Trachsel

22. Who was the last batter at Shea Stadium?
a. Brian Schneider   b. Ryan Church   c. Fernando Tatis
d. Damion Easley

23. In 2009, which Mets catcher stunned the Red Sox with a ninth-inning homer to beat Boston at Fenway Park?
a. Ronny Paulino   b. Mike Nickeas   c. Omir Santos   d. Henry Blanco

24. Who led the 2009 Mets with 12 home runs?
a. Daniel Murphy   b. Gary Sheffield   c. Fernando Tatis
d. Jeff Francoeur

25. Which Met pitched a shutout on the final day of the 2009 season?

a. Liván Hernandez   b. Pat Misch   c. Nelson Figueroa
d. Tim Redding

ANSWERS

1. b. Benny Agbayani

The outfielder's 11th-inning grand slam off Danny Young gave the Mets a 5–1 lead at the Tokyo Dome on March 30, 2000. It was the first at-bat of the season for Agbayani who almost didn't make the team out of spring training. He wouldn't hit another home run until another road game against the Cubs, this time at Wrigley Field on June 14. Agbayani hit 14 home runs in 1999 and 15 more in 2000. He was one of seven Mets in double-digit homers in 2000. His 13th-inning homer off Aaron Fultz won Game 3 of the NLDS against the Giants.

2. a. Melvin Mora

The versatile Mora played all three outfield positions and every infield position except first base. When Rey Ordoñez was lost for the season with an injury, Mora was tasked with replacing the Gold Glove winner who made four errors in 1999. Mora made six errors in his final month as Mets shortstop, including one in Boston on a potential game-ending double play. The Mets traded him for the sure-handed Mike Bordick, who helped the Mets win the pennant before returning to the Orioles as a free agent in 2001. Mora went on to become a two-time All-Star as an outfielder and third baseman.

3. c. Bill Pulsipher

After a stint with the Brewers, Pulsipher returned to the Mets in 2000 looking to earn a spot in the rotation. He didn't make the Opening Day roster but returned when Bobby Jones strained his right calf. Pulsipher started against the Giants on May 1, giving up four runs in three and one-third innings. Five days later, he gave up five runs on nine hits in three and one-third innings against the

Marlins. It was his final appearance with the Mets, though he would later pitch briefly for the Red Sox, White Sox, and Cardinals. He retired with a 13–19 record and a 5.15 ERA.

4. c. Armando Benitez
Benitez saved 41 games in 2000, the first Met to hit the 40-save mark. Benitez also led the league with 68 games finished. He saved 43 more the next season. He took over the closer role when John Franco was injured during the 1999 season, with Franco serving as set-up man when he returned. Franco's season high as a Met was 38 saves, set in 1998. As a member of the Marlins, Benitez led the league with 47 saves in 2004 and received some MVP votes. Benitez retired with 289 saves in his 15 seasons.

5. a. Bruce Chen
The lefty gave up one unearned run over seven innings in New York's 3–2 win over the Braves on September 21. Chipper Jones scored in the fourth when Mike Piazza was unable to handle Edgardo Alfonzo's throw from right after Ken Caminiti's double past first base. Chen, who made his debut with the Braves against the Mets in 1998, was acquired in late July 2001 from the Phillies for Turk Wendell and Dennis Cook as the Mets looked for starting pitching. He went 3–2 in 11 starts. The well-traveled Chen pitched for 11 teams in his 17 seasons and finished 82–81 with a 4.62 ERA in 400 games, including 227 starts.

6. a. Lenny Harris
With a single off the bench on October 6, 2001, off Montreal's Carl Pavano, Harris had his 151st career pinch-hit breaking Manny Mota's record in the Mets' 4–0 win at Shea. It was his third pinch-hit of the week, allowing him to set the record before the end of the season. Harris was a Met in 1998, played against them in the 1999 playoffs, and then was reacquired during the 2000 season. Harris was hitting .188 for Arizona at the time of the deal but hit .304 for the Mets the rest of the season. He played for eight teams in 17 seasons and finished with 212 pinch-hits.

7. c. Mike Bacsik

Bacsik, who came to the Mets from Cleveland along with Roberto Alomar, won each of his first two starts as a Met in July 2002, both against the Marlins, the second being a complete game at Shea. He was the first Mets rookie to pitch a complete game since Masato Yoshii in 1998. And he was the first Mets pitcher to win his first two major league starts since Robert Person in 1995–1996. Bacsik went 4-4 with a 5.77 ERA in two seasons with the Mets. The southpaw, whose father pitched in the majors for five seasons between 1975 and 1980, is best remembered for giving up Barry Bonds's record-breaking 756th home run while pitching for the Nationals in 2007.

8. a. Dan Wheeler

The 26-year-old reliever pitched one and one-third innings in an 18–10 loss to the Braves on April 7, 2004, and then was asked by Art Howe to make an emergency start the next night. Scott Erickson was slated to make his Mets debut but strained his left hamstring during his warm-up session leading to Wheeler, who threw 28 pitches the night before, taking the ball. He gave up three runs on six hits in four-plus innings, throwing 57 pitches in a game eventually won by Atlanta 10–8. Wheeler would pitch 13 seasons in the majors and appeared in the World Series for the Astros and Rays.

9. c. Mike Cameron

On June 18, 2004, Cameron homered off Danny Patterson to beat the Tigers 3-2. The next night, he singled against Patterson in the 10th to give the Mets a 4-3 win over Detroit. An All-Star outfielder with the Mariners, Cameron was signed by the Mets before the 2004 season and hit 30 homers in his first season in Queens, though he batted .231 with 143 strikeouts. Injuries limited him to 76 games in 2005 and he was traded to the Padres for Xavier Nady. Cameron retired after playing for eight teams in 17 seasons, winning three Gold Gloves and hitting 278 home runs.

10. d. Eric Valent

Valent, whom the Mets had taken in the Rule 5 draft the previous offseason, hit for the cycle in Montreal on July 29, 2004. In the second inning, Valent beat out an infield single and in the third, he doubled to left off starter Rocky Biddle. In the fifth he homered off Sun-Woo Kim. Facing Roy Corcoran in the seventh, Valent roped one down the right field line which he turned into a triple to complete the cycle. It was the second and final triple of Valent's career. The former Phillie and Red also hit all 13 home runs of his five-year career in 2004.

11. b. Richard Hidalgo

An in-season pickup from the Houston Astros, for whom he homered 44 times in 2000, Hidalgo went deep in five straight games for the 2004 Mets. He homered on July 1 in Cincinnati and then in each game of a sweep of the Yankees at Shea Stadium, followed by a long ball in Philadelphia. Hidalgo hit 21 home runs in just 86 games as a Met, despite a .228 batting average. He retired with 171 home runs, making him part of a rare group of players to hit 40 homers in a season but finish with fewer than 200 in their career. The list includes former Mets manager Davey Johnson.

12. a. Marlon Anderson

Pinch-hitting with the Mets down 2–1 to the Angels on June 11, 2005, Anderson hit Francisco Rodriguez's 3-1 pitch into the gap in right-center. Steve Finley's diving attempt failed and he incidentally kicked the ball away, leading to Anderson beating a play at the plate to tie the game. Cliff Floyd's walk-off homer an inning later gave the Mets a 5–3 win. It was one of 11 home runs Anderson hit in parts of four seasons with the Mets, seven of which came in 2005. Anderson hit a home run in his first major league at-bat as a member of the Phillies off Mel Rojas of the Mets in September 1998.

13. d. Dae-Sung Koo

Standing comically far from the plate in what Fox's Tim McCarver had just called "the biggest give-up at-bat" of the year, the lefty reliever and swinger lined a Randy Johnson pitch to deep center for a double against the Yankees and their future Hall of Famer on May 21, 2005. With Koo on second after only his second big-league at-bat (he looked at three strikes in his first one), José Reyes dropped a bunt in front of home to advance Koo to third. When the neophyte baserunner saw that catcher Jorge Posada had vacated his station to field the sacrifice, the pitcher known as Mr. Koo beat second baseman Robinson Cano's throw from first to the plate to give the Mets a seventh-inning 3–0 lead en route to a 7–1 Subway Series victory at Shea Stadium. The 35-year-old rookie from Korea received a standing ovation after striking out Cano to end the pitching portion of his afternoon in the eighth, but it turned out Mr. Koo's brilliant day in the Queens sunshine contained a dark underside, as he injured his shoulder on his slide home. Koo posted a 3.91 ERA with no decisions or saves in his brief big-league career to go with his .500 batting average.

14. a. Paul Lo Duca

The former Dodgers and Marlins All-Star was the first Mets Opening Day catcher not named Mike Piazza since Tim Spehr in 1998. He drove in the Mets' first run of the 2006 season with a third-inning single off Washington's Liván Hernandez in the Mets' 3–2 win. Lo Duca would make the All-Star team and bat .318, helping the Mets win the NL East for the first time since 1988. The 2006 season also marked the fifth in a row that Lo Duca caught at least 1,000 innings. He would spend two seasons with the Mets before splitting 2008 with the Nationals and Marlins.

15. d. Steve Trachsel

The slow-working right-hander pitched six and one-third shutout innings in the 4–0 win against the Marlins as the Mets clinched the division on September 18 at Shea. José Valentin homered twice to support Trachsel, who would finish the season 15–8 despite a 4.97 ERA. He even helped his own cause in a June 20 win against the Reds with a home run, his first in eight years. The division-clinching win was the last of 66 in six seasons as a Met for Trachsel. He spent the next two seasons with the Orioles and Cubs before retiring with a 143–159 record.

16. a. Carlos Beltrán

The center fielder tied Todd Hundley's team record with 41 home runs. His best power months were May and July when he hit 10 home runs. Beltrán didn't seem to love Shea Stadium, as he batted .317 with 26 homers and 78 RBIs on the road while batting .224 with 15 homers and 38 RBIs at home. He had 39 homers through August and hit number 40 on September 11 in Florida. On September 28, he homered off Atlanta's Peter Moylan in New York's 7–4 win. Beltrán slugged 149 home runs in seven seasons with the Mets, including the final one hit by a Met at Shea Stadium.

Carlos Beltrán

17. b. Jorge Sosa

The starter-reliever was invited to camp with the hopes of making it as a starter. When he joined the team in May 2007, he won each of his first three starts. After a loss to the Braves, he won three more, culminating with eight shutout innings against a dangerous Tigers lineup in Detroit. Unfortunately, Sosa would struggle over the next month-and-a-half, and Willie Randolph moved him to the bullpen. He went 2–2 with a 4.18 ERA in 28 games in relief. Sosa returned to the Mets in 2008, going 4–1 despite a whopping 7.06 ERA in 20 appearances.

18. a. José Reyes

The speedy shortstop shattered Roger Cedeño's previous record of 66 with 78 stolen bases in 2007. Reyes stole 60 and 64 the previous two seasons. Reyes tied and set the team record on August 22 in a loss to the Padres. In the bottom of the third, he stole second and third off Jake Peavy for steals 65 and 66. Then, in the fifth, he stole third again as part of a double steal with David Wright. Reyes was also caught stealing a league-high 21 times in 2007. His 408 stolen bases are the team record, ahead of Mookie Wilson's 281.

19. b. Moises Alou

The 41-year-old outfielder had the longest hitting streak of any New York player since Joe DiMaggio's legendary run of 56 consecutive games, spanning August 31 through September 27, 2008. While the Mets struggled in the final month of the season, Alou thrived, batting .402. His six-game hitting streak in late August was broken only by an unsuccessful pinch-hit appearance before beginning his 30-game streak. Injuries limited his time in New York and his 15 games in 2008 were the last of his career. The six-time All-Star retired with a .303 average and 332 home runs. His half-brother Luis Rojas later managed the Mets for two seasons.

20. b. Carlos Delgado

Serving as the designated hitter, Delgado drove in nine runs in the Mets' 15–6 romp at Yankee Stadium on June 27, 2008. In the fifth, Delgado drove in two runs with a double off Edwar Ramirez. The next inning, Delgado launched a grand slam versus Ross Ohlendorf. In the eighth, he hit a three-run homer off LaTroy Hawkins. The slugger had been slumping a bit and his average was down to .229 heading into the first game of a day-night doubleheader that would be played in both the Bronx and Queens, but Yankee Stadium seemed to get him back on track and he followed with a big July. Delgado finished the season, his last full season, with a .271 average, 38 homers, and 115 RBIs.

21. b. Oliver Perez

The erratic lefty made 34 starts for the Mets in 2008 but also walked 105 batters, leading the NL in both categories. He walked at least five batters in a game seven times, including eight walks in one game against the Rockies. His up-and-down season saw him finish 10–7 with a 4.22 ERA. He would struggle mightily in 2009 and 2010 but would reinvent himself as a crafty reliever. Perez became a hired gun, pitching in the postseason for Houston, Washington, and Cleveland. He played for eight teams in a 20-season career, ending with the 2022 Diamondbacks, by which time he was the last active member of the 2006 Mets NL East Division champs.

22. b. Ryan Church

The Mets' right fielder flied out against Matt Lindstrom to end New York's 4–2 loss, the team's 2008 playoff hopes, and 45 seasons at Shea Stadium all at once. New York trailed, 2–0, before Carlos Beltrán's homer tied it. But in the eighth, Wes Helms and Dan Uggla hit back-to-back homers to put the Marlins on top. With the Brewers' win, it meant the Mets needed to win Game 162 to force a Game 163 showdown with Milwaukee. Instead, the Mets failed to rally, leaving two runners on in the eighth and one in the ninth. Church was traded to the Atlanta Braves during the 2009 season for another outfielder, Jeff Francoeur.

23. c. Omir Santos

The light-hitting catcher, who would retire with seven home runs, took Jonathan Papelbon over the Green Monster to give the Mets a 3–2 lead and a shocking win on May 23, 2009. Mike Pelfrey and Josh Beckett dueled most of the night after Boston took a 2–1 lead in the first. In the ninth, Papelbon walked Gary Sheffield but then fanned two before Santos jumped on the first pitch from the Boston closer. Santos played parts of five seasons with Baltimore, the Mets, Detroit, and Cleveland. He played 96 of his 122 career games with the 2009 Mets. Six days after his homer at Fenway, he beat the Marlins with a walk-off single.

24. a. Daniel Murphy

It was the first season of Citi Field and Mets batters had to deal with the 15-foot-high Great Wall of Flushing in left field and outfield dimensions less inviting than they were accustomed to at Shea, so many would-be home runs either stayed in play or died on the warning track. There were also injuries to Carlos Beltrán and Carlos Delgado. Murphy had seven home runs through August but hit five the rest of the way to lead the team. Beltrán, David Wright, Gary Sheffield, and Jeff Francoeur hit 10 apiece. Wright led the team with 72 RBIs. In 1977, John Stearns, John Milner, and Steve Henderson led the Mets with 12 home runs apiece, meaning Murphy's final home run prevented the 2009 club from claiming a slice of power-depleted infamy.

25. c. Nelson Figueroa

In his final game with the Mets, Figueroa pitched a four-hit shutout while striking out seven and walking none in a 4–0 win over the Astros. Carlos Lee flied out to left to end the afternoon, as Jerry Manuel left the veteran pitcher in for 113 pitches. The Brooklyn native went 6–11 with a 4.28 ERA as a starter-reliever in two seasons. Figueroa was in the minors with the Mets in the 1990s before being traded to Arizona and played with four major league teams before pitching for his hometown Mets in 2008. He later worked as a pre- and postgame analyst for the club's games on SNY.

2010s

1. Which Met returned to Queens in 2010 after a four-year hiatus and hit his 100th home run?
a. Angel Pagan   b. Mike Jacobs   c. Ramon Castro
d. Jeff Keppinger

2. Who appeared in two games for the Mets in 2002 and was their Opening Day center fielder in 2010?
a. Jeff Duncan   b. Jason Tyner   c. Gary Matthews Jr.
d. Shane Spencer

3. Who was the Mets' Opening Day second baseman in 2011?
a. Luis Castillo   b. Daniel Murphy   c. Brad Emaus   d. Kaz Matsui

4. Which pitcher tossed a shutout on the final day of the 2011 season?
a. Miguel Batista   b. Nelson Figueroa   c. Johan Santana
d. R. A. Dickey

5. Who was the only Mets pitcher to homer in 2012?
a. Chris Young   b. Jeremy Hefner   c. Jon Niese   d. Collin McHugh

6. Who was the Mets catcher for Matt Harvey's debut in 2012?
a. Josh Thole   b. Travis d'Arnaud   c. Mike Nickeas   d. Rob Johnson

7. Who hit a grand slam on Opening Day in 2013?
a. Mike Baxter   b. Collin Cowgill   c. Omar Quintanilla
d. Lucas Duda

8. This Mets catcher hit nine home runs in April 2013. Who is he?
a. John Buck   b. Travis d'Arnaud   c. Ronny Paulino
d. Brian Schneider

9. Which pitcher finished the 2013 season with 14 consecutive scoreless outings, including eight saves?
a. Bobby Parnell   b. Frank Francisco   c. LaTroy Hawkins
d. Jeurys Familia

10. Which Met homered in the first inning of the 2014 opener off Stephen Strasburg?
a. Kirk Nieuwenhuis   b. Andrew Brown   c. Curtis Granderson
d. David Wright

11. Which Mets catcher hit a grand slam in his first game with the team?
a. Taylor Teagarden   b. Johnny Monell   c. Devin Mesoraco
d. Jason Phillips

12. Which Mets pitcher went five innings in a start after pitching out of the bullpen the night before?
a. Scott Rice   b. John Lannan   c. Daisuke Matsuzaka
d. Carlos Torres

13. Which two Mets led the 2015 team with 73 RBIs?
a. Yoenis Céspedes and Daniel Murphy
b. Lucas Duda and Daniel Murphy
c. Yoenis Céspedes and Lucas Duda
d. Curtis Granderson and Yoenis Céspedes

14. Which two Mets pitchers led the 2015 NL champions with 14 wins apiece?
a. Matt Harvey and Noah Syndergaard
b. Steven Matz and Matt Harvey
c. Bartolo Colón and Jacob deGrom
d. Noah Syndergaard and Jacob deGrom

15. In 2015, who became the first Met to homer three times in a home game?

a. Curtis Granderson   b. Kirk Nieuwenhuis   c. Lucas Duda
d. Yoenis Céspedes

16. Jeurys Familia struck out a future Mets teammate to clinch the 2015 NL East title. Who was he?

a. Neil Walker   b. Joe Panik   c. José Bautista   d. Jay Bruce

17. Which Met collected his first career hit off future Met José Quintana?

a. Ty Kelly   b. Matt den Dekker   c. Josh Thole   d. Jeurys Familia

18. Which Met tied a team record with six hits in a game against the Cubs in 2016?

a. Daniel Murphy   b. Yoenis Céspedes   c. Wilmer Flores
d. José Reyes

19. Which Met once hit a grand slam off Madison Bumgarner?

a. Justin Ruggiano   b. James Loney   c. T. J. Rivera
d. Alejandro De Aza

20. Which pitcher had to make an emergency start when Matt Harvey was suspended by the team?

a. Tommy Milone   b. Jamie Callahan   c. Sean Gilmartin
d. Adam Wilk

21. Which Met hit a walk-off grand slam against Tampa Bay in 2018?

a. Brandon Nimmo   b. José Bautista   c. Jordanny Valdespin
d. Jeff McNeil

22. Which Met hit a walk-off double in David Wright's final game?

a. Amed Rosario   b. José Reyes   c. Austin Jackson
d. Kevin Plawecki

23. Which two Mets homered in their first at-bat with the team two days apart in 2019?
a. Joe Panik and Adeiny Hechavarria
b. Rajai Davis and Aaron Altherr
c. René Rivera and Keon Broxton
d. Marcus Stroman and Sam Haggerty

24. Which Met hit .354 with 16 home runs in 71 games at Citi Field in 2019?
a. J. D. Davis   b. Pete Alonso   c. Robinson Cano   d. Jeff McNeil

25. Who hit a walk-off home run to end the 2019 season?
a. Pete Alonso   b. Joe Panik   c. René Rivera   d. Dom Smith

ANSWERS

1. b. Mike Jacobs
Jacobs was with the Mets early in the 2010 season and hit home run number 100 off Washington's Brian Bruney on April 11 at Citi Field. Jacobs hit .310 with 11 home runs in 30 games for the 2005 Mets, including one in his first major league at-bat, before being traded to the Marlins for Carlos Delgado after that season. The Mets signed Jacobs to a minor league deal for the 2010 season and he was the Opening Day first baseman after Daniel Murphy was injured. The 100th homer was the final one for Jacobs in his career, which ended with the Arizona Diamondbacks in 2012.

2. c. Gary Matthews Jr.
In 2002, Matthews pinch-hit for Al Leiter and pinch-ran for Mo Vaughn before being traded to the Orioles. The Mets reacquired Matthews from the Angels in January 2010 to compete with Angel Pagan for the starting center field job with Carlos Beltrán injured. Matthews hit .190 in 36 games before being released in mid-June. He played for seven teams in his 12-season career, including an All-

Star season with the Texas Rangers in 2006. His father was the 1973 NL Rookie of the Year with the Giants and was a 1979 All-Star as a member of the Braves.

3. c. Brad Emaus

Luis Castillo had been let go. Daniel Murphy struggled in the field. Luis Hernandez struggled at the plate. Justin Turner had minor league options. So Emaus, a Rule 5 pickup who hit .294 in spring training, was the Opening Day second baseman, batting seventh in the lineup. He was in the majors for only two-and-a-half weeks before being returned to the Toronto Blue Jays. Emaus hit .162 in 14 games for the Mets, his only major league service. But he did have a 1.000 fielding percentage in 53 chances. Turner became the primary second baseman in 2011, playing 78 games at the position.

4. a. Miguel Batista

The veteran right-hander threw a two-hit shutout against the Reds in a 3–0 win at Citi Field, a game in which Mike Baxter hit his first career homer. The journeyman threw 123 pitches in the victory. In his 18-year career, Batista went 102–115 with 11 teams, including the World Champion 2001 Diamondbacks. A starter-reliever, Batista pitched in the ninth inning of Game 2 of that year's NLDS and then started Game 3 and pitched six innings for the win. He also tossed seven and two-thirds shutout innings in Game 5 of the World Series at Yankee Stadium. The 2011 shutout was the fifth and final one of his career.

5. b. Jeremy Hefner

On May 29, 2012, Jeremy Hefner helped his own cause with a fourth-inning solo home run off Phillies righty Joe Blanton to extend the Mets' lead to 4–2. Hefner gave up three runs in six innings in the 6–3 victory, earning the first win of his major league career. In two seasons with the Mets, he would go 8–15 with a 4.65 ERA, returning to the team in 2020 as pitching coach after serving as a coach in the Twins organization.

6. d. Rob Johnson

Johnson was behind the plate in Arizona on July 26, 2012, when Harvey pitched five and one-third shutout innings and fanned 11 Diamondbacks. A former Mariner and Padre, Johnson signed a minor league deal with the Mets and was called up in May when Josh Thole suffered a concussion. He pitched against the Blue Jays late in a blowout loss. He went back and forth between the majors and minors, playing in 17 games for the Mets. Johnson spent 2013 with the Cardinals before trying to hang on with the Padres as a pitcher before arm injuries ended his career.

7. b. Collin Cowgill

Cowgill delivered a grand slam in the seventh inning off future Met Brad Brach in an 11–2 Mets thrashing of the Padres at Citi Field. The former A's and Diamondbacks outfielder was in his first game as a Met. He would play only 23 games with the Mets before being traded to the Angels in June, hitting a mere .180 with two home runs and eight RBIs while with New York. His other dinger also came at home during the first week of the season, a solo shot against the Marlins. Seven years after he wound down his big-league playing career in 2016, Cowgill reached the majors anew as first-base coach for the Cincinnati Reds.

8. a. John Buck

Buck made a good first impression after being acquired from Toronto in the deal which saw R. A. Dickey go to the Blue Jays for Noah Syndergaard and Travis d'Arnaud. Buck hit nine home runs and drove in 25 runs in April. His nine homers tied the record for a catcher in that month with Johnny Bench (1971) and Charles Johnson (2001). It was Buck's only season as a Met; he would finish with 15 home runs and 60 RBIs. He hit 134 homers in his 11-year career, which included a 2010 All-Star appearance.

9. c. LaTroy Hawkins

An underrated performer on a forgettable 2013 Mets team, Hawkins pitched to a 2.93 ERA in 72 appearances. He was one of the few bright spots in the second half, with a September ERA of zero.

Hawkins pitched 21 seasons in the majors, going 75–94 with a 4.31 ERA. Hall of Famer Kirby Puckett was the starting right fielder in his major league debut with the Twins in 1995 and his career ended with an appearance in the 2015 ALCS with the Blue Jays. Hawkins's 1,042nd and final regular-season appearance came against Tampa Bay, a franchise that did not exist when he entered the majors.

10. b. Andrew Brown

An outfielder who had previously spent time with St. Louis and Colorado, Brown showed some pop, hitting seven homers for the Mets in 2013. When Chris Young (the outfielder signed from the A's, not to be confused with the tall pitcher of the same name and era) tweaked a quad running out a grounder at the end of spring training in 2014, Brown found himself in Terry Collins's starting lineup. With two on and two out in the first, Brown swung at a 2-2 Strasburg pitch and sent it over the Citi Field wall in left center. The Nats would come back to win, 9–7, in ten innings, beginning a season of domination over the Mets, when they'd go 15–4. Brown would hit .182 in 19 games in what proved to be the final action of his big-league career.

11. a. Taylor Teagarden

Signed to a minor league deal in 2014, the Mets called up Teagarden two months into the season. On June 10, he hit an opposite-field grand slam off Milwaukee's Marco Estrada to give the Mets a 6–1 lead in what would be an eventual 6–2 victory. The former Rangers and Orioles catcher would bat .143 with one homer and five RBIs in nine games with the Mets before being sidelined with a strained hamstring. He would also play in eight games for the Cubs in 2015, finishing his career with 21 home runs.

12. d. Carlos Torres

A solid reliever for the Mets from 2013 to 2015, Torres was pressed into starting on August 18, 2014, against the Cubs. Torres had pitched one-third of an inning the day before. But for the Monday afternoon game, scheduled starter Bartolo Colón flew to the Dominican Republic to see his mother who was in critical condition.

With the Mets' Triple-A team located in Las Vegas, too far away to bring in an emergency starter on such short notice, Torres was tabbed. The multipurpose righty pitched five shutout innings, but his bullpen mates squandered his efforts in a 4–1 loss. Torres would go 17–18 in three seasons as a Met.

13. b. Lucas Duda and Daniel Murphy
The two lefty hitters led the division champs with 73 RBIs apiece. Duda had 27 home runs and Murphy hit 14. Duda recorded 17 RBIs during a 13-game stretch from late July to early August, including several clutch hits against the Nationals as the NL East race heated up. Murphy drove in 73 runs despite missing almost all of June with injury. Curtis Granderson had 70 RBIs and led the slow-footed Mets with 11 steals. Wilmer Flores was fourth on the team in RBIs with 59, while Céspedes had driven in 44 runs in 57 games after being acquired at the trading deadline.

Daniel Murphy

14. c. Bartolo Colón and Jacob deGrom
For deGrom, it was his first full season and it resulted in an All-Star appearance and a 14–8 record with a 2.54 ERA and 205 strikeouts,

good enough to place seventh in National League Cy Young voting. Colón had an up-and-down season: he won his first four starts; staggered to 10–11; and then won four straight decisions before losing his final two to finish 14–13 with a 4.16 ERA. The 42-year-old did have some throwback performances to his 2005 AL Cy Young winning season, like his September shutout in Miami, when he blanked the Marlins on 100 pitches *and* made highlight reels everywhere by tossing out a runner with a behind-the-back flip to first base.

15. b. Kirk Nieuwenhuis
The left-handed-hitting outfielder started the season in New York, was acquired by the Angels, but then returned to the Mets in July. On July 12, he hit his first homer of the season. And second. And third. In the second inning, he homered to left off Arizona's Rubby De La Rosa. The next inning, he took De La Rosa deep to left center. In the fifth, he homered to right off Randall Delgado. He drove four of the Mets' runs in the 5–3 win. Unbelievably, after no Met had accomplished the feat in more than 50 years, Duda hit three home runs at Citi Field on July 29 (a power display that got lost in the night's bigger story, Wilmer Flores shedding tears at shortstop when it was reported—prematurely and erroneously—that he'd been traded to the Brewers).

16. d. Jay Bruce
On September 26, 2015, Familia fanned Bruce to end the Mets' 10–2 laugher in Cincinnati and gave the Mets the division crown for the first time since 2006. Lucas Duda hit a grand slam in the first and Curtis Granderson added a solo shot in the second. Michael Cuddyer's two-run double made it 7–2 and David Wright added the exclamation point with a three-run homer in the ninth. Bruce would hit 46 home runs in parts of three seasons in two tours of duty with the Mets, including 29 in 2017 before being traded to Cleveland in August. He was back with the Mets after signing as a free agent for the 2018 season and was traded to the Seattle Mariners in a deal that brought Edwin Diaz and Robinson Cano to the Mets that December. Bruce, a three-time All-Star, hit 319 home runs in his 14-season career.

17. a. Ty Kelly

The utility infielder delivered his first hit on Memorial Day 2016 with a fifth-inning single up the middle off the White Sox All-Star. Matt Harvey outdueled Quintana, with Neil Walker homering in the 1–0 win. Kelly spent eight seasons in the minors before being called up to the majors, playing 855 minor league games and having 3,000 at-bats while awaiting his big break. Kelly would also start at third base for Team Israel in the World Baseball Classic. He retired from pro baseball in 2019, but continued to play for Team Israel and competed in the 2020 Summer Olympics.

18. c. Wilmer Flores

Flores went 6-for-6 in a 14–3 shellacking of the Cubs at Citi Field on July 3, 2016. In the second inning, he homered off Jon Lester and then added an RBI single off the tall lefty later in the inning. In the fourth, he singled off Spencer Patton, and in the fifth, he took him deep for a two-run homer. In the seventh, he singled off Joel Peralta. Facing Cubs catcher Miguel Montero, who was working as a mop-up pitcher, Flores singled to left in the eighth for his sixth hit. The Mets' popular Venezuelan infielder tied his countryman Edgardo Alfonzo's record, which had been set on August 30, 1999, in a 17–1 drubbing of Houston. Alfonzo was 6-for-6 with three home runs in that game at the Astrodome.

19. a. Justin Ruggiano

The outfielder who the Mets picked up shortly after he was released by the Texas Rangers a month earlier took the Giants' southpaw star over the wall at the San Francisco stadium formerly known as AT&T Park in the third inning of his fourth game with the Mets on August 18, 2016. The Giants came back to win, 10–7, with Bumgarner hitting a home run off Jacob deGrom. Ruggiano was with six teams before the Mets signed him in response to center fielder Juan Lagares's thumb injury. Ruggiano himself went on the disabled list, as it was then called, with a strained hamstring at the beginning of August. His homer off Met-killer MadBum came in his first game following that DL stint. The journeyman couldn't stay healthy, however, and he played in only eight games as a Met. The shoulder injury that curtailed his regular season also kept him out of the Wild Card game when the Mets were blanked by Bumgarner in a classic pitchers' duel.

20. d. Adam Wilk
With Matt Harvey suspended three games for violating team rules, the Mets called on southpaw Adam Wilk to make his first start since 2015 (when he was a member of the Angels) on Sunday, May 7, 2017, against the Marlins at Citi Field. Wilk, who had been with Triple-A Las Vegas, flew on Saturday from Las Vegas to Denver to Albuquerque, where he found out he would be needed the next afternoon in New York. Wilk gave up a first-inning three-run homer to Giancarlo Stanton and would be tagged for six runs (five earned) in three and two-third innings in his only appearance as a Met. The Mets were shut out on one hit, a sixth-inning single by René Rivera against starter José Urena in the 7–0 loss.

21. b. José Bautista
Acquired by the Mets late in his career, Bautista hit nine homers in 83 games with the Mets. On July 6, 2018, the slugger crushed a two-out grand slam in the ninth inning to give the Mets a 5–1 win over the Rays. With runners on second and third and two outs, Tampa Bay decided to intentionally walk Brandon Nimmo to load the bases and have Chaz Roe go after the Mets' right fielder, who sent the first pitch over the left-center-field fence and into Citi Field's second deck. Bautista was a six-time All-Star who twice led the American League in homers as a Blue Jay, but this was his first-ever walk-off home run. He retired with 344 home runs, including seven grand slams.

22. c. Austin Jackson
September 29, 2018, was an emotional sendoff for David Wright in the captain's final game. The Mets and Marlins apparently didn't want it to end, playing a scoreless game into the 13th inning. With runners on first and second and one out, Jackson lined Javy Guerra's first pitch to left center for the winning run. It was the final hit of Jackson's nine-season career, which saw him play for

seven teams. He had been drafted by the Yankees and was sent to the Tigers in a deal that included Curtis Granderson going to the Yankees and Max Scherzer landing with the Tigers. In 57 games with the Mets, Jackson hit .247 with three home runs.

23. b. Rajai Davis and Aaron Altherr
Davis was not a home run threat, having hit 62 in his 14-season career, though he did famously tie Game 7 of the 2016 World Series for Cleveland with an eight-inning long ball, but on May 22, 1999, against the Nationals, he delivered a pinch-hit three-run homer off Sean Doolittle in New York's 6–1 win at Citi Field (a game he made by investing in a $243 Uber ride from Allentown, Pennsylvania, on the afternoon he was summoned from Triple-A). Altherr—who Mets fans might remember making the last out of the game that clinched their club's 2016 wild card—hit 37 homers in his six-season career, though he showed pop by hitting 19 for the 2017 Phillies. On May 24, against the Tigers, Altherr's pinch-hit homer off Buck Farmer gave the homestanding Mets a 7–6 lead, though Detroit would rally to win. The righty swinger had no more homers left in his bat as a major leaguer but baseball-starved early risers during the COVID-19 pandemic woke to watch him star in Korean Baseball Organization games ESPN televised around dawn every morning in its quest to give sports fans something/anything fresh to consume. As a member of the 2020 NC Dinos, Altherr belted 31 long balls out of KBO parks.

24. a. J. D. Davis
The Mets acquired Davis, a part-time third baseman and outfielder for the Houston Astros, before the 2019 season. He hit .307 with 22 homers and 57 RBIs, saving his best for the fans at Citi Field. In only the second home game of the year, he hit two homers against Washington. On August 21, he beat Cleveland with a walk-off hit against future Met Brad Hand. The following week, he homered in three consecutive games against the Cubs. Davis would hit .278 with 37 home runs in four seasons with the Mets before being traded to the Giants for Darin Ruf during the 2022 campaign.

25. d. Dom Smith

Down to their last out, Dom Smith's three-run homer off Atlanta lefty Grant Dayton gave the Mets a 7–6 win on September 29, 2019. It was a fitting end for a Mets team that pulled off a number of late wins and went from 40–50 at the All-Star break to a 46–26 second half of the season. It was Smith's 11th homer for the year. In the top of the 11th, Chris Mazza induced an inning-ending double play on the first pitch he threw, meaning the righty recorded a win while throwing just one pitch. Smith would hit 46 home runs in six seasons as a Met, including 10 in the COVID-shortened 2020 season.

2020s

1. Who homered on Opening Day 2020 in the Mets' 1–0 win?
a. Pete Alonso   b. Yoenis Céspedes   c. Rene Rivera
d. Michael Conforto

2. Which Met set the team record with a .616 slugging percentage in 2020?
a. Pete Alonso   b. Wilson Ramos   c. Dom Smith
d. Michael Conforto

3. Which former Cy Young winner went 1–7 with a 5.64 ERA for the Mets in 2020?
a. Rick Porcello   b. Dallas Keuchel   c. Max Scherzer
d. Justin Verlander

4. In 2021, which Met became a brief folk hero with two walk-off fielder's choices?
a. Jonathan Villar   b. Chance Sisco   c. Patrick Mazeika
d. Albert Almora

5. Which Met hit six homers in 2021, with five either tying games or giving the Mets the lead?
a. José Peraza   b. Billy McKinney   c. Brandon Drury
d. Mason Williams

6. Which Met went 6–0 with a 0.95 ERA in 2021?
a. Miguel Castro   b. Aaron Loup   c. Edwin Diaz   d. Drew Smith

7. Which Mets pitcher batted .364 in 2021?
a. Jacob deGrom   b. Marcus Stroman   c. Taijuan Walker
d. Trevor Williams

8. Which Mets pitcher collected his first base hit in his 14th major league season?
a. Carlos Carrasco   b. Tommy Hunter   c. Joey Lucchesi   d. Rich Hill

9. Which Mets pitcher gave up 10 earned runs in a loss to the Braves in 2021?
a. Joey Lucchesi   b. Corey Oswalt   c. Jerad Eickhoff
d. Jordan Yamamoto

10. Who was the Mets' Opening Day starter in 2022?
a. Max Scherzer   b. Chris Bassitt   c. Carlos Carrasco
d. Tylor Megill

11. Which Met homered in the 2022 home opener but was let go at the end of April?
a. Nick Plummer   b. Travis Blankenhorn   c. Matt Reynolds
d. Robinson Cano

12. Which Met earned a save against the Dodgers by retiring Mookie Betts, Freddie Freeman, and Will Smith in a one-run extra-inning game in 2022?
a. José Butto   b. Adonis Medina   c. Colin Holderman
d. Chasen Shreve

13. Which Mets position player pitched two scoreless innings in a 2022 game against the Braves?
a. Travis Jankowski   b. Darin Ruf   c. Michael Perez
d. Daniel Vogelbach

14. Which Met set a career high with 15 wins in 2022?
a. Taijuan Walker   b. Carlos Carrasco   c. Marcus Stroman
d. Chris Bassitt

15. Which Met hit for the cycle in 2022?
a. Francisco Lindor   b. Brandon Nimmo   c. Starling Marte
d. Eduardo Escobar

16. Which Met beat the Yankees with a walk-off single in 2022?
a. Brandon Nimmo   b. Starling Marte   c. Francisco Lindor
d. Luis Guillorme

17. Who pitched six innings of perfect ball as the Mets clinched a 2022 playoff spot?
a. Carlos Carrasco   b. Taijuan Walker   c. Max Scherzer
d. Chris Bassitt

18. Which Met had a 30–30 season in 2023?
a. Francisco Lindor   b. Brandon Nimmo   c. Starling Marte
d. Pete Alonso

19. Which former Yankees star played three games for the 2023 Mets?
a. Luke Voit   b. Dellin Betances   c. Greg Bird   d. Gary Sanchez

20. Who was the only pitcher to win at least 10 games for the 2023 Mets?
a. Kodai Senga   b. Tylor Megill   c. Max Scherzer   d. José Quintana

21. Which Met had the team's only hit on Opening Day 2024?
a. Joey Wendle   b. DJ Stewart   c. Starling Marte   d. Zack Short

22. In 2024, which three-time All-Star surrendered Pete Alonso's 200th career home run?
a. Sonny Gray   b. Liam Hendriks   c. Mike Mikolas   d. Corbin Burnes

23. Which Mets catcher helped turn the first game-ending 2-3 double play in major league history in 2024?
a. Francisco Alvarez   b. Tomás Nido   c. Luis Torrens
d. Omar Narváez

24. Which pitcher led the Mets in wins in 2024?
a.   Luis Severino   b. Sean Manaea   c. Jose Quintana
d. David Peterson

25. Which Met hit a two-run homer in the ninth to beat the Braves and help the Mets clinch a 2024 wild card berth?
a.   Francisco Lindor   b. Mark Vientos   c. Brandon Nimmo
d. Pete Alonso

ANSWERS

1. b. Yoenis Céspedes
After missing the 2019 season, Céspedes hit the seventh-inning homer off Atlanta's Chris Martin that accounted for all the scoring in New York's Opening Day win on July 24 at an empty Citi Field. Four pitchers combined to blank Atlanta in manager Luis Rojas's debut. The good times wouldn't last for Céspedes. After batting .161 in eight games, he went AWOL for a game in Atlanta before it was announced that he was opting out of the season over COVID concerns. It was the last action for him in the majors. The outfielder hit 165 home runs in eight seasons.

2. c. Dom Smith
The first baseman-outfielder posted a .616 slugging percentage in 50 games, hitting 10 home runs in 177 at-bats. In August, Smith batted .329 with six home runs and 21 RBIs, earning him enough MVP support to finish 13th in NL balloting despite the Mets finishing out of that COVID-shortened year's expanded playoff picture. The former first-round draft pick wouldn't be able to capture that success in either of his next two seasons with the Mets as his playing time dwindled. In 2022, he hit .194 with no homers before moving on to the Nationals and later the Red Sox. The Mets' slugging percentage record for a 162-game season is held by Mike Piazza, who had a .614 mark in 2000. Piazza hit 38 home runs during that pennant-winning campaign and finished third in the MVP voting.

3. a. Rick Porcello

The 2016 AL Cy Young winner, who narrowly edged out Justin Verlander, struggled mightily in 12 starts with the Mets. Considered a low-risk, one-year signing, the right-hander was crushed by the Braves in his first start of the season and never improved much from there. Porcello's lone bright spot came in Washington on August 5 when he beat the Nationals, 3–1, for the 150th win of his career. But the native New Jerseyan and lifelong Mets fan lost his final six decisions of the COVID-shortened season, his final year in the majors. The 2020 team made a similar addition with former Cardinals All-Star Michael Wacha, who compiled results similar to those posted by Porcello: 1–4 with a 6.62 ERA in eight games, including seven starts.

4. c. Patrick Mazeika

The backup catcher had two walk-off RBIs before even collecting his first career hit. In the 10th inning, with the bases loaded and one out against Arizona on May 7, Mazeika hit one between the mound and home. Diamondbacks pitcher Stefan Crichton's desperation flip to the plate was late and offline, allowing Pete Alonso to score. Four days later, batting in a tie game with runners on the corners and one out, Mazeika hit a chopper to first. Trey Mancini's throw home was too late to get Jonathan Villar and Mazeika had another walk-off RBI. He was the first player in 100 years to record multiple walk-off RBIs before his first hit.

5. a. José Peraza

You might say this was a second baseman suited for his times, for José Peraza demonstrated a unique ability to reset his internal clock and get himself in sync with a peculiarity of pandemic-era baseball. Doubleheaders were shortened to seven innings apiece in 2020 and 2021 in deference to health concerns, and twice Peraza came through with big hits in the seventh innings that were designed to be final innings. In the opener of a July 4 doubleheader at Yankee Stadium, his seventh-inning two-run double thrust the Mets ahead en route to a 10–5 Subway Series win. Three days later at Citi Field, in another of those *the seventh is the new ninth* situations, Peraza homered off Brewers closer Josh Hader to ensure New York would take Milwaukee to "extra innings," in this case the eighth (when the Mets would emerge victorious). Unfortunately for Peraza, the Mets didn't play abbreviated twinbills every day, and the well-traveled journeyman wound up batting only .204 in 2021, his final season in the majors.

6. b. Aaron Loup

The lefty reliever had the year of his life in 2021, pitching to a 0.95 ERA in 65 outings. After giving up runs in three straight May appearances, his only slump of the season, Loup became practically unhittable, surrendering six earned runs the entire season and only two after May 21 (one of those on an ultimately harmless homer to then Nationals wunderkind Juan Soto). Loup had previously pitched for four teams before joining the Mets, but never with this kind of success. His sub-one ERA in more than fifty innings of work was only the 13th in major league history. Relievers residing in that statistical pantheon include Hall of Famer Dennis Eckersley and 300-save men Fernando Rodney and Jonathan Papelbon. Loup, a free agent after 2021, turned his great season into a two-year, $17 million deal with the Angels, with whom his ERA returned to a more pedestrian level.

7. a. Jacob deGrom

In addition to being the game's most dominant pitcher, deGrom also helped himself at the plate. While always a respectable hitting pitcher during his career, the ace was a genuine two-way threat in 2021, going 12-for-33 at the plate with six RBIs. He had at least one hit in 10 of his first 13 starts, including a pair of multi-hit games. In his best performance of the year, a 15-strikeout shutout against the Nationals in which he gave up two hits, he also notched two hits of his own, an RBI, and scored two runs. All that was missing from his offensive ledger in 2021 was a home run. DeGrom hit three long balls in his career, the last of them coming in August 2019 against the Braves.

Jacob deGrom

8. b. Tommy Hunter

The reliever who debuted in 2008 had been 0-for-4 in his career at the plate before a clean single against the Braves on May 18, 2021. In the final season before the designated hitter came to the National League to stay, Hunter singled to left off Atlanta's Tucker Davidson. Hunter even scored when Jonathan Villar homered two batters later. Hunter was 13-4 in 2010 as a starter with the Rangers but was later converted to the bullpen during his time with the Orioles. The last Mets pitcher with a base hit before the permanent DH rule went into effect was Tylor Megill, who doubled off Atlanta's Huascar Ynoa on October 1, 2021.

9. c. Jerad Eickhoff

With Mets pitching stretched thin, the right-hander made a spot start against the Braves on July 27, 2021, and gave up 10 runs in three and one-third innings. He walked five and gave up seven hits, including three home runs in a 12-5 loss to Atlanta. Austin Riley's grand slam was the big blow. The game was part of a critical five-game series before the trade deadline when the Mets missed an opportunity to put some distance between themselves and the Braves. Instead, the Braves took three of five to jump-start what became a rush toward another division title, while the Mets fell out of contention. This game turned out to be Eickhoff's Met swan song. The former Phillies starter was 0-2 with an 8.69 ERA in five appearances, including four starts.

10. d. Tylor Megill

With Jacob deGrom out with a stress reaction in his right scapula and Max Scherzer pushed back a game with hamstring soreness, Megill made the Opening Day start in 2022. Megill pitched five shutout innings in Washington in a 5-1 win over the Nationals on April 7. He retired the last eight hitters he faced and fanned six batters to begin the Buck Showalter era in style. Megill went 4-0 in April, including the night he threw five shutout innings at the front of a combined no-hitter against the Phillies. But Megill wouldn't win a game the rest of the season, missing substantial time due to injuries. He pitched out of the bullpen late in the year, finishing with a 4-2 record.

11. d. Robinson Cano

The veteran second baseman homered off Arizona's Zach Davies in the 2022 home opener, a 10–3 Mets win on April 15. Cano, who was suspended for the 2021 season for using performance-enhancing drugs, started 2022 going 8-for-41 in the first month of the season and was designated for assignment. He played with the Padres and Braves in 2022 but batted only .150. In his career, the eight-time All-Star hit 335 home runs and won two Gold Gloves. Cano was acquired from the Mariners in the deal that also brought Edwin Diaz to Queens. In letting Cano go, the team ate most of the $40 million he was owed.

12. b. Adonis Medina

The rookie righty who had pitched a handful of games for the Philadelphia Phillies the previous two seasons earned his first career save at Dodger Stadium in a 5–4 win on June 5, 2022. Edwin Diaz pitched a scoreless eighth, but Seth Lugo blew the save in the ninth. New York scored in the 10th and Buck Showalter called on Medina and his 5.19 ERA for the final three outs. With Gavin Lux on second base to start the frame (automatic runners in extra innings having become the MLB standard in 2020), Medina retired Mookie Betts on a flyout and Freddie Freeman on a groundout. Trea Turner reached on catcher's interference and stole second, but Medina fanned Will Smith to end the game and secure his only major league save as of 2024.

13. b. Darin Ruf

After Mets pitchers gave up 13 runs in six innings of an eventual 13–1 loss at Atlanta on August 15, Buck Showalter called on the outfielder and first baseman to save the bullpen. Ruf pitched a 1-2-3 seventh inning, retiring Ronald Acuña Jr., Dansby Swanson, and Austin Riley in order. He also pitched a scoreless eighth, working around a two-out single. Ruf, who began his career with the Phillies, was acquired from the San Francisco Giants in August 2022 for J. D. Davis and three minor leaguers. Ruf, who hit a career-high 16 home runs in 2021 (and had starred in Korea for a few years before that), would struggle mightily with the Mets, batting .152 with no homers in 28 games. He went back to the Giants in 2023 before moving on to the Brewers, where a knee injury ended his season in June.

14. d. Chris Bassitt

In his lone season with the Mets, Bassitt won a career-high 15 games after being acquired from the A's. He was 7–7 at the end of July before winning eight of nine decisions, including two straight against the Phillies and one against the Dodgers. Unfortunately, his Mets tenure ended on a down note. He failed to make it out of the third inning in his final regular season start in a critical loss to the Braves and then lost the deciding game of the Wild Card series against the Padres. He signed with the Blue Jays as a free agent following the season.

15. d. Eduardo Escobar

The third baseman accomplished the feat on June 6 in an 11–5 win at San Diego. He singled off Blake Snell in the first inning and doubled off him in the fourth. In the eighth, he hit a two-run homer off Craig Stammen. With one more chance in the ninth, Escobar tripled to right off Tim Hill. He had a season-high six RBIs in the West Coast win. Though he struggled for much of the year, he enjoyed a hot September, batting .321 with eight home runs and 25 RBIs. Escobar was traded to the Angels during the 2023 season.

16. b. Starling Marte

Marte's single off Wandy Peralta gave the Mets a 3–2 win on July 27. The Mets led, 2–0, with Max Scherzer pitching seven shutout innings before reliever David Peterson gave up a two-run homer to Gleyber Torres in the eighth. In the ninth, Eduardo Escobar doubled and moved to third on a bunt. With runners on the corners and one out, Marte brought home Escobar. The hit raised Marte's average to .300. His regular season, in which he was named to the NL All-Star team, ended after he was hit by a pitch in Pittsburgh on September 6 (he would return for the postseason). The Mets lineup slumped without him, and the Braves overtook New York to win the division.

17. c. Max Scherzer

The Mets clinched a playoff berth for the first time in six years with a 7–2 win over the Brewers on September 19. Mad Max retired all 18 Brewers he faced, striking out nine. Tylor Megill gave up a leadoff double in the seventh to spoil the combined no-hit bid. In his first season as a Met, Scherzer went 11–5 with a 2.29 ERA and 173 strikeouts. He asked for a trade during the 2023 season and was sent to the Rangers, where he helped Texas win its first World Series despite missing time due to various injuries.

18. a. Francisco Lindor

The Mets' star shortstop had the first 30–30 season of his career with 31 home runs and 31 stolen bases. He stole his 30th base in

D. BENJAMIN MILLER, CCO, VIA WIKIMEDIA COMMONS

Francisco Lindor

late September against the Phillies, the first time he reached 30 in his career. In the final homestand of the season, Lindor hit his 30th home run in a two-homer performance against the Marlins, both off Johnny Cueto. He was the first Met since David Wright with a 30–30 season and finished in the top 10 of the NL MVP voting for his season. Lindor also became the third Puerto Rican–born player to accomplish the feat.

19. d. Gary Sanchez
The former Yankees phenom who was an October regular in the Bronx was signed to fill a catching void when Tomás Nido sat on the injured list with dry-eye syndrome. Sanchez's time with the Mets lasted six at-bats. In his last game with the Mets, he was charged with a passed ball and also dropped a popup. Nido's return from the IL made Sanchez expendable. Rookie Francisco Alvarez's emergence also factored into the team's decision to drop the ex-star. Sanchez was picked up by the Padres for whom he hit six home runs in his first two weeks. Sanchez would hit 19 home runs in 72 games with San Diego in 2023.

20. a. Kodai Senga
Due to injuries, ineffectiveness, and trades that depleted the rest of the rotation, the MLB rookie who starred in Japan was the only Met with at least 10 wins, going 12-7 when all was said and done. The ghost fork specialist won three straight starts in August to improve to 10-6. Senga received run support unfamiliar to most Mets pitchers in recent years, with the team scoring 31 runs in the three games, capped off by a 13-run outburst in St. Louis on August 19. Max Scherzer tied for second in the team with nine wins despite being suspended for 10 games for using a sticky suspension on his hand against the Dodgers in late April and being traded away in late July.

Kodai Senga

21. c. Starling Marte

The right fielder, who returned to the lineup after an injury-plagued 2023 season, homered in the second inning off Milwaukee's Freddy Peralta to give the Mets a 1–0 lead. Unfortunately, it would be the final Mets hit of the day as the Brewers came back to win, 3–1. It was the first Opening Day loss for the Mets since 2019. The game also marked the first time the Mets opened the season against the Brewers. Only two other Mets reached base, including DJ Stewart, who was picked off following a second-inning walk. The quiet Mets bats would begin the season 0–5 with only a ninth-inning rally against the Tigers sparing them the indignity of an 0–6 start.

22. a. Sonny Gray

Alonso, the Mets' slugging first baseman, launched his 200th homer off the Cardinals' starter in the fifth inning on April 27 in a 7–4 St. Louis win at Citi Field, a day otherwise marked by the debut of the Mets' slate-gray and purple-accented City Connect uniforms. Alonso entered 2024 hitting at least 40 home runs three times in his career, including 53 in his rookie season of 2019, when Alonso led walk-off celebrations by tearing off his teammates' jerseys, whatever color those shirts happened to be. The milestone shot was his eighth homer of the month. The blast was also Alonso's first career hit against Gray, who made for an apt mound presence on the afternoon the Mets unveiled their new concrete-themed look. Gray previously put together All-Star seasons with the A's, Reds, and Twins; pitched in three postseasons; and finished second in 2023's AL Cy Young voting when he was with Minnesota. He was also on the 2017 Yankees playoff team. The right-hander finished second in the 2023 AL Cy Young voting with the Twins.

23. c. Luis Torrens

The Mets held a most tenuous 6–5 lead in London on June 9 against the Phillies. Alec Bohm had just walked with the bases loaded, which meant the sacks were still full when slugger Nick Castellanos came to bat with only one out. Castellanos proceeded to dribble a Drew Smith pitch a bit in front of the plate. Torrens pounced on the ball; turned around to step on home; and then threw to first to complete the game-ending double play that earned the Mets a split of their first-ever UK series. Smith was awarded the save, but it was the quick-acting catcher who really rescued the Mets. Torrens's nifty fielding in London, along with a knack for throwing out opposing baserunners and a bat more powerful than initially anticipated (he'd crushed two home runs in a game against the Nationals in Queens shortly before the Mets crossed the pond), helped the recently promoted pickup supplant both Tomás Nido and Omar Narváez as primary backup to Francisco Alvarez.

24. b. Sean Manaea

After joining the Mets as a free agent in the offseason, the lefty won a team-high 12 games, going 12–6 with a 3.47 ERA in 32 starts. He was the model of consistency, going 6–3 with a 3.46 ERA in the first half of the season and 6–3 with a 3.48 ERA in the second. Manaea was 6–3 at Citi Field and 6–3 on the road. He led the team with 184 strikeouts, including a game high of 11, accomplished against the Twins and Diamondbacks. Luis Severino won 11 games, while Jose Quintana and David Peterson won 10 apiece. Reed Garrett won eight games out of the bullpen.

25. a. Francisco Lindor

The star shortstop's two-run homer off Atlanta's Pierce Johnson on September 30 gave the Mets an 8–7 lead they would hold on to in the 161st game of the season to clinch a playoff berth. The Mets needed one win in a doubleheader against the Braves on the final day of the regular season to clinch. In the opener, the Mets trailed, 3–0, after seven innings before exploding for six runs on six hits in the eighth. After the Braves rallied back with four runs in the bottom of the frame to take a 7–6 lead, Lindor's 33rd home run of the season put the Mets back on top to stay.

ALL-STARS

1. Who was the first Met selected to an All-Star team?
a. Richie Ashburn   b. Duke Snider   c. Chris Cannizzaro
d. Al Jackson

2. Ron Hunt was the first Met to start an All-Star Game in 1964, at Shea Stadium. Who is the only other second sacker to start an All-Star Game in a Mets uniform?
a. Felix Millan   b. Jeff McNeil   c. Edgardo Alfonzo   d. Jeff Kent

3. Who did Tom Seaver strike out to close out the 1967 All-Star Game?
a. Tony Conigliaro   b. Carl Yastrzemski   c. Bill Freehan
d. Ken Berry

4. Who did Jerry Koosman strike out to end the 1968 All-Star Game?
a. Mickey Mantle   b. Carl Yastrzemski   c. Bill Freehan
d. Reggie Jackson

5. Off which Orioles pitcher did Cleon Jones get a base hit in the 1969 All-Star Game, several months before facing him in the World Series?
a. Dave McNally   b. Jim Palmer   c. Mike Cuellar   d. Pat Dobson

6. Which one of these catchers did not represent the Mets in the All-Star Game at least four times?
a. Jerry Grote   b. John Stearns   c. Gary Carter   d. Mike Piazza

7. Who was the first Mets pitcher to start an All-Star Game?

a. Tom Seaver   b. Jerry Koosman   c. Jon Matlack
d. Dwight Gooden

8. Which future Met struck out Willie Mays in the 1972 All-Star Game?

a. Dean Chance   b. Mike Marshall   c. Mike Torrez   d. Mickey Lolich

9. Who was the first Met to record an All-Star victory?

a. Tom Seaver   b. Tug McGraw   c. Jon Matlack   d. Sid Fernandez

10. True or False: Tom Seaver wore a Dodgers batting helmet in the 1976 All-Star Game.

11. Which Met acquired in the 1977 trade for Tom Seaver made the 1978 All-Star team?

a. Pat Zachry   b. Doug Flynn   c. Steve Henderson   d. Dan Norman

12. Which Met tied the 1979 All-Star Game with an eighth-inning homer and gave the NL the lead with a ninth-inning bases-loaded walk?

a. Lee Mazzilli   b. John Stearns   c. Joel Youngblood
d. Willie Montañez

13. Who homered off Dwight Gooden in the 1986 All-Star Game?

a. Don Mattingly   b. Cal Ripken Jr.   c. Lou Whitaker
d. Wally Joyner

14. Which former Met teammate homered off Tom Seaver in the 1981 All-Star Game?

a. Rusty Staub   b. Ken Singleton   c. Dave Kingman   d. Amos Otis

15. Which Met earned the save in the 1987 All-Star Game?

a. Dwight Gooden   b. Ron Darling   c. Sid Fernandez
d. Jesse Orosco

16. Which former Met gave up a hit to Bobby Bonilla in the 1993 All-Star Game?

a. Rick Aguilera   b. David Cone   c. Ron Darling   d. Jesse Orosco

17. Which future Mets batterymate did Mike Piazza, then with the Dodgers, homer off in the 1995 All-Star Game?

a. Al Leiter   b. David Cone   c. Orel Hershiser   d. Kenny Rogers

18. Which Met struck out Ken Griffey Jr. and Mark McGwire back-to-back in the 1997 All-Star Game?

a. John Franco   b. Rick Reed   c. Bobby Jones   d. Al Leiter

19. Which Mets pitcher was selected to two All-Star Games but didn't pitch in either one?

a. Al Leiter   b. Rick Reed   c. Armando Benitez   d. Turk Wendell

20. Who is the only Mets player to start an All-Star Game as a designated hitter?

a. Darryl Strawberry   b. Mike Piazza   c. Carlos Beltrán
d. David Wright

21. Which starting pitcher did Mike Piazza catch in the 2004 All-Star Game?

a. Roger Clemens   b. Tom Glavine   c. Randy Johnson
d. Greg Maddux

22. Which former Met did David Wright homer off in the 2006 All-Star Game?

a. Scott Kazmir   b. Kenny Rogers   c. Kris Benson   d. Mike Hampton

23. Matt Harvey started the first All-Star Game played at Citi Field in 2013. Who was the Dark Knight's mound opponent on that occasion?

a. Max Scherzer   b. Felix Hernandez   c. Justin Verlander
d. Yu Darvish

24. Mets skipper Terry Collins managed the National League All-Star team in 2016 but neither of his available Mets players got into the game. One was Jeurys Familia. Who was the other Met who didn't make an appearance?
a. Matt Harvey   b. Jacob deGrom   c. Curtis Granderson
d. Bartolo Colón

25. Which one of the following players never represented the Mets in an All-Star Game?
a. Ed Kranepool   b. Joel Youngblood   c. Kevin McReynolds
d. Daniel Murphy

ANSWERS

1. a. Richie Ashburn
The Hall of Fame outfielder was in New York for just one season, but on two All-Star Game rosters with the Mets. The 1962 season was the last of four in which two All-Star Games were played to increase the money going into the players' pension fund. Ashburn didn't play in the first game, a 3–1 NL win in Washington. Twenty days later, Ashburn had a pinch-hit single off Detroit's Hank Aguirre and came around to score on a Dick Groat single in the AL's 9–4 win at Wrigley Field. Ashburn retired after the 1962 season, in which he batted .306.

2. b. Jeff McNeil
After Ron Hunt in 1964, it would be 58 years until another Mets second baseman started the Midsummer Classic as McNeil replaced injured Marlins second baseman Jazz Chisholm. Comfortable at several positions, McNeil had two plate appearances—he was hit by a pitch from Toronto's Alex Manoah and grounded out against Texas' Martin Perez in the American League's 3–2 win at Dodger Stadium. McNeil finished the season with a league-best .326 batting average. Edgardo Alfonzo in 2000 and Daniel Murphy in 2014 previously represented the Mets at second base in the All-Star

Game, but the respective starters for the NL in those years were Jeff Kent and Chase Utley.

3. d. Ken Berry

It took a 15th inning, but the Mets' lone representative finally entered the All-Star Game to close out a 2–1 win. After Tony Perez's homer gave the NL the lead, the 22-year-old rookie Seaver got Tony Conigliaro to fly out, walked Carl Yastrzemski, and got Bill Freehan to fly out before striking out Ken Berry. It was the 30th strikeout of the game. The 1967 contest was the only All-Star appearance for Berry, the White Sox outfielder who would later play for the Angels, Brewers, and Indians. For Seaver, it was the first of 12 All-Star appearances, including nine in a Mets uniform.

4. b. Carl Yastrzemski

It was fitting in the Year of the Pitcher that the All-Star Game would finish 1–0. With two outs in the ninth, Jerry Koosman came in to replace Ron Reed and fanned the Red Sox star to end the game. Willie Mays scored the only run of the game in the first inning by singling; taking second on an error and third on a wild pitch; and scoring on a double play. The game at the Astrodome also saw Tom Seaver strike out five batters in two innings, including Mickey Mantle, making his final All-Star Game appearance. Koosman would also be an All-Star in 1969.

5. a. Dave McNally

Three months before the "shoe polish" play in the World Series, Jones and McNally faced off in Washington with Jones singling to center in the sixth inning. It was a good Midsummer Classic for Jones, who earlier singled off Mel Stottlemyre and scored two runs in the Senior Circuit's 9–3 victory. He became the first Met with two base hits in an All-Star Game. Bud Harrelson did it in 1970, but it wouldn't be accomplished again until Lance Johnson matched the total in 1996. It was the lone All-Star appearance of Jones's career. He batted .340 in 1969, good for third in the NL.

6. a. Jerry Grote

The longtime Mets catcher was a two-time All-Star, getting the start in 1968 at his old home in the Astrodome and making the 1974 squad before injuries ended his season early. He caught five shutout innings from Juan Marichal and Don Drysdale in the 1968 game. John Stearns represented the Mets four times between 1977 and 1982, a bright spot in the dark days of the franchise. Gary Carter made the All-Star team in each of his first four seasons with the Mets from 1985 to 1988. Mike Piazza was a seven-time All-Star while a Met, being selected for the team each year he was with the team except for 2003.

7. a. Tom Seaver

Gil Hodges tabbed his ace to start the 1970 All-Star Game (despite using him for a batter out of the bullpen in the game before the break). Coming off the World Series title, Seaver was 14–5 with a 2.40 ERA at the break. Tom Terrific pitched three shutout innings in Cincinnati, striking out four and only allowing one hit. The NL would win, 5–4, scoring three in the ninth to tie it and winning in the 12th when Pete Rose ran over Ray Fosse in a play at the plate. Seaver would lead the league in ERA and strikeouts in 1970.

8. d. Mickey Lolich

In his first All-Star Game with the Mets, Willie Mays went hitless in two at-bats including a strikeout against Tigers ace Mickey Lolich. It was the 23rd of 24 career All-Star Games for the Say Hey Kid, who made 24 rosters in 20 seasons because of the two-game format from 1959 to 1962. Only Hank Aaron made the All-Star roster in more seasons. Mays was a sentimental choice in his later seasons and appeared in the 1973 game as a pinch-hitter, striking out against Sparky Lyle. Lolich would pitch for the Mets in 1976 after being acquired for Rusty Staub, going 8–13 with a 3.22 ERA.

9. b. Tug McGraw

The Mets' lefty fireman pitched scoreless ninth and 10th innings in the 1972 All-Star Game, recording the win in the 4–3 victory at Atlanta Stadium. He struck out three batters in the ninth, including

Tug McGraw

Reggie Jackson, to keep it 3–2. The NL tied the game off Wilbur Wood in the bottom of the frame. McGraw pitched a 1-2-3 10th and won when Joe Morgan's single off Dave McNally drove in Nate Colbert with the winning run. McGraw finished the season with a 1.70 ERA. He would make the 1975 star as a member of the Phillies, though he didn't appear in the NL's 6–3 victory.

10. True
Tom Seaver was almost traded to the Dodgers before the 1976 season, and though that didn't happen, he did wear a Dodgers helmet while batting in the Midsummer Classic. In the 1970s and 1980s it was fairly common for pitchers who weren't expecting to hit to wear an All-Star teammate's helmet. Seaver came to the plate wearing Steve Garvey's helmet though he didn't bat like Garvey, striking out against Catfish Hunter. Over the years, Nolan Ryan batted wearing a Padres helmet, Lee Smith batted in an Expos helmet, Dave Stieb batted in a Mariners helmet, and Charles Nagy batted wearing a Rangers helmet. The Mets' 1981 representative, outfielder Joel Youngblood, also grabbed a non-Mets helmet (Braves) before coming to the plate and popping out.

11. a. Pat Zachry
Acquired in the deeply unpopular Midnight Massacre, Zachry won 10 games in the first half of the season, reaching 10-3 with a 2.90 ERA after a two-hit shutout against the Phillies on July 4. He was the lone Mets All-Star, but he didn't get into the game. His season ended later in July when, in a moment of frustration, he tried kicking a batting helmet in the dugout, missed, caught his spike in the wooden steps, and wound up with a hairline fracture in his foot. Zachry went 41–46 in six seasons with the Mets. The righty pitched for the Phillies and Dodgers before retiring.

12. a. Lee Mazzilli
With the National League trailing 6–5, Mazzilli led off the eighth inning with a home run off Texas closer Jim Kern. Then, with two outs in the ninth inning, Mazzilli worked a bases-loaded walk

against reigning Cy Young winner Ron Guidry to put the NL on top. Bruce Sutter then closed out the AL in the bottom of the ninth at the Kingdome. Despite Mazzilli's heroics, the game is best remembered for two great throws from Dave Parker—one to nail Jim Rice at third in the seventh and one to get Brian Downing at the plate to preserve the tie in the eighth.

13. c. Lou Whitaker
The Tigers' second baseman launched a two-run homer to right off Gooden at the Astrodome in the AL's 3–2 win. It was the fourth of five consecutive All-Star Games for the Brooklyn-born Whitaker, who spent his entire 19-season career with Detroit. For Gooden, it was his third All-Star Game in three seasons but he would only make one more team, in 1988. The Midsummer Classic matchup was a preview of the Fall Classic, as Gooden pitched against Roger Clemens, who also would face him in Game 2 of the World Series at Shea. The two would later become teammates with the Yankees.

14. b. Ken Singleton
The veteran outfielder homered off the Reds' Tom Seaver, his Mets teammate from 1970 to 1972, before he was traded to the Expos in the Rusty Staub deal. The 1981 All-Star Game in Cleveland was the first game following the end of the players' strike, and the fans at Cleveland Stadium jeered the players during introductions. Baltimore's Singleton, a three-time All-Star, did his best to earn cheers by breaking a scoreless tie with the second-inning homer, but it was a future Met who was the hero. Gary Carter, the MVP, hit two home runs in the NL's comeback, and Mike Schmidt's two-run shot off Rollie Fingers allowed a 5–4 win.

15. c. Sid Fernandez
It took about three-and-a-half hours, but El Sid finally made it into the 1987 All-Star Game, with Davey Johnson calling on the lefty to close out the National League's 2–0 win in the 13th inning. Tim Raines's two-run triple broke the scoreless tie and Fernandez got Dave Winfield on a forceout to end the game. The NL improved

to 8–0 in extra-inning games in All-Star history. Fernandez had shown his ability to pitch out of the bullpen in 1986 when his two-and-one-third shutout relief innings in Game 7 of the World Series kept Met hopes alive.

16. a. Rick Aguilera
Though not beloved by the Flushing faithful, Bonilla made the 1993 All-Star team, a bright spot on the field for a Mets team that would lose 103 games. Bonilla replaced his former Pirates teammate Barry Bonds in left and singled off former Met Rick Aguilera in the top of the eighth in the AL's 9–3 win in Baltimore. It was the third straight All-Star appearance for Aguilera, who went to Minnesota in the 1989 deal that brought Frank Viola to the Mets. Bonilla would again represent the Mets in the 1995 All-Star Game in Texas, less than three weeks before being traded to the Orioles.

17. d. Kenny Rogers
Piazza tied the 1995 Midsummer Classic in the seventh inning with an opposite-field shot off the Rangers southpaw. The NL was held to three hits in the game, but won, 3–2, on solo home runs by Craig Biggio, Piazza, and Jeff Conine in the sixth, seventh, and eighth innings. It was the third straight All-Star appearance for Piazza. The game marked Rogers's first appearance; he would wait nine years before making it back in his third tour of duty with the Rangers. After joining the Mets, Piazza would catch Rogers once the team acquired the lefty for their 1999 playoff run.

18. c. Bobby Jones
Jones got his money's worth in his lone All-Star Game appearance, getting out of the eighth inning by striking out Griffey and McGwire in the AL's 3–1 win in 1997. He was the first Met to pitch in an All-Star Game since David Cone five years earlier. Jones was 12–3 with a 2.29 ERA after a 1–0 win over the Pirates on June 20, but he wouldn't earn another decision in his favor for nearly two months, finishing the season 15–9. Jones would win 74 games in eight seasons with the Mets before signing with the Padres, where he spent two seasons.

19. b. Rick Reed

The pitcher known as a poor man's Greg Maddux was a two-time All-Star, in 1998 and 2001. Reed won seven of eight starts in May and June 1998, including one against the Marlins managed by Jim Leyland, who selected him for the All-Star team. Reed pitched on the Sunday before the Midsummer Classic and didn't appear in the slugfest at Coors Field, won 13–8 by the AL. Bobby Valentine selected Reed for the 2001 game in Seattle, but the righty didn't appear because of a stiff neck. Reed posted a 59–36 record with the Mets from 1997 until he was traded to the Minnesota Twins for outfielder Matt Lawton a few weeks after his 2001 All-Star Game selection.

20. c. Carlos Beltrán

Batting second as the starting designated hitter for the National League in the 2011 All-Star Game, Carlos Beltrán went 1-for-2 in their 5–1 victory at Chase Field in Phoenix. After striking out and batting left-handed against Jered Weaver of the Los Angeles Angels of Anaheim in his first at-bat, Beltrán switched to the right side and reached on an infield single against Texas Rangers lefty C. J. Wilson leading off the fifth inning. He eventually scored on Prince Fielder's three-run homer later in the inning. It was Beltrán's fourth and final All-Star appearance as a Met (he was selected to the game nine times in his 20-year career), as he was traded to the San Francisco Giants for then-minor league pitcher Zack Wheeler two weeks later.

21. a. Roger Clemens

The Rocket jumped out to a 9–0 start in his first year as an Astro and was a no-brainer to start in Houston. And when Mike Piazza was voted as the starting catcher, it made for strange bedfellows as the heated rivals had been through a July 2000 beaning and Clemens throwing a piece of Piazza's bat at the catcher in the World Series later that year. Working together didn't go much better. Clemens gave up six runs on five hits in his one inning of work. Manny Ramirez and Alfonso Soriano both homered. Piazza also didn't help Clemens offensively, going 0-for-2 with a strikeout.

22. b. Kenny Rogers

After finishing as runner-up to Ryan Howard in the 2006 Home Run Derby, David Wright hit the first pitch he saw from Kenny Rogers in the All-Star Game for a home run. Wright became the first Met since Lee Mazzilli to homer in the Midsummer Classic. The game marked the first of seven All-Star appearances for Wright, who would become a staple at the Senior Circuit hot corner for much of the next decade. The AL would win, 3–2, with a two-out ninth-inning rally against Trevor Hoffman. Wright hit 19 homers in the first half of the season and only seven after the break, with some people blaming the Home Run Derby for his power outage.

23. a. Max Scherzer

While Matt Harvey's start at Citi Field received most of the attention, Jim Leyland tabbed his Detroit Tigers ace Max Scherzer, who raced out to a 13–0 record in 2013, to start for the American League. He was the first pitcher to start 13–0 since Roger Clemens was 14–0 for the 1986 Red Sox. The Detroit star pitched a 1-2-3 inning, setting down Brandon Phillips, Carlos Beltrán, and Joey Votto in the AL's 3–0 win. Scherzer would finish the season 21–3, including a win over Harvey and the Mets at Citi Field in late August. He was rewarded with his first of three Cy Young Awards.

24. d. Bartolo Colón

The Mets were the only National League team not to have a player appear in the 2016 All-Star Game at San Diego's Petco Park, won by the American League, 4–2. Mets manager Terry Collins, who skippered the National League stars by virtue of winning the 2015 pennant, didn't use Jeurys Familia or Bartolo Colón. He said after the game that he would have only used Familia if the Nationals were leading and held back Colón in the event the game went into extra innings. Two other Mets, Yoenis Céspedes, voted in as a starting outfielder, and pitcher Noah Syndergaard, had been selected to the game, but were nursing injuries and could not participate in the Midsummer Classic.

25. c. Kevin McReynolds

Left fielder Kevin McReynolds was a durable and consistent member of the Mets after joining the team in a blockbuster trade with the San Diego Padres after the 1986 championship season. In his first three seasons in New York, he averaged 148 games played, 26 home runs, 90 RBIs, and 15 stolen bases and led National League outfielders in assists on two occasions. In 1988, he helped the Mets win a division title, setting career highs with 99 RBIs and 21 stolen bases (and wasn't caught once). He hit two home runs in the seven-game NLCS loss to the Dodgers. His numbers dipped a bit in 1991, and he was traded after that season to the Kansas City Royals in a deal for former Cy Young Award winner Bret Saberhagen. McReynolds returned to the Mets in 1994 for his final major league season.

POSTSEASON

1. Which Met batted .538 in the 1969 National League Championship Series?
a. Cleon Jones   b. Art Shamsky   c. Wayne Garrett   d. Al Weis

2. Which Met had a team-high five RBIs in the 1969 NLCS?
a. Tommie Agee   b. Ed Kranepool   c. Ken Boswell   d. Rod Gaspar

3. Which Mets pitcher had two singles in a 1969 NLCS game?
a. Tom Seaver   b. Jerry Koosman   c. Gary Gentry   d. Nolan Ryan

4. Which Met batted .455 in the 1969 World Series?
a. Al Weis   b. Donn Clendenon   c. Ron Swoboda   d. Tommie Agee

5. Who scored the winning run in Game 4 of the 1969 World Series?
a. Ed Charles   b. Rod Gaspar   c. J. C. Martin   d. Cleon Jones

6. Which Met pitched a two-hit shutout against the Reds in the 1973 NLCS?
a. Tom Seaver   b. Jerry Koosman   c. Jon Matlack   d. George Stone

7. Who delivered the go-ahead single in the 12th inning of Game 2 of the 1973 World Series?
a. Willie Mays   b. Rusty Staub   c. Bud Harrelson   d. Tom Seaver

8. Which Met won Game 3 of the 1986 NLCS with a ninth-inning home run?
a. Wally Backman   b. Mookie Wilson   c. Tim Teufel
d. Lenny Dykstra

9. Which Met pitched five shutout innings of relief in Game 6 of the 1986 NLCS?
a. Jesse Orosco   b. Roger McDowell   c. Rick Aguilera   d. Doug Sisk

10. Which Met was the first designated hitter for the team in a World Series game?
a. Danny Heep   b. Kevin Mitchell   c. Howard Johnson
d. Gary Carter

11. True or False: Jesse Orosco drove in the last run of the 1986 World Series.

12. Which Met batted .429 in the 1988 NLCS?
a. Gregg Jefferies   b. Lee Mazzilli   c. Lenny Dykstra
d. Howard Johnson

13. Who hit the walk-off home run to clinch the 1999 NLDS?
a. Edgardo Alfonzo   b. Rickey Henderson   c. Todd Pratt
d. Matt Franco

14. Who is the Mets' all-time leader in postseason hits, runs, and RBIs?
a. Darryl Strawberry   b. Edgardo Alfonzo   c. Mike Piazza
d. David Wright

15. Who hit two of the Mets four homers in the 1999 NLCS?
a. Robin Ventura   b. Mike Piazza   c. John Olerud   d. Melvin Mora

16. Which Met was the winning pitcher in the "Grand Slam Single" game in the 1999 NLCS?
a. Octavio Dotel   b. Orel Hershiser   c. Kenny Rogers
d. Pat Mahomes

17. Which Met delivered a bases-clearing double to put the 2000 NLCS out of reach?

a. Benny Agbayani   b. Timo Perez   c. Mike Hampton   d. Todd Zeile

18. Which Met hit a three-run homer in the ninth inning off Mariano Rivera in Game 2 of the 2000 World Series?

a. Jay Payton   b. Kurt Abbott   c. Bubba Trammell   d. Todd Pratt

19. Which former Dodger delivered the go-ahead single in the clinching game of the 2006 NLDS?

a. Shawn Green   b. José Valentin   c. Paul Lo Duca
d. Marlon Anderson

20. Who hit two home runs in one 2006 NLCS game?

a. Carlos Delgado   b. Carlos Beltrán   c. David Wright   d. Cliff Floyd

21. Which Met hit four home runs in the 2015 NLCS and was named MVP?

a. Yoenis Céspedes   b. Daniel Murphy   c. David Wright
d. Kelly Johnson

22. Which former Met won Game 1 of the 2015 World Series out of the bullpen?

a. LaTroy Hawkins   b. Shaun Marcum   c. Chris Young   d. Oliver Perez

23. Who was the first Met to reach base against Madison Bumgarner in the 2016 wild card game?

a. T. J. Rivera   b. René Rivera   c. Ty Kelly   d. James Loney

24. Which Met pitched in all three games of the 2022 Wild Card Series and recorded a save?

a. Seth Lugo   b. Edwin Diaz   c. Adam Ottavino   d. Trevor May

25. In 2024, which Mets infielder set a team record with 14 RBIs in one postseason?

a. Francisco Lindor   b. Mark Vientos   c. Jose Iglesias   d. Pete Alonso

ANSWERS

1. b. Art Shamsky

The lefty-swinging right fielder went 7-for-13 starting against right-handed pitchers in Gil Hodges's platoon system. He went 3-for-4 in Game 1, 3-for-5 in Game 2, and 1-for-4 in the series-clincher. Shamsky hit 13 of his 14 home runs in the regular season off right-handers, though he was no slouch against southpaws, batting .409 (9-for-22) when given the chance. Despite his tremendous performance against the NL West champion Braves, he started only one game in the World Series against Baltimore's lefty-heavy rotation. In the NLCS, several Mets had their proverbial hitting shoes on—Cleon Jones batted .429 and Ken Boswell, Tommie Agee, and Wayne Garrett each batted .333 or higher.

2. c. Ken Boswell

The second baseman, who drove in 32 runs all season, had five RBIs in the final two games against the Braves. Boswell drove in 11 runs during the final month of the season, and his hot hitting carried into the NLCS. His two-run homer off Milt Pappas gave the Mets an 8–0 lead in Game 2 and his two-run blast off Pat Jarvis gave the Mets a fourth-inning lead in Game 3. He also added an RBI single off George Stone in his next at-bat. Yet Gil Hodges stuck to his successful platooning ways, and Boswell would sit on the bench in four of the five World Series games, going 1-for-3 without an RBI in Game 3.

3. d. Nolan Ryan

In 27 seasons, Ryan had three postseason hits, and two of them came in Game 3 of the 1969 NLCS. Ryan hit .103 (3-for-29) in 1969, but in the bottom of the fifth, he led off with a single versus Pat Jarvis and scored when Wayne Garrett homered to give the Mets a 5–4 lead. In the bottom of the eighth, Ryan singled off Cecil Upshaw. Coincidentally, the light-hitting Ryan would again have a multi-hit game against the Braves (two singles) in a 20–6 win in Atlanta on August 7, 1971. The pitching legend would retire with a .110 career batting average.

4. a. Al Weis

The "mighty mite" of the Mets who batted .215 in 1969 could have won World Series MVP for his offensive heroics. With two on and two out in the ninth inning of Game 2, Weis delivered the go-ahead single off Dave McNally as the Mets evened the Series. Down 3–2 in the seventh inning of Game 5, Weis homered off McNally to tie the game, allowing the on-deck batter, Jerry Koosman, to stay in the game and setting the stage for a 5–3 win. Weis had only six career homers to that point, but one had come off McNally in 1964.

5. b. Rod Gaspar

Gaspar came around to score from second when Orioles pitcher Pete Richert's throw to first on J. C. Martin's bunt hit Martin's wrist and rolled away from Davey Johnson covering first base. The play was controversial, as replays showed Martin was running inside the baseline. The rookie outfielder was pinch-running for Jerry Grote, who led off the inning with a pop-fly double. Al Weis was then intentionally walked, and Martin pinch-hit for Seaver. Gaspar was a standout defensively for the 1969 Mets, leading the team in outfield assists with 12 despite starting in only 44 games. He also led National League outfielders in double plays with six.

6. c. Jon Matlack

The young lefty helped the Mets bounce back from a heartbreaking Game 1 defeat with a two-hit shutout in New York's 5–0 Game 2 win. Cincinnati right fielder Andy Kosco's two singles were the only hits off the Mets southpaw. Matlack, who threw three shutouts in the regular season, dueled Don Gullett with the Mets leading, 1–0, through eight innings on Rusty Staub's fourth-inning home run. The Mets broke it open with four runs in the ninth against Tom Hall and Pedro Borbon. The performance was even more impressive, given that during the regular season Matlack went 1–3 with a 4.26 ERA in four regular season starts against the Big Red Machine.

7. a. Willie Mays

It was the Say Hey Kid who singled off Rollie Fingers to bring in Bud Harrelson and give the Mets a 7–6 lead in Game 2. The Mets would go on to win the wild four-hour-and-13-minute game, 10–7, to even the Series. Mays would have only one more at-bat in the final five games of the Series. The all-time great went 3-for-10 in the 1973 postseason, his last hurrah before retiring. He helped the Mets clinch the pennant against the Reds in Game 5 of the NLCS, delivering an infield RBI single and coming around to score in New York's four-run fifth inning.

8. d. Lenny Dykstra

Nails's two-run homer off Dave Smith gave the Mets a 6–5 win in the first playoff game at Shea in 13 years and a 2–1 lead in the NLCS. Dykstra didn't show much power with eight home runs in the regular season, but one had been a ninth-inning homer at the Astrodome off Mike Scott. The center fielder would continue to prove himself as a clutch October performer with two homers in the World Series against Boston. He also homered in the 1988 NLCS against the Dodgers. In the 1993 postseason, Dykstra homered six times for the Phillies, with two dingers against the Braves in the NLCS and four home runs in the World Series against the Blue Jays.

9. b. Roger McDowell

The right-hander held the Astros scoreless from the ninth through the 13th inning when any hiccup would have put the Mets in a Game 7 against Mike Scott. He retired 14 of the 15 batters he faced, with lone baserunner Kevin Bass being caught stealing after singling. The sinkerballer recorded 10 outs by groundout. The reliable McDowell had been 0–3 with a 4.15 ERA in six regular-season appearances against Houston. He went 14–9 during the year, pitching 128 innings and even received some MVP votes. McDowell was also the winning pitcher in Game 7 of the World Series. He also had a solid season for the 1988 division champs before being traded to the Phillies alongside Lenny Dykstra in June 1989.

10. a. Danny Heep

In Game 3 of the 1986 World Series, the Mets' first Series game using the designated hitter, it's fitting it was a batter with the initials DH doing the hitting. And in the first inning with the bases loaded,

Heep singled to score Keith Hernandez and Gary Carter after they escaped a botched Boston rundown. It was the only hit of the Series for Heep, who batted .091 in the Fall Classic. Heep would win another World Series with the 1988 Dodgers and was also on the 1990 AL East champion Red Sox team. Despite 1973 being the first season of the DH in the American League, pitchers hit for themselves in that year's Mets–A's World Series.

11. True

Davey Johnson put on a butcher boy play with Orosco faking a bunt and swinging away against Al Nipper. Orosco's bouncing ball went up the middle, which had been vacated by the Red Sox infielders. Orosco had shown himself to be capable with the bat, with three hits and two sacrifice bunts in nine plate appearances in 1985. The sacrifice situation in Game 7 was seemingly obvious; NBC's Joe Garagiola saying you could bet the house Orosco would bunt. After the single, his partner Vin Scully replied that Garagiola lost his house. Orosco would play through 2003 without collecting another hit, though he did draw a walk in a 1997 game during his tenure with the Orioles.

12. c. Lenny Dykstra

Dykstra had six hits in the 1988 NLCS, including five in the final three games. His three-run homer off Tim Belcher in the Mets' 7–4 Game 5 loss cut the Dodgers' 6–0 lead in half in the fifth inning, and in the eighth, he doubled and came around to score to cut it to 6–4. In Game 6, he singled and scored a run as the Mets pushed the lead to 5–1 for David Cone. He later singled off former teammate Jesse Orosco. He also singled off Orel Hershiser in Game 7. The following June, Dykstra was sent to Philadelphia with Roger McDowell for Juan Samuel in one of the worst trades in team history.

13. c. Todd Pratt

Todd Pratt hit a home run in his very first Met at-bat, in 1997 versus the Marlins (off 1999 NLDS Game 4 starter Al Leiter, no less) and he hit a home run in his very last Met at-bat, in 2001 against the Phillies, the team the Mets were days away from trading him to.

But no long ball off the bat of the backup catcher his teammates called Tank meant more in Met lore than the one that defeated the Diamondbacks and catapulted the Mets into an NLCS showdown with the Braves. Despite his moment of pure playoff thunder and those blasts that bookended his New York stay, Pratt wasn't exactly a slugger, having hit all of 17 home runs in five seasons as a Met reserve, including a mere three homers in the season leading up to his autumnal swing for the ages, none since that April. He figured to sit behind Mike Piazza throughout October, but the superstar got hurt; the understudy was pressed into service; and the next thing Shea Stadium knew, a Matt Mantei pitch was disappearing over the center-field wall, just out of the reach of the outstretched glove of defensive whiz Steve Finley. The Mets had earned their first postseason series win since they secured the 1986 World Championship, and the name "Todd Pratt" became synonymous with home runs in Flushing. As a fitting enough postscript, Pratt returned to Shea with the Phillies about a month after his departure from Queens and reminded the fans what he could do now and then by homering off Mets lefty Bruce Chen.

14. b. Edgardo Alfonzo
Fonzie was one of the most reliable Mets in October, with 26 hits, 17 RBIs, and 15 runs scored in the 1999 and 2000 postseasons. He hit two homers in his first playoff game, including the game-winning grand slam in Arizona. The ever-smooth infielder also homered in the Game 4 clincher. Alfonzo hit safely in 12 of New York's 14 playoff games in 2000, posting a .444 average in the NLCS, and drove in a run in each of the Mets' four wins against the Cardinals. As a member of the Giants, he hit .529 in their 2003 NLDS loss to the Marlins.

15. c. John Olerud
The first baseman homered off John Smoltz and Greg Maddux during the NLCS. Olerud's home run off Smoltz broke a scoreless tie in Game 4 and his two-run homer in the first inning of Game 5 off Maddux would produce the only Mets runs scored until the

15th inning. Olerud had slugged a grand slam off Maddux at Shea two-and-a-half weeks earlier in a game critical to the Mets' playoff chances. The only other Mets homers in the pitching-dominated series were Melvin Mora's shot in Game 2 (giving Mora a home run in the postseason before he ever hit one in the regular season) and Mike Piazza's game-tying blast amidst the drama of Game 6—a home run that scored Olerud directly after Olerud himself had plated Rickey Henderson with a key single of his own. This epic faceoff versus the Mets' archrivals marked Olerud's final action as a Met, as the Washington state native returned home and signed with the Mariners in the offseason.

16. a. Octavio Dotel

The rookie right-hander gave up one near-fatal run in three innings and picked up the win when the Mets rallied in the bottom of the 15th. Dotel had been largely overlooked on Bobby Valentine's depth chart, pitching only in Game 2 of the NLDS and failing to retire four of the five batters he faced. When Game 5 of the NLCS reached the 13th, Dotel was summoned for what amounted to the long haul. The righty, Valentine's *ninth* pitcher of the rain-soaked marathon, escaped damage in his first inning of work when a relay from the outfield cut down a potential run at the plate. But Keith Lockhart's RBI triple in the 15th put the Braves three outs from the World Series and positioned Dotel as the pitcher of record, pending what the Mets did in the bottom of the inning. It was Dotel's final appearance with the Mets before he was traded to Houston after the season as part of the deal that brought Mike Hampton and Derek Bell to New York. The Dominican native would prove an enduring figure in the majors, pitching for a total of 13 different teams in 15 seasons, finally reaching and winning a World Series as a member of the 2011 Cardinals.

17. d. Todd Zeile

Zeile doubled home three runs off Pat Hentgen to give the Mets a 6–0 lead in the fourth inning of Game 5 in an eventual pennant-clinching 7–0 win. After struggling in the NLDS, Zeile batted .368

with eight RBIs in the NLCS. He also delivered a two-run double with the bases loaded in Game 4. His hot bat continued to smolder in the World Series, where he hit .400 against the Yankees, producing multi-hit performances in the first four games. The well-traveled Zeile was no stranger to the playoffs or Yankee Stadium, having been an October visitor to the Bronx with the 1996 Orioles and 1998 and 1999 Rangers. Despite a distinguished career that encompassed more than 2,000 hits and time with 11 different teams across 16 seasons, the 2000 World Series represented Zeile's lone opportunity to play for all the marbles.

18. a. Jay Payton

The outfielder went the other way with a Rivera pitch, depositing a three-run blast in the right field seats to cut the Yankees' lead to 6–5. Homering off Rivera in the postseason was no small feat. It was the second and final homer the Hall of Fame closer allowed in his postseason career that spanned 141 innings and 96 appearances over 16 seasons. The only other player to homer off Rivera in the postseason was Sandy Alomar Jr.—a member of the 2007 Mets—who did so with Cleveland in 1997. Payton had homered at Yankee Stadium during the 2000 regular season, off Andy Pettitte on June 10.

19. c. Paul Lo Duca

The All-Star catcher's sixth-inning single off Jonathan Broxton gave the Mets a 6–5 lead en route to a 9–5 win and a series sweep of the Dodgers. Neither Steve Trachsel nor Greg Maddux made it past the fourth inning in the three-hour, 51-minute game that featured 30 combined hits. The Mets jumped out to a 4–0 lead but the Dodgers rallied to grab a 5–4 edge before the Mets poured it on. Lo Duca batted .455 with three RBIs in the sweep, which memorably featured him tagging out two Dodgers on one play at the plate in Game 1.

20. b. Carlos Beltrán

Though his taking of strike three to end the NLCS remained a staple of Mets debate for years to come, Beltrán homered twice in the Mets' 12–5 laugher in Game 4 in St. Louis. His third-inning home run off Anthony Reyes tied the game at one, and his seventh-inning homer off former Met teammate Braden Looper finished the scoring. Beltrán batted .296 in the series with three home runs, his first snapping a scoreless tie in New York's 2–0 Game 1 victory. The star center fielder helped lead the Mets to the doorstep of the World Series in his second season with the club, but 2006's trip to mid-October represented the only significant team success during his seven years in Flushing before being traded to the Giants in 2011. Beltrán would make the World Series with the Cardinals in 2013 and win a World Championship in his twentieth and final major league campaign as a member of the 2017 Houston Astros.

21. b. Daniel Murphy

Murph homered three times against the Dodgers in the NLDS and then, as an encore, homered in each game of the NLCS sweep against the Cubs. He homered off Jon Lester and Cy Young winner Jake Arrieta at Citi Field. He homered to give the Mets the lead off Kyle Hendricks in Game 3, and his Game 4 home run off Fernando Rodney provided the exclamation point. Murphy, who batted .529, was named MVP of the series. After the season, he signed with the division-rival Nationals, where he helped Washington win the division and was voted runner-up in 2016's MVP voting, no doubt buoyed by his .413 batting average versus the Mets.

22. c. Chris Young

The six-foot-ten right-hander went 5–9 over two injury-shortened seasons with the Mets but resurfaced as a reliable swingman with Kansas City. He pitched three shutout innings in Game 1, striking out four and earning the victory when the Royals won in the bottom of the 14th. Young also returned to start Game 4 at Citi Field, giving up two runs in four innings in a game the Royals would rally to capture. The Mets did beat Young, 2–0, in KC for New York's first win of the 2016 season, the pitcher's second to last in the big leagues. Young would next see the Fall Classic as general manager and architect of the 2023 World Champion Rangers.

23. b. René Rivera

In the 2016 NL wild card game at Citi Field, Noah Syndergaard squared off with Giants ace Madison Bumgarner, who came into the contest with a postseason record of 7–3 (and a five-inning save in Game 7 of the 2014 World Series) with a 2.14 ERA. Thor went seven scoreless innings, allowing just two hits and three walks, while striking out 11. Meanwhile, the Mets were being shut down by MadBum, who set down the first six batters before catcher René Rivera led off the bottom of the third with a single to center before he was erased on a double play. It was one of just four hits and two walks MadBum allowed as he went the distance, striking out six batters in the Giants' 3–0 victory, with all the scoring coming on eighth-place hitter Conor Gillaspie's home run off Jeurys Familia in the ninth inning.

24. a. Seth Lugo

Appearing in each game against the Padres, Lugo threw two shutout innings over three appearances in his only playoff series with the Mets. His most important outing came with Game 2 on the line. The Mets entered the ninth up 7–2, but Adam Ottavino hit a batter and walked three to bring up Josh Bell as the tying run. Lugo came in and got Bell to ground out. After the season, Lugo joined the Padres where he was given a chance to start, something he wanted to do for years in Queens. He signed with the Royals before the 2024 season and earned the first All-Star berth of his career.

25. b. Mark Vientos

The third baseman, who began the season as a Syracuse Met, drove in 14 runs in 13 games against the Brewers, Phillies, and Dodgers as the Mets came within two wins of playing in the World Series. Vientos hit .327 with five home runs during the Mets' run to the NLCS. He hit two homers and drove in four runs in Game 2 of the NLDS against the Phillies. In Game 2 of the NLCS, he hit a second-inning grand slam off Dodgers righty Landon Knack. Vientos also went deep in Games 4 and 6 against the Dodgers. Despite not making the Opening Day roster, Vientos belted 27 home runs in 111 games during the regular season, which included walk-off blasts against the Cardinals and Reds.

AWARDS
AND HONORS

1. Which Hall of Famer was the first batter in Mets history?
a. Richie Ashburn   b. Gil Hodges   c. Frank Thomas
d. Don Zimmer

2. Which Hall of Famer represented the Mets at the 1963 All-Star Game?
a. Gil Hodges   b. Yogi Berra   c. Duke Snider   d. Warren Spahn

3. Which player was named MVP of the 1969 World Series?
a. Jerry Koosman   b. Donn Clendenon   c. Tom Seaver   d. Al Weis

4. Who became the first Met to win a Gold Glove, doing so in 1970?
a. Tommie Agee   b. Rod Gaspar   c. Jerry Grote   d. Tom Seaver

5. Who was the first Mets infielder to win a Gold Glove?
a. Ken Boswell   b. Bud Harrelson   c. Ed Kranepool
d. Wayne Garrett

6. Who was the first Met to win a Silver Slugger Award?
a. Darryl Strawberry   b. Keith Hernandez   c. Gary Carter
d. Dwight Gooden

7. Which Met was named NL Comeback Player of the Year in 1986?

a. Lee Mazzilli   b. Ray Knight   c. Mookie Wilson   d. George Foster

8. Which Met was named NL Player of the Month in September 1988?

a. Kevin McReynolds   b. Darryl Strawberry   c. David Cone
d. Randy Myers

9. Who is the only Mets pitcher to win a Gold Glove?

a. Dwight Gooden   b. Frank Viola   c. Bob Ojeda   d. Ron Darling

10. Who was the first Met to win Rolaids Relief Man of the Year award?

a. Neil Allen   b. Jesse Orosco   c. Randy Myers   d. John Franco

11. Which one of these players hit his 400th career home run while playing for the Mets?

a. Dave Kingman   b. Eddie Murray   c. Carlos Beltrán   d. Mike Piazza

12. Which Mets pitcher was NL Player of the Week in early May 1997?

a. Cory Lidle   b. Dave Mlicki   c. Rick Reed   d. John Franco

13. Which Mets pitcher was NL Player of the Week in July 1999?

a. Al Leiter   b. Orel Hershiser   c. Masato Yoshii   d. Octavio Dotel

14. Which Met won Comeback Player of the Year honors in 1999?

a. John Franco   b. Orel Hershiser   c. Rickey Henderson
d. Pat Mahomes

15. Which pitcher won the Silver Slugger in 2000?

a. Mike Hampton   b. Rick Reed   c. Bobby Jones   d. Al Leiter

16. Who was the MVP of the 2000 NLCS?

a. Timo Perez   b. Mike Hampton   c. Mike Piazza
d. Edgardo Alfonzo

17. Which Met collected the 2,500th hit of his career in 2002?
a. Mo Vaughn   b. Jeromy Burnitz   c. Mike Piazza
d. Roberto Alomar

18. Which Met was NL Pitcher of the Week in August 2003?
a. Tom Glavine   b. Al Leiter   c. Steve Trachsel   d. Armando Benitez

19. This Met won his 200th career game in 2006. Who is he?
a. Tom Glavine   b. Pedro Martinez   c. David Cone   d. Orel Hershiser

20. Which Met outfielder won three consecutive Gold Gloves?
a. Carlos Beltrán   b. Shawn Green   c. Mike Cameron
d. Juan Lagares

21. Which Met was NL Player of the Month for June 2006?
a. José Reyes   b. Carlos Beltrán   c. Carlos Delgado
d. David Wright

22. Who was NL Comeback Player of the Year in 2015?
a. Daniel Murphy   b. Yoenis Céspedes   c. Matt Harvey
d. Jeurys Familia

23. True or False: No Met has won the Trevor Hoffman Award for the NL's top reliever.

24. Which Met won a Silver Slugger in 2022?
a. Pete Alonso   b. Francisco Lindor   c. Jeff McNeil
d. Starling Marte

25. Who was the first Met skipper to be named Manager of the Year?
a. Bobby Valentine   b. Willie Randolph   c. Terry Collins
d. Buck Showalter

ANSWERS

1. a. Richie Ashburn

The Hall of Fame center fielder played 12 seasons in the City of Brotherly Love with the Phillies before spending two seasons with the Cubs. The two-time batting champion led the league in hits three times, walks four times, triples twice, and stolen bases once. On April 11, 1962, he led off for the Mets and flied out to center off St. Louis' Larry Jackson. Ashburn went 1-for-5 in the game, singling and scoring the first run in team history in the third inning of New York's 11–4 loss. Ashburn hit .306 and was an All-Star in what was his final season in the majors.

2. c. Duke Snider

The beloved Duke of Flatbush returned to New York in 1963 after 16 seasons with the Dodgers in Brooklyn and Los Angeles, with the Mets purchasing his contract for $40,000. Snider made his eighth and final All-Star Game, appearing as a pinch-hitter in the ninth inning and striking out against Boston's Dick Radatz in the NL's 5–3 win as the Mets' lone representative. Snider played in 129 games in 1963, his highest total since 1957. He collected his 2,000th career hit and 400th home run during the season. Snider would play one more year, spending 1964 with the Giants and sharing the outfield with Willie Mays.

3. b. Donn Clendenon

The big first baseman was named MVP for his three-homer performance in the Series. Clendenon was a Pirate from 1961 to 1968 and was taken by the Expos in the expansion draft. Montreal had a deal to send him to Houston, but he refused to report and, after spending two months with the Expos, he was dealt to the Mets in mid-June. The Mets had lacked a power bat, but once they had Clendenon's, his 12 homers helped the team overtake the Cubs in the NL East race. In the World Series, he homered off Dave McNally twice and Mike Cuellar once. His five hits and four RBIs led the team in the low-scoring Fall Classic.

4. a. Tommie Agee

In 1970, the speedy center fielder became the first African American player to win a Gold Glove in both leagues as well as the first non-pitcher to win a Gold Glove in each league. Agee showed off his range, much as he did in Game 3 of the 1969 World Series with his two iconic catches. The other 1970 outfield Gold Glove recipients in the NL were Roberto Clemente and Pete Rose. Agee won a Gold Glove as a member of the White Sox in 1966, his Rookie of the Year season. Ironically, Agee committed a career-high 13 errors in 1970.

5. b. Bud Harrelson

After posting a .978 fielding percentage, Harrelson was awarded a Gold Glove in 1971. His outstanding glove work earned him a spot on the All-Star team and he received a few MVP votes despite batting .252 with no home runs. The popular shortstop had shown much improvement since committing 32 errors in 1967, his first full season. Harrelson played in 142 games in 1971, the last time he would appear in more than 120 in a year. In his 13 seasons as a Met, Harrelson never played another position. After joining the Phillies in 1978, he also played second base, third base, and even one inning in left field.

6. b. Keith Hernandez

In 1984, his first full season as a Met, Hernandez became the franchise's first recipient of the Silver Slugger, an award that was inaugurated four years earlier. Hernandez batted .311, seventh-best in the NL, with 15 homers and 94 RBIs. He also won a Gold Glove and finished second in the MVP voting to Chicago's Ryne Sandberg. Hernandez was the first NL first baseman to win a Silver Slugger in 1980 when he was a member of the Cardinals. The man, known in his playing days as Mex, was the heart of the 1984 Mets team that won 90 games, the team's first winning season since 1976. His 31 doubles were the most by a Met since Lee Mazzilli in 1980.

Keith Hernandez

7. b. Ray Knight

The veteran third baseman batted .298, an 80-point improvement from his 1985 average, and his 11 home runs were his most since 1980. Knight began his career with the Reds and became their starting third baseman in 1979 after Pete Rose left for the Phillies, finishing fifth in the MVP voting and helping the Reds to the 1979 NL West title. He was named to the All-Star team in 1980. Before the 1982 season, Knight was sent to the Astros where he again made the All-Star team and earned some MVP votes. The Mets acquired him late in the 1984 season, but after undergoing surgery he slumped in 1985. Knight bounced back in 1986 and would be World Series MVP.

8. a. Kevin McReynolds

The left fielder, who had come over in a big deal with the San Diego Padres involving Kevin Mitchell after the 1986 season, batted .326 with seven home runs, 22 RBIs, and four stolen bases as the Mets put the division out of reach for good and wrapped up their second NL East title in three seasons. Some highlights included driving in three runs in a 3–0 win over the Expos, a two-homer game at Shea against the Phillies, and a four-RBI outburst in a drubbing of the Cardinals. McReynolds finished third in the MVP voting behind Dodgers outfielder Kirk Gibson and Mets teammate Darryl Strawberry.

9. d. Ron Darling

In his sixth full season with the Mets, the smooth right-hander became the first Mets pitcher to win a Gold Glove. After leading the league in double plays started by a pitcher with five in 1987, Darling finished second in 1989 with five. Earlier in his career, he led the league in assists twice. Darling also owned one of the best pickoff moves in the game. It was an impressive all-around season for Darling, who won 14 games with a 3.52 ERA, hit the only two home runs of his career, and was even inserted as a pinch-runner twice. Starting in 1990, Greg Maddux was awarded the first of 13 consecutive Gold Gloves for NL pitchers, a streak snapped by former Met Mike Hampton, pitching and fielding for the Braves in

2003. Maddux then won five straight from 2004 to 2008, by which time Darling was ensconced in the SNY broadcast booth.

10. d. John Franco
After joining the Mets in a trade for fellow southpaw Randy Myers the previous offseason, Franco notched a league-high 33 saves. He also went 5–3 with a 2.53 ERA and was selected to the All-Star team. He'd won the Rolaids award as a member of the Reds in 1988. The Mets traded their own lefty closer Randy Myers to the Reds in exchange for the native Brooklynite. Franco saved 30 games by the end of August 1990 and despite a shaky September, was rewarded with the Rolaids Relief Man of the Year honors. The award, which began in 1976, was discontinued following the 2012 season, and was reincarnated as the Trevor Hoffman (NL) and Mariano Rivera (AL) Relief Man of the Year Award in 2014.

11. b. Eddie Murray
On May 3, 1992, the Hall of Fame first baseman hit the milestone homer to left off Atlanta's Marvin Freeman in a 7–0 Mets win. Murray had 398 career homers when the season began but had to wait nearly a month to reach the magic number. It took more than two weeks for his first homer as a Met, a walk-off shot against the Cardinals. Murray would hit 43 home runs in two seasons with the Mets and would finish his career with 504. Murray was the second of three Mets to hit their 400th dinger in a Mets uniform, the others being Duke Snider in 1963 and Carlos Delgado in 2006.

12. c. Rick Reed
Reed won the honor by going 2–0 with a 0.60 ERA in victories over the Reds and Cardinals in late April and early May. The right-hander had bounced around with the Pirates, Royals, Rangers, and Reds before spending the 1996 season in the Mets minor league system. He would become the best pitcher on the 1997 team, finishing 13–9 with a 2.89 ERA on the first Mets club with a winning record since 1990. Reed made the 1998 and 2001 All-Star teams and went 11–5 for both the 1999 and 2000 Mets playoff teams.

13. d. Octavio Dotel

The hard-throwing righty made his debut in late June, taking Jason Isringhausen's spot in the rotation and in late July was named Player of the Week for tossing victories against the Orioles and Cubs. He gave up two runs in 14⅓ innings, finishing by striking out Sammy Sosa in the eighth inning of a one-run game at Shea Stadium. The Mets were the first stop in Dotel's somewhat nomadic career during which he would play for 13 teams. He was traded to Houston after the 1999 season in the Mike Hampton deal and spent most of his career as a reliever. He would win a World Series with the Cardinals in 2011.

14. c. Rickey Henderson

At 40 years old, the Hall of Fame left fielder provided a spark at the top of the lineup, batting .315 with a .423 on-base percentage and 37 stolen bases. His batting average was his highest since his MVP season of 1990 with the A's and 79 points higher than his 1998 average. Unfortunately, his time with the Mets might be best remembered for his playing cards with Bobby Bonilla in the clubhouse in Atlanta during Game 6 of the NLCS after he was taken out for defense. Henderson would be cut loose from the Mets in May 2000, touring the Mariners, Padres, Red Sox, and Dodgers through 2003 before returning to Queens as first-base coach under former Yankees teammate Willie Randolph in 2007.

15. a. Mike Hampton

When the Mets acquired Hampton in a blockbuster trade after the 1999 season, they not only added an ace pitcher but a solid bat. Hampton, who also won the award in 1999 with Houston, hit .274 with the Mets. The lefty pitcher who swung as a righty notched five multi-hit games on the season, including a three-hit performance at the plate against the Marlins. He also drove in eight runs. All 20 of his hits on the season were singles. Hampton would later win Silver Slugger awards with the Rockies and Braves (and swat 16 homers in his post-Mets career). Rick Reed also batted over .200 for the 2000 Mets, though Glendon Rusch, Al Leiter, and Bobby Jones each hit .060 or below.

16. b. Mike Hampton

Hampton pitched 16 shutout innings against the Cardinals to help lead the Mets to the World Series for the first time since 1986. He pitched seven shutout innings on the road in Game 1 and then a complete game three-hit shutout in clinching Game 5 at Shea Stadium. Timo Perez made a strong case for the award, scoring eight runs, collecting seven hits, and keeping the pressure on the Cardinals with his speed. Perez scored in the first inning in three of the Mets victories. Edgardo Alfonzo batted .444 with four RBIs and Mike Piazza hit .412 with two homers and four RBIs.

17. d. Roberto Alomar

Leading off the bottom of the first inning of the July 26, 2002, game with the milestone single off Cincinnati's Elmer Dessens, the Hall of Fame second baseman would go 3-for-3 with two walks in the 3–2 victory. Alomar made 12 consecutive All-Star teams with San Diego, Toronto, Baltimore, and Cleveland prior to joining the Mets. But Alomar would hit only .266 in 2002, 70 points lower than the year before, matching his career low posted as a rookie in 1988. Alomar's 11 homers were also his lowest total since the strike-shortened 1994 season. The Mets would trade him to the White Sox during the 2003 season.

18. c. Steve Trachsel

One of the bright spots on the 2003 Mets, the right-hander pitched 16⅓ scoreless innings over two starts in August. He pitched a one-hit shutout against the Rockies at Shea and followed it with seven and one-third scoreless innings at Dodger Stadium. Trachsel won 16 games that season, including another one-hit shutout against the defending World Series champion Angels in Anaheim. Trachsel would win 66 games in six seasons with the Mets, with 15 coming for the 2006 division champs. He's remembered mainly for his deliberate pace, tagged with the nickname "The Human Rain Delay" for his slow work on the mound. He won 143 games in his 16-season career.

19. b. Pedro Martinez

On April 17, 2006, the three-time Cy Young winner beat the Braves, 4–3, for his 200th career victory. He gave up three runs in six and two-thirds innings, with Duaner Sanchez and Billy Wagner closing the door on the milestone victory. Martinez got off to a 5–0 start in April, but spotty run and bullpen support, injuries, and diminishing effectiveness combined to limit him to nine wins in 2006. A season later, he'd reach another career milestone in a Met uniform: his 3,000th strikeout. Martinez went 32–23 in four seasons as a Met, and finished his career with 219 wins, going 5–0 for the 2009 Phillies NL championship team after leaving the Mets. Martinez was enshrined in the Hall of Fame in 2015.

20. a. Carlos Beltrán

Beltrán won three consecutive Gold Gloves from 2006 to 2008. Signed by the Mets for $119 million before the 2005 season, he added not only power and speed to the lineup but was a terrific fielder. He also solidified center field for a team that seemed to have a different primary center fielder each year in the early 2000s from Jay Payton to Timo Perez to Jeff Duncan to Mike Cameron. In his third Gold Glove campaign, he registered a .993 fielding percentage on a league-high 429 chances. Beltrán only made 10 errors in those three seasons combined. Beltrán also added Silver Sluggers to his trophy case in 2006 and 2007.

21. d. David Wright

The Mets' All-Star third baseman hit .327 with 10 homers and 29 RBIs in June as the club began to pull away with the division, extending their lead from 4½ to 10½ games. He had a pair of multi-homer games, with one against the Giants and another against the Reds. Wright homered in all three games in a sweep of the Phillies in Philadelphia during which the Mets pounded out 23 runs. He collected 35 hits in June and his batting average soared as high as .339. The eventual team captain slowed down right after the All-Star break with some pointing to the Home Run Derby ruining his

David Wright

swing, but Wright would bounce back to hit .371 in September. He'd finish ninth in NL MVP balloting.

22. c. Matt Harvey

After undergoing Tommy John surgery and missing the 2014 season, Harvey returned in 2015 with a 13–8 record and 2.71 ERA. The Dark Knight won his first five starts of the year, including two against the Nationals in which he threw 13 shutout innings. He also pitched eight and two-thirds innings in a victory at Yankee Stadium. Harvey was the winning pitcher on September 26 at Cincinnati when the Mets clinched the NL East title for the first time since 2006. But injuries would stop Harvey from having another great season with the Mets. He would go a combined 9–19 with a 5.93 ERA from 2016 through early 2018 when he was traded to the Reds.

23. False

Edwin Diaz went 3–1 with a 1.31 ERA and 118 strikeouts in 62 innings to win the award in 2022. His average of 17.1 strikeouts per nine innings set the record for highest single-season rate by any pitcher with at least 60 innings. Diaz finished in the top 10 of the Cy Young voting and top 20 in MVP voting. On April 29, he struck out Philadelphia's Bryce Harper, Nick Castellanos, and J. T. Realmuto to finish off a combined no-hitter (following up on the hitless work of Tylor Megill, Drew Smith, Joely Rodriguez, and Seth Lugo). He didn't blow a save after May 24, converting his final 22 opportunities. Unfortunately, Diaz would miss the 2023 season after sustaining an injury celebrating in the World Baseball Classic.

24. c. Jeff McNeil

The Mets' All-Star second baseman led the league with a .326 batting average and earned himself a Silver Slugger Award. It was a bounce-back season for The Squirrel after he batted a career-low .251 in 2021, a far cry from the output of the player who hit .300 each of his first three seasons. He came out of the gate hot in 2022, batting .361 in early May. His average dropped as low as .287 in late July, but he turned it back on late in the season. McNeil had

20 hits in his final 10 starts of the season, allowing him to edge out Dodgers first baseman Freddie Freeman for the batting title.

25. d. Buck Showalter

Showalter won the award in his first year as Mets skipper. He previously had taken the honors with the Yankees, Rangers, and Orioles. He led the Mets to 101 wins, the second-most in franchise history, and a 24-game improvement over 2021. The Mets made the postseason for the first time since 2016 but lost in the wild card round to the Padres. The Mets were the fourth franchise Showalter took to the postseason, joining the Yankees, Diamondbacks, and Orioles. Showalter became the first Mets manager to win the BBWAA (Baseball Writers' Association of America) managerial award, which was first handed out in 1983. Earlier, Davey Johnson (twice) and Willie Randolph finished as runners-up. Showalter's encore in orange and blue didn't go nearly as well, and he was let go after the Mets dropped to 75 victories in 2023.

UNIFORM NUMBERS

1. What was Duke Snider's first number with the Mets?
a. 1   b. 4   c. 11   d. 41

2. Though closely identified with number 7, which number did Ed Kranepool wear in his early days as a Met?
a. 6   b. 10   c. 17   d. 21

3. Who was the first Met to wear number 41?
a. Clem Labine   b. Grover Powell   c. Jim Bethke
d. Gordie Richardson

4. Who was the first Met to wear number 42?
a. Felix Mantilla   b. Larry Elliot   c. Ron Taylor   d. Ron Hodges

5. Which player gave up number 24 to Willie Mays in 1972?
a. Art Shamsky   b. Don Hahn   c. Jim Beauchamp   d. Craig Swan

6. Who was the first Met to wear number 36 after Jerry Koosman?
a. Wayne Twitchell   b. Ed Lynch   c. John Gibbons   d. Joe Sambito

7. Who wore number 8 before Gary Carter?
a. Bruce Bochy   b. John Gibbons   c. Joe Torre   d. José Oquendo

8. Who was the first Met to wear 0?
a. Rey Ordoñez   b. Terry McDaniel   c. Chuck Carr   d. Juan Lagares

9. Who had to change his number from 16 upon coming to the Mets because Dwight Gooden wouldn't give it up?

a. Bobby Bonilla   b. Eddie Murray   c. Bret Saberhagen
d. Frank Viola

10. Which Met wore five different numbers?

a. Jeff McKnight   b. Rick Cerone   c. Chris Donnels
d. Mark Carreon

11. What number did Lance Johnson wear the day Mookie Wilson was inducted into the Mets Hall of Fame in 1996?

a. 11   b. 24   c. 51   d. 99

12. Who gave up 45 when John Franco switched after giving up his number 31 to Mike Piazza?

a. Jerry Dipoto   b. Randy Niemann   c. Mauro Gozzo
d. Cookie Rojas

13. What number did Benny Agbayani wear before he was number 50?

a. 39   b. 49   c. 51   d. 74

14. Who was the first Met to wear 73?

a. Kenny Rogers   b. Ricardo Rincon   c. Chris Mazza
d. Joe McEwing

15. Who was the last Met to wear 42?

a. Butch Huskey   b. Roger McDowell   c. Mo Vaughn
d. Rigo Beltrán

16. Who gave up number 47 to Tom Glavine?

a. Jeff D'Amico   b. Steve Trachsel   c. Joe McEwing
d. Jason Phillips

17. Who was the only Met to wear 00?

a. Tony Clark   b. Rey Ordonez   c. Brian McRae   d. Steve Bieser

18. Who was the last Met to wear 5 before David Wright?

a. Mark Johnson   b. Tsuyoshi Shinjo   c. John Olerud   d. Art Howe

19. Who wore number 12 to honor Met Ken Boswell?

a. Felix Millan   b. Jeff Kent   c. Roberto Alomar   d. Willie Randolph

20. Which Met was not allowed to wear his former number 42 in 2006?

a. Carlos Delgado   b. José Lima   c. José Reyes   d. Carlos Beltrán

21. Who was the last Met to wear 17?

a. Dae-Sung Koo   b. José Lima   c. David Newhan
d. Fernando Tatis

22. Who gave up number 7 to José Reyes upon the shortstop's return to the Mets in 2016?

a. Kevin Plawecki   b. Brandon Nimmo   c. Eric Campbell
d. Travis d'Arnaud

23. What number did Mickey Callaway wear during his final week as Mets manager?

a. 6   b. 26   c. 46   d. 56

24. What number did Buck Showalter wear when he managed the Mets?

a. 11   b. 26   c. 35   d. 86

25. What number did Max Scherzer wear as a Met?

a. 12   b. 21   c. 22   d. 45

ANSWERS

1. c. 11

Snider was closely identified with number 4 which he wore as a beloved Brooklyn Dodger and then in Los Angeles. But when the Mets brought Snider back to New York, Charlie Neal was wearing that number. Snider wore number 11 instead. The Duke reached some milestones wearing number 11, including his 2,000th career hit on April 16, off Cincinnati's Jim Maloney, and his 400th career homer, off the Reds' Bob Purkey, on June 14. He also hit a game-winning three-run homer at the Polo Grounds to stun the Cardinals, 3–2, on June 7. When Neal was traded to the Reds in July, Snider claimed number 4, which he wore for the rest of the season.

2. d. 21
Ed Kranepool wore 21 from 1962 to 1964. But when the Mets acquired legendary Braves pitcher Warren Spahn, winner of 356 career games to date, Kranepool gave Spahn number 21 and switched to 7. Spahn wore 21 for 19 seasons with the Boston and Milwaukee Braves, during which he was a 17-time All-Star, eight-time wins leader, three-time ERA leader, and four-time strikeout leader. Spahn made his debut wearing number 16 for the 1942 Braves, managed by Casey Stengel. He pitched in four games before serving in World War II. When he returned for the 1946 season, Spahn wore 21. The old lefty would finish 4–12 in 20 games with the Mets in 1965 before moving on to the Giants in July.

3. a. Clem Labine
The longtime Dodgers relief ace pitched in the first game of Mets history wearing the number 41. The right-hander was a part of five Dodgers pennant winners in the 1950s and also pitched in three games of the 1960 World Series with the Pirates. He was also selected to two All-Star teams. Labine pitched one inning in the Mets' team debut, an 11–4 loss to the Cardinals on April 11, 1962, giving up one unearned run in the bottom of the eighth. A week later, the Cardinals tagged him for five runs in one inning amidst a 15–5 blowout at the Polo Grounds. He pitched one scoreless inning in Cincinnati six days later in what would be the final appearance in the career of this Boy of Summer.

4. b. Larry Elliot
Now the most famous number in baseball, 42 was given to left-handed outfielder Larry Elliot when the former Pirate joined the

Mets in 1964. In July, he became the first Met to homer in four consecutive games, accomplishing the feat with three dingers in Cincinnati against the Reds and one back home at Shea Stadium against the Braves. He spent 1965 in the minors and wore 17 when he returned to the big club in 1966. In 1967, he was traded to the Kansas City A's, with the Mets receiving third baseman Ed Charles in the deal.

5. c. Jim Beauchamp

A first baseman and outfielder, Beauchamp was acquired by the Mets in the October 1971 deal that saw Art Shamsky return to his hometown of St. Louis. Beauchamp was given Shamsky's number 24. But he only played a handful of games as 24 before the Mets acquired "Say Hey Kid" Willie Mays, who had worn that number for the Giants since 1951. When the trade was announced, manager Yogi Berra told the Mets' equipment manager, "I guess you'd better get 24 off Beauchamp." Beauchamp, who had just taken batting practice wearing number 24, was assigned number 5. A veteran of ten major league seasons, Beauchamp, like Mays, saw his final major league action in the 1973 World Series.

6. a. Wayne Twitchell

With Jerry Koosman in Minnesota in 1979, number 36 was available and given to veteran pitcher Wayne Twitchell. The right-hander was a 1973 All-Star with the Phillies, going 13–9 with a 2.50 ERA and five shutouts. Twitchell struggled as a Met, going 5–3 with a 5.23 ERA in 33 games. His highlight was pitching five and one-third innings of shutout relief to get the win in a 3–2 victory over the Reds on June 11, in relief of starting pitcher Jesse Orosco. Twitchell was sold to the Mariners late in the 1979 season, where he ended his career.

7. b. John Gibbons

Gibbons wore number 8 in ten games with the 1984 Mets in an injury-shortened campaign. He was a highly touted catching prospect, but on December 10, 1984, the Mets traded for Gary Carter, the Expos' perennial All-Star catcher who was closely associated with 8. After spending 1985 in the minors, Gibbons returned to the majors in August 1986 wearing number 35. He was memorably part of a game-ending 8-2-5 double play in a 6–5 win over San Diego. He also went 4-for-4 with two doubles and a homer in a 9–5 win over the Phillies. Gibbons would later manage the Blue Jays to two American League Championship Series appearances and returned to the Mets as manager Carlos Mendoza's bench coach in 2024.

8. b. Terry McDaniel
A Mets farmhand since 1986, when he was drafted in the sixth round, the switch-hitting outfielder was called up to the Mets in August 1991. McDaniel was inserted in seven games as a pinch-runner by Bud Harrelson and his interim replacement, Mike Cubbage. Harrelson took criticism for using McDaniel as a pinch-hitter for Daryl Boston late in a game against the Pirates in which Boston had three hits, including a grand slam. McDaniel struck out. The first zero in team history played 23 games in the majors, batting .207 with two stolen bases. McDaniel played in the Reds system in 1992 and later toured the independent leagues for three seasons.

9. d. Frank Viola
The Mets acquired the 1988 AL Cy Young winner at the 1989 trading deadline in a deal that saw Rick Aguilera and Kevin Tapani go to Minnesota. Viola wore number 16 with the Twins. Doc Gooden was asked if he'd give it up. "I don't care how much money he makes," the good Doctor replied. "He can have my locker, I'll take him to all the best restaurants and show him New York. He can even have my wife, but he can't have my number, no way." Viola wore 26, which had been Tapani's number, for the rest of the 1989 season before switching to 29.

10. a. Jeff McKnight
A utility player in the late 1980s and early 1990s, McKnight wore 15 upon his arrival in 1989. After two seasons in Baltimore, he returned to Queens in 1992 as number 5. Jeremy Burnitz was given that number the following season, so McKnight switched to 7. When the coaching staff was shaken up once Dallas Green

was named manager in late May, Bobby Wine wanted 7; McKnight switched to 17. And when Bret Saberhagen wanted 17 in 1994, McKnight wore 18, which Saberhagen had worn for the Mets the previous two seasons. McKnight played parts of four years with the Mets, batting .250 with four home runs in 173 games, including 105 games in 1993. His father, Jim, played in 63 games for the Cubs in the early 1960s.

11. c. 51

For Mookie's induction into the Mets Hall of Fame on September 1, 1996, Johnson switched from 1 to 51, not wanting to wear Mookie's number on Wilson's big day. The brief trip to Area 51 also allowed the former Cardinal to salute one of his past teammates, Willie McGee. Johnson in unfamiliar digits produced familiar 1996 results, as the National League's base hit leader went 3-for-5 with two RBIs and a run scored in the Mets' 6–5 extra-inning triumph over the Giants. Ironically, when Wilson joined the Mets' coaching staff in 1997, he wore 51 until Johnson was traded in early August. Wilson grabbed the 1 he'd modeled throughout the 1980s and Mel Rojas, who was acquired from the Cubs in the same deal that sent Johnson to Chicago, took 51. That number was later worn by several relievers, most notably Paul Sewald, as well as several coaches including Dave Engle, Chris Chambliss, and Rick Peterson.

12. b. Randy Niemann

When the Mets acquired Mike Piazza, John Franco surrendered the 31 that—until that moment—had been synonymous with the closer his entire lengthy career in favor of 45, a tribute to Tug McGraw. Lefty Franco had grown up in Brooklyn, a fan of lefty McGraw, so it was a natural fit. All that stood in Franco's way was bullpen coach Randy Niemann's hold on Tugger's old number. Let's just say Johnny made Randy an offer the coach didn't wish to refuse (he reportedly sprung for a set of golf clubs). As a pitcher, Niemann wore 46 in 1985 and 40 during the 1986 season. On Bobby Valentine's staff, he wore 45 and then switched to 48, which remained his until he was dismissed in the mass firing of coaches in June 1999. Niemann returned to the staff in 2001 and wore 52 until the end of the 2002 season. In 2009, the old southpaw came back as part of Jerry Manuel's staff, wearing 55 through the 2010 season.

13. a. 39
Agbayani, a fan favorite, was first called up to the majors in 1998, after five years in the minors. He played in only 11 games, starting three, and batted .133. But when he was called back up to the Mets in May 1999, he was wearing 50, a tribute to his home state, Hawaii, the 50th (and still most recent) state to enter the union in 1959. Agbayani hit 10 home runs in his first 73 at-bats, and 50 became synonymous with the Honolulu native. He would hit 14 home runs on the season while sharing outfield time with his boyhood hero Rickey Henderson. Agbayani also wore 50 with the Rockies and Red Sox in 2002.

14. a. Kenny Rogers
Rogers wore 37 in Texas and Oakland, but with that number retired for Casey Stengel, he switched to 73. Coincidentally, when the southpaw joined the Yankees in 1996, he took 17 because 37 was retired for Stengel. Rogers went 5–1 with a pair of complete games in 12 starts for the Mets but is mostly remembered for walking Andruw Jones to force in the game-losing run in the 11th inning of Game 6 of the NLCS. The first four Mets to wear 73—Rogers, Ricardo Rincon, Robert Carson, and Daniel Zamora— were all left-handed pitchers. In 2021, infielder-outfielder Travis Blankenhorn wore 73, and he was followed by right-handed relievers Jimmy Yacabonis (2023) and Matt Festa (2024).

15. c. Mo Vaughn
Butch Huskey was wearing 42 for the Mets when Major League Baseball retired the number en masse for Jackie Robinson in 1997. Huskey was traded to the Mariners after the 1998 season. Before the 2002 season, the Mets acquired Mo Vaughn from the Angels for starting pitcher Kevin Appier. The fearsome slugger was with Boston in 1997 and kept 42 when he went to Anaheim and later New York. Vaughn, the 1995 AL MVP and a three-time All-Star, hit 26 home runs for the 2002 Mets, including the 300th of his career. But injuries limited him to 27 games in 2003 and ended his career.

16. c. Joe McEwing

McEwing, the super utility man for the Mets, wore 47 for his first three seasons with the team. But that changed when New York acquired Tom Glavine in free agency from the Braves. The two-time Cy Young and five-time 20-game winner took the 47 he was identified with in Atlanta. But it wasn't for free. Glavine and his wife financed a baby nursery in McEwing's home. "If you play long enough, that number becomes your identity," Glavine said. Four and seven add up to 11, which was Super Joe's new number. McEwing, who wore 48 as a rookie in St. Louis, then switched to 47 as a tribute to his former Cardinals teammate John Mabry before joining the Mets.

17. a. Tony Clark

In 2003, Clark became the first Met to wear 00. Well, the first Mets player, because Mr. Met is indelibly 00. But given the choice of 83, 88, or 00, Clark chose 00. A former All-Star with the Tigers, Clark was asked by children why he was wearing Mr. Met's number, so in early June, Clark switched to 52. The first baseman became the first Mets player to wear that number as it had only been issued to coaches, including Solly Hemus, Don Heffner, Harvey Haddix, Joe Pignatano, Greg Pavlick, Dave Wallace, and Randy Niemann.

18. b. Tsuyoshi Shinjo

The charismatic outfielder was a seven-time All-Star in Japan and was given 5, his number in Japan, when he joined the Mets for the 2001 season. He quickly won over fans, especially after hitting a home run in the home opener, a win over the Braves. He went to San Francisco for the 2002 season, helping the Giants win the pennant while lefty bench player Mark Johnson wore 5 for the Mets. But Shinjo and his number 5 returned to Queens in 2003. He hit .193 in 62 games, the final action of his major league career. David Wright's would begin the next year, and 5 would never be up for grabs again.

19. d. Willie Randolph

While being introduced as Mets manager, Randolph mentioned that had worn number 12 as a Dodgers and Mets player to honor

Ken Boswell, the Mets' second baseman from 1967 to 1974. Boswell, who set a record with an 85-game errorless streak during the 1970 season, was the favorite player of Randolph, who grew up in Brooklyn. Randolph indeed wore 12 with the Mets during the 1992 season, the 18th and final season of his big-league career, and returned to the Boswell signifier during a Mets managerial tenure that stretched from 2005 to 2008. Other second basemen to wear 12 for the Mets include Jeff Kent, Roberto Alomar, and Danny Garcia. It's also worth noting that veteran Shawon Dunston—like Randolph, a Mets fan in his Brooklyn youth—acknowledged Boswell as one of his numerical predecessors when he was assigned 12 upon joining his childhood team of choice for their 1999 playoff push.

20. b. José Lima

When Jackie Robinson's 42 was retired across baseball in 1997, MLB allowed any player who was wearing it at that moment—including Butch Huskey, then of the Mets, and Mo Vaughn, eventually of the Mets—to keep wearing it. In Houston, Astros righty José Lima was indeed stuck with 42, but as his big-league journey unfolded, he switched numbers, as players often do. For the 2005 Royals, the entertaining if erratic Lima wore 33. Despite his coming off a 5–16 record and 6.99 ERA, the Mets found him attractive enough to sign ahead of the 2006 season. When Lima, who'd won 21 games in 1999, arrived in Port St. Lucie, he asked if he could have 42 again. Alas, the "grandfathering" rule didn't apply if a player hadn't maintained a hold on 42 continuously from 1997 forward. Lima, a popular figure among teammates, took 17 as a Met and, unfortunately, a shellacking from opposing batters, going 0–4 in four starts and posting an ERA close to 10. The former All-Star died four years later at the age of 37.

21. d. Fernando Tatis

Fifteen players inexplicably wore 17 following Keith Hernandez's departure. David Cone fanned 19 Phillies wearing the number, which he did to honor Hernandez. Mike Bordick homered in his first at-bat in 2000 wearing the number. Dae-Sung Koo doubled off Randy Johnson wearing the number. But Mex's 17 was also handed out to

Satoru Komiyama, Wilson Delgado, and David Newhan. Tatis, best remembered for hitting two grand slams in one inning in 1999 as a Cardinal, wore 17 as a Met from 2008 to 2010, hitting 21 homers. The number was pulled out of circulation and *finally* retired in honor of Hernandez in 2022.

22. d. Travis d'Arnaud

Reyes wore 7 from 2003 to 2011 before signing with the Marlins. Coach Bob Geren wore it next, but switched with Travis d'Arnaud before the 2015 season, taking the catcher's 15 in the process. D'Arnaud wore 7 until July 2016 when Reyes returned to Citi Field. Reyes gave d'Arnaud a Rolex watch in exchange for the number. D'Arnaud, an Indianapolis Colts fan, switched to 18 to honor Peyton Manning. Reyes wore 7 through the end of the 2018 season, his last in the majors. Marcus Stroman was the next Met to wear the number, donning it for the final two months of the 2019 season after being acquired from Toronto. He switched to 0 for the remainder of his Mets career, citing respect for Reyes's association with 7 as a motivation (Stroman and Reyes had been Blue Jays teammates).

23. b. 26

Callaway wore 36 for almost the entirety of his two seasons as Mets manager. In late September 2019, the team announced that 36 would be retired the following year for Jerry Koosman. Callaway switched to 26 for what was left of 2019. He didn't get too used to the new number as he was fired days after the season ended despite New York going 46–26 after the All-Star break and making a run at the National League's second wild card spot. Because of the pandemic and empty 2020 stadiums, Koosman's number retirement ceremony was pushed back to 2021.

24. a. 11

Though it was rarely seen under his windbreaker, Buck Showalter wore number 11 as Mets manager in 2022 and 2023. Showalter previously wore the number as skipper of the Yankees, Diamondbacks, and Rangers. As manager of the Orioles, he wore 26 as a tribute to Johnny Oates, who managed Showalter in the

Yankees system. Oates later managed the Rangers and Orioles. Showalter was the first Mets manager to be named NL Manager of the Year, winning the award in 2022. Coincidentally, Showalter's first-base coach with the Mets, Wayne Kirby, wore number 11 when he was a Mets outfielder in 1998. Kirby hit .194 in 26 games in Flushing at the end of his eight-year major league career.

25. b. 21
The right-handed ace Scherzer wore 21 with the Mets. He was number 31 for seven seasons with the Nationals (and a few months with the Dodgers), but the Mets retired that number in honor of Mike Piazza in 2016. Scherzer wore 37 in his five seasons with the Tigers, a number long retired by the Mets for Casey Stengel. He wore 39 at the start of his career with the Diamondbacks, well before his reputation as the fiercest of competitors took hold. The three-time Cy Young winner went 11–5 with a 2.29 ERA in 2022, his only full season with the Mets, winning his 200th career game in September, retiring all 18 Brewers he faced to help the Mets clinch a playoff berth on September 19.

PITCHING GEMS

1. Who was the first pitcher to no-hit the Mets?
a. Juan Marichal   b. Sandy Koufax   c. Bob Gibson
d. Warren Spahn

2. Which Mets batter made the last out of Jim Bunning's perfect game on Father's Day 1964?
a. Charley Smith   b. George Altman   c. Jesse Gonder
d. John Stephenson

3. In 1965, which Mets pitcher shut out the Reds for eight innings the night Jim Maloney no-hit the Mets for 10 innings but lost in the 11th?
a. Jack Fisher   b. Al Jackson   c. Warren Spahn   d. Frank Lary

4. Which Phillies pitcher struck out 18 Mets in 15 scoreless innings in 1965?
a. Jim Bunning   b. Ray Culp   c. Chris Short   d. Bo Belinsky

5. Which pitcher set a then major league record with 19 strikeouts against the 1969 Mets?
a. Don Drysdale   b. Nolan Ryan   c. Steve Carlton   d. Phil Niekro

6. Who had a no-hit bid broken up in the eighth inning by the Cubs' Ernie Banks in 1970?
a. Jerry Koosman   b. Gary Gentry   c. Jon Matlack   d. Nolan Ryan

7. Which Padre broke up Tom Seaver's 1972 no-hit bid in the ninth inning?
a. Fred Kendall b. Leron Lee c. Cito Gaston d. Ed Spiezio

8. Later in the 1972 season, which Montreal Expos pitcher blanked the Mets in the first no-hitter pitched outside the United States?
a. Carl Morton b. Bill Stoneman c. Ernie McAnally
d. Balor Moore

9. Which Giants pitcher no-hit the Mets at Candlestick Park in 1975?
a. Mike Caldwell b. John Montefusco c. Ed Halicki d. Jim Barr

10. Who pitched 10 innings of one-hit shutout ball for the Mets' last win of the 1982 season?
a. Charlie Puleo b. Terry Leach c. Pete Falcone d. Mike Scott

11. Which Met fanned 16 batters in consecutive starts?
a. Dwight Gooden b. Sid Fernandez c. Ron Darling
d. David Cone

12. In 1991, which Met pitched a complete-game one-hit shutout in his fourth career start?
a. Wally Whitehurst b. Pete Schourek c. Doug Simons
d. Anthony Young

13. Who no-hit the Mets at the Astrodome in 1993?
a. Mike Scott b. Nolan Ryan c. José Lima d. Darryl Kile

14. Which Met once fanned 15 Cubs in seven innings at Wrigley Field?
a. David Cone b. Sid Fernandez c. Al Leiter d. Kenny Rogers

15. Which Met pitched a one-hit shutout to clinch the 2000 NLDS?
a. Mike Hampton b. Al Leiter c. Bobby Jones d. Rick Reed

16. Which 2001 Met pitched eight innings of one-hit ball against the Red Sox at Shea?
a. Kenny Rogers   b. Octavio Dotel   c. Glendon Rusch
d. Masato Yoshii

17. Which Met tossed a one-hit shutout against the Brewers at Shea in 2002?
a. Shawn Estes   b. Jeff D'Amico   c. Kris Benson   d. Pedro Astacio

18. Which Met pitched six and two-third innings of one-hit ball against the Marlins in 2003 one day after the Mets were one-hit by Florida?
a. Jae Weong Seo   b. David Cone   c. Mike Bacsik   d. Tom Glavine

19. Which Met pitched a one-hit shutout against the Marlins a month before being converted into a reliever in 2005?
a. Kaz Ishii   b. Aaron Heilman   c. Victor Zambrano   d. Juan Padilla

20. Which Met pitched the first no-hitter in team history?
a. Hideo Nomo   b. Dwight Gooden   c. Johan Santana   d. Matt Harvey

21. Who pitched nine innings of one-hit ball against the White Sox in a combined shutout in 2013?
a. Noah Syndergaard   b. Matt Harvey   c. Jon Niese   d. Daisuke Matsuzaka

22. Which former Met tossed seven no-hit innings against the Mets at Citi Field in a 2014 game?
a. Aaron Harang   b. Shaun Marcum   c. Miguel Batista
d. Collin McHugh

23. Which Met struck out 15 Nationals in a two-hit shutout early in the 2021 season?
a. Jacob deGrom   b. Matt Harvey   c. Justin Verlander
d. Chris Bassitt

24. Also in 2021, who pitched eight innings of one-hit ball against the Reds in a combined shutout?
a. Jason Vargas   b. Steven Matz   c. Marcus Stroman   d. Rich Hill

25. Which Mets starter pitched five no-hit innings in New York's combined no-hitter against the Phillies in 2022?
a. Tylor Megill   b. Carlos Carrasco   c. Trevor Williams   d. José Butto

ANSWERS

1. b. Sandy Koufax
On June 30, 1962, Koufax no-hit the Mets in a 5–0 win, working around five walks and striking out 13. Koufax fanned seven in the first three innings, while the Dodgers staked him to a 4–0 lead in the first. Koufax got Felix Mantilla to ground into a forceout to end the game. It was the Dodgers' first no-hitter since moving to Los Angeles in 1958 and the first of the four Koufax pitched. He would throw one each year from 1962 to 1965, including a perfect game against the Cubs in 1965, which was caught by future Mets skipper Jeff Torborg.

2. d. John Stephenson
The Mets rookie catcher pinch-hit for pitcher Tom Sturdivant and struck out swinging to end Jim Bunning's perfect game. The Phillies ace righty struck out 10 batters in the opening game of the Father's Day doubleheader and even helped his own cause with a two-run double. Fortunately, the Mets would get three hits in the second game. Stephenson would spend ten seasons in the majors, seeing action with the Cubs, Giants, and Angels. When Nolan Ryan made his debut on September 11, 1966, Stephenson was his catcher. He would later reunite with Ryan on the Angels. Stephenson eventually coached college baseball and for the Mets organization.

3. d. Frank Lary
On June 14, 1965, Maloney, the Reds' right-handed ace, hurled 10 no-hit innings and struck out 18 batters, but lost in the 11th.

Larry Bearnarth took over from Lary in the ninth and pitched three scoreless innings to pick up the victory after Johnny Lewis, who had struck out three times, led off the top of the 11th with a home run. While Maloney was fanning 18 Mets, Lary (three) and Bearnarth (one) combined for just four strikeouts. Maloney would pitch a 10-inning no-hitter later in 1965 in a 1–0 win against the Cubs. And in 1969, he only had to throw *nine* no-hit innings in a 10–0 win over the Astros.

4. c. Chris Short
The Phillies' southpaw fanned 18 batters in 15 innings at Shea Stadium on October 2, 1965, in what finished as a scoreless tie after 18 innings. Short and Mets starter Rob Gardner both went 15. It was the second game of a twi-night doubleheader. The Mets lost the first game, 6–0, to Jim Bunning, who only allowed two hits. An inning could not start after a 1:00 a.m. curfew, and the game ended 0–0. That meant the game needed to be made up the next day, creating another doubleheader on the last day of the season. A day after playing 27 innings, the teams went 22 more. The Mets lost both games by the same score of 3–1, with the finale lasting 13 innings.

5. c. Steve Carlton
Carlton set a then modern-day record with 19 strikeouts in a nine-inning game, but a pair of Ron Swoboda home runs gave the Mets a 4–3 win over the Cardinals on September 15, 1969. "Lefty" got off to a quick start with six strikeouts in the first two innings. Swoboda gave the Mets a 2–1 lead in the fourth, but the Cardinals fought back to take a 3–2 lead against Gary Gentry before Swoboda's eighth-inning homer. Carlton struck out the side in the ninth to get to 19, with Amos Otis the final strikeout victim. Tug McGraw pitched three scoreless innings to gain credit for the victory.

6. b. Gary Gentry
Ten months after Tom Seaver's near-perfect game, Gentry flirted with history against the Cubs. On May 13, 1970, at Wrigley Field, the young right-hander was four outs away from a no-hitter when Ernie Banks lined a single just out of left fielder Dave Marshall's

reach. Gentry would toss another shutout two weeks later in a 3–0 win against the Cardinals. Though Gentry was a reliable starter for his first few major league seasons, he was traded to the Braves after the 1972 season and injuries would limit his time in the majors. He was re-signed by the Mets in 1975 but retired after one start in the minors.

7. b. Leron Lee
Though not as famous as his July 9, 1969, "imperfect game," Seaver was two outs away from a no-hitter on July 4, 1972, when San Diego left fielder Leron Lee singled to center. The Franchise had walked four but allowed no hits when he took the mound for the ninth. After Dave Roberts grounded out, Lee, apparently determined to play the role of Jimmy Qualls, broke up history before Nate Colbert hit into a double play to end the game. Lee was the only hitter on the offensively challenged Padres to bat .300 in 1972. San Diego had the second-lowest batting average in the National League at .227, ahead of only the Mets at .225.

8. b. Bill Stoneman
During the final week of the 1972 season, the Mets traveled to Montreal and were no-hit by Bill Stoneman in a 7–0 Expos win in the first game of an October 2 doubleheader. Stoneman worked around seven walks, retiring Don Hahn on a forceout to end the game. Future longtime Mets announcer Tim McCarver was Stoneman's catcher. This was Stoneman's final start of his All-Star season and the second no-hitter of his career, having no-hit the Phillies in 1969. The season before he finished in the top 10 in Cy Young voting. For all his success, he would retire with a career record of 54–85. Stoneman would later serve as the general manager of the 2002 Angels World Series Championship team.

9. c. Ed Halicki
The Giants' second-year righty no-hit the Mets, who may have worn themselves out by scoring nine runs on 12 hits in the first game of the doubleheader. Halicki walked two and fanned 10 in the game of his life, getting Wayne Garrett to ground out to first

to end it. Rusty Staub had reached in the fifth after a bobble by second baseman Derrel Thomas, but the official scorer ruled it an error. It was the final Giants no-hitter at Candlestick Park and the team's last no-hitter at home until Jonathan Sanchez no-hit the Padres in 2009. Halicki later pitched for the Angels and retired with a 55–66 record.

10. b. Terry Leach

The sidearmer made a spot start in the final series of the year, pitching a 10-inning one-hit shutout in Philadelphia. Luis Aguayo's fifth-inning triple was the only hit off Leach. John Denny matched zeroes with Leach and both teams were scoreless on one hit through nine. In the 10th, the Mets scored off Porfi Altamirano as Hubie Brooks delivered a sacrifice fly. Leach stranded Aguayo on third to end the game. Leach went 24–9 in seven seasons with the Mets, including an 11–1 mark in 1987. He went 7–1 as a starter as injuries ravaged the team that season. Leach pitched for the Royals, Twins, and White Sox before retiring.

11. a. Dwight Gooden

The 19-year-old phenom didn't tire late in his rookie season of 1984. He won eight of his last nine starts, almost pitched a no-hitter, and fanned 16 batters in consecutive starts. On September 12, five days after his one-hitter against the Cubs, Gooden fanned 16 Pirates in a 2–0 win at Shea. He also set the rookie strikeout record, surpassing Herb Score's mark. For an encore, Dr. K struck out 16 Phillies at Veterans Stadium on September 17, but lost, 2–1, on an eighth-inning balk. Gooden finished with a whopping 276 strikeouts, finishing second in the Cy Young voting and winning Rookie of the Year.

12. b. Pete Schourek

The rookie lefty spent most of 1991 in the bullpen but moved to the rotation late in the year and tossed a one-hit shutout against the Expos at Shea on September 10. Montreal outfielder Ken Williams had the lone hit. Schourek would go 16–24 in three seasons as starter and reliever with the Mets. Schourek's best season in the majors came with the Reds in 1995 when he went 18–7 for the NL

Central champs and was runner-up to Greg Maddux in Cy Young voting. He also made a postseason start for the Red Sox in 1998.

13. d. Darryl Kile

Houston's All-Star right-hander no-hit the Mets on September 8, 1993, in a 7–1 win. Kile struck out Chico Walker to end the game, the first time the Mets had been no-hit in 18 years. Butch Huskey struck out three times in his major league debut. The Mets did score a run in the fifth as Jeff McKnight walked and came around on a wild pitch and error. The game also marked Frank Tanana's second-to-last start as a Met before being traded to the Yankees. Kile, a three-time All-Star, passed away during the 2002 season of a heart attack at the age of 33.

14. c. Al Leiter

The veteran southpaw had never struck out a dozen batters in a game but fanned 15 Cubs in seven innings on August 1, 1999, the most strikeouts for a Met since David Cone blew away 19 Phillies in 1991. Leiter was removed with a 3–2 lead after throwing 136 pitches but had to settle for a no decision when Armando Benitez blew the save in the ninth. The Mets would win in 13 innings on Pat Mahomes's RBI single. Leiter had an up-and-down 1999 but ended the season on a high note by beating the Braves in a critical late-September showdown and then shutting out the Reds in Game 163 to send the Mets to the NLDS.

15. c. Bobby Jones

The right-hander who hadn't tossed a shutout since 1997 sent the Giants home by firing a one-hitter on 116 pitches in a 4–0 win at Shea. He set down the Giants in order in eight of nine innings. Jeff Kent doubled to lead off the fifth, and two walks loaded the bases for pitcher Mark Gardner. San Francisco skipper Dusty Baker opted not to use a pinch-hitter and Gardner popped up. Jones struck out five. Barry Bonds, who struck out twice, flied out to center to end the game and send the Mets to the NLCS. Jones also scored a run in the fifth on Edgardo Alfonzo's two-run double after reaching base on a third-strike wild pitch.

16. c. Glendon Rusch

Rusch pitched eight innings of one-hit ball, with Trot Nixon's bunt single in the first the only hit of the afternoon in front of 52,006 at Shea on July 14, 2001. The lefty also struck out 10 Red Sox before being removed after 117 pitches. Armando Benitez pitched a 1-2-3 ninth inning, striking out Nixon to end the game. Mark Johnson drove in both runs in the 2–0 win, highlighted by a solo home run off Rolando Arrojo. After appearing in one game in relief for the Mets following a late-season trade in 1999, Rusch made 63 starts for the Mets in 2000 and 2001 and served as Bobby Valentine's go-to long reliever during the 2000 postseason, picking up a win in the NLCS and posting a 1.08 ERA across eight and one-third innings versus the Giants, Cardinals, and Yankees.

17. a. Shawn Estes

The former San Francisco Giants lefty earned his first win as a Met on April 26, 2002, with a one-hit shutout in a pitchers' duel against ex-Met Glendon Rusch that lasted one hour and 53 minutes. Estes retired the first 18 Brewers before Eric Young Sr. singled to left to lead off the seventh. Young made the final out of the game, a groundout to third. Rusch also pitched a gem, allowing one run on three hits, most decisively a second-inning home run by Jay Payton, in eight innings against his old team. The following day, Pedro Astacio took a no-hitter one out into the seventh before Milwaukee's Geoff Jenkins broke it up with a single.

18. a. Jae Weong Seo

The rookie right-hander gave up one hit in six and two-third innings against the Marlins on June 17, 2003, in the *third consecutive* one-hitter the Mets played, all on the road. Two days earlier at Anaheim, David Eckstein's sixth-inning single was the only safety Steve Trachsel allowed as he shut out the Angels, 8–0. The next night at Pro Player Stadium, Florida's electrifying freshman Dontrelle Willis held the Mets to a lone hit in a 1–0 shutout, marred only by a single to Ty Wigginton in the fourth inning. Seo, the first Korean-born Met, surrendered just a fifth-inning single to Juan Encarnacion, who was caught stealing, and didn't walk a batter. David Weathers and

Armando Benitez then combined to retire all seven batters they faced. The Mets faced the minimum 27 batters in the 5–0 victory, the first time in franchise history that Met pitching went through an opposing lineup exactly three times and no more, with Jeromy Burnitz's solo homer in the seventh putting the Mets in front.

19. b. Aaron Heilman

Heilman earned his first win of 2005 with a 4–0 win over the Marlins on April 15. Luis Castillo's fourth-inning infield single was the only hit off the right-hander, while the Mets scored four times off Josh Beckett. Heilman was moved to the bullpen in mid-May with Willie Randolph having six possible starters to work with. Heilman, to his chagrin, never made another start in the majors. Although his assigned role might not have matched his preference, Heilman did, for more than a spell, contribute positively in the Mets bullpen, setting up effectively for Braden Looper in 2005 and Billy Wagner during much of 2006. (The ninth inning of the seventh game of the 2006 NLCS was a different story.) Overall, Heilman's career as a Mets starter shook out to a record of 5–13, an ERA of 5.93, and one fabulous one-hit night.

20. c. Johan Santana

No, the answer has not changed since June 1, 2012. In the 8,020th game in Mets history, Santana threw the franchise's first-ever no-hitter, delivering a 134-pitch effort at Citi Field against the defending World Champion Cardinals. David Freese's strikeout ended the 8–0 exercise in mass catharsis and put Santana in the history books. Though Met-watchers had never experienced their own no-hitter, they knew that sometimes a few extraordinary events have to transpire to bring one to life, and "Nohan" was no exception. Old friend Carlos Beltrán's liner in the sixth hit the left-field foul line if you believe video evidence, but third-base umpire Adrian Johnson called it foul, and there was not yet any mechanism for a manager to challenge such a ruling. In the seventh, Mike Baxter's running catch and crash into the left-field wall to haul in Yadier Molina's fly ball saved the day. An eighth-inning pitch seemingly hit Shane Robinson on the hand but wasn't called (again, no replay rule existed in 2012), and Robinson went on to strike out. Santana walked five, struck out eight, and put an end to more than a half-century of Mets fan heartbreak and deprivation.

21. b. Matt Harvey
On May 7, 2013, the Dark Knight flirted with perfection, retiring the first 20 White Sox he faced before Alex Rios's infield single with two outs in the seventh inning. Shortstop Ruben Tejada made a strong throw to first which Rios barely beat out. Harvey also fanned a dozen batters this night in Flushing, throwing strikes on 76 of 105 pitches. The Mets won in 10 innings on Mike Baxter's single, with reliever Bobby Parnell gaining credit for the win. The performance came three weeks after Harvey held Minnesota hitless for six and two-third innings before Justin Morneau homered off Target Field's foul pole. Harvey won his first four starts of 2013, and the gem against the White Sox lowered his ERA to 1.28. His blazing first half earned him the honor of starting the All-Star Game at Citi Field.

22. a. Aaron Harang
The veteran righty, who made four starts with the 2013 Mets, returned to Citi Field to pitch seven no-hit innings in a Braves uniform on April 18, 2014. Leading 1–0 in the seventh with two on and two outs, Harang struck out Andrew Brown with his 121st and final pitch of the night. Harang walked six and struck out five. The Braves won, 6–0, but David Wright singled off Luis Avilán with two outs in the eighth to break up the combined no-hit effort. As a Red, Harang tied for the league lead with 16 wins in 2006. The following season he finished fourth in NL Cy Young voting.

23. a. Jacob deGrom
At a Citi Field whose attendance was limited by COVID restrictions, the Mets ace filled scorebooks with K's and zeroes. The Mets ace fanned 15 Nationals in a two-hit shutout masterpiece on April 23, 2021, a contest he also dominated with his bat (2-for-4 and the RBI double that put the Mets ahead to stay). It was the two-time Cy Young winner's first blanking since his one-hitter in Philly in 2016. DeGrom now had 50 strikeouts in his first four starts, topping the

previous record of 48 held by Nolan Ryan and Shane Bieber. It was also his third straight start with at least 14 strikeouts; Pedro Martinez and Gerrit Cole had been the only previous pitchers to accomplish the feat. DeGrom's 15-strikeout performance was the first by a Met since Al Leiter in 1999. DeGrom was having the best season of his extraordinary career in 2021, going 7–2 with a 1.08 ERA in 15 starts, when injuries halted his campaign come July. The Mets not coincidentally fell from first place in midsummer to completely out of contention by September.

24. c. Marcus Stroman

On July 21, 2001, Stroman went eight innings, allowing only a third-inning single to Aristides Aquino. Jeurys Familia pitched a scoreless ninth and Dom Smith hit a grand slam in the 7–0 win over the Reds at Cincinnati. Stroman led the league with 33 starts in 2021, though he had only a 10–13 record to show for his 3.02 ERA. The righty had some tough luck during his two seasons with the Mets, going 14–15 with a solid 3.21 ERA. Stroman, who was previously an All-Star with the Blue Jays, had another All-Star season in 2023 with the Cubs before signing with the Yankees.

25. a. Tylor Megill

Megill started and threw five no-hit innings against the Phillies at Citi Field on April 29, 2022, walking three and striking out five before being removed after 88 pitches. Drew Smith, Joely Rodriguez, Seth Lugo, and Edwin Diaz combined to complete the no-hitter in the 3-0 win. The victory improved Megill to 4-0 with a 1.93 ERA in the first month of the season, but it proved his final win of the year. Injuries would limit him to only four more starts and six late-season relief appearances. The hitless performance by Megill & Co.'s victims served as something of a foreshadowing for the postseason: Philadelphia would also lose Game 4 of the 2022 World Series on a combined no-hitter.

ROOKIES

1. Which rookie was the first Mets pitcher to defeat Sandy Koufax?
a. Al Jackson   b. Tug McGraw   c. Darrell Sutherland
d. Tom Seaver

2. Which Met hit 15 home runs by the All-Star break of his rookie season?
a. Ed Kranepool   b. Cleon Jones   c. Ron Swoboda   d. Ken Boswell

3. Which Mets pitcher threw a shutout in his debut, the only win of his major league career?
a. Al Schmelz   b. Bill Hepler   c. Dick Rusteck   d. Larry Miller

4. Who was the first Met to win NL Rookie of the Year?
a. Tom Seaver   b. Jerry Koosman   c. Jerry Grote   d. Bud Harrelson

5. Which Met tossed seven shutouts as a rookie?
a. Jerry Koosman   b. Dick Selma   c. Jim McAndrew   d. Craig Swan

6. Which rookie won Game 3 of the 1969 World Series?
a. Nolan Ryan   b. Gary Gentry   c. Jack DiLauro   d. Jim McAndrew

7. This Hofstra product and future three-time All-Star made his debut with the Mets in 1970. Who is he?
a. Amos Otis   b. Jim Bibby   c. Ken Singleton   d. Leroy Stanton

8. Which Met was named Rookie of the Year in 1972?
a. Jon Matlack   b. John Milner   c. Ted Martinez   d. Buzz Capra

9. Which one of these Mets hit a home run in his first major league at-bat?
a. Cleon Jones   b. Bruce Boisclair   c. Duffy Dyer   d. Benny Ayala

10. Which Met stole seven bases in 1980 after making his debut in September?
a. Mookie Wilson   b. Wally Backman   c. Hubie Brooks
d. Dan Norman

11. Which Mets pitcher was injured in his major league debut?
a. Ed Lynch   b. Jesse Orosco   c. Mike Scott   d. Tim Leary

12. Which 1983 Met hit a home run in his first at-bat in the majors?
a. Ron Darling   b. José Oquendo   c. Mike Fitzgerald
d. Ron Gardenhire

13. Which Met collected three hits in the 1986 division-clincher against the Cubs on the night he made his first career start?
a. Kevin Mitchell   b. Kevin Elster   c. Rafael Santana
d. Dave Magadan

14. A future All-Star who won 109 games in 14 seasons, this Met made his debut as a reliever in 1995.
a. Mike Remlinger   b. Paul Byrd   c. Jerry Dipoto   d. Doug Henry

15. This rookie, who played 13 games for the Mets in 2000, would go 1,220 at-bats in the majors before hitting his first home run.
a. Melvin Mora   b. Jay Payton   c. Jason Tyner   d. Vance Wilson

16. Which player was a Mets teammate of a Hall of Fame brother?
a. Rich Murray   b. Ramon Martinez   c. Mike Glavine
d. Sandy Alomar Jr.

17. Who hit a home run in his first at-bat in the majors in 2004?
a. José Reyes   b. Kaz Matsui   c. Ty Wigginton   d. Jeff Duncan

18. Against which team did David Wright make his debut?
a. Boston Red Sox   b. Atlanta Braves   c. Montreal Expos
d. Pittsburgh Pirates

19. Which Met had three doubles at Coors Field in his major league debut in 2008?
a. Edgardo Alfonzo   b. Jeff Keppinger   c. Timo Perez
d. Nick Evans

20. Which Met rookie hit 19 home runs in 2010?
a. Ike Davis   b. Daniel Murphy   c. Lucas Duda   d. Wilmer Flores

21. Which pitcher set the Mets team record for most strikeouts in a debut?
a. Matt Harvey   b. Steven Matz   c. Jacob deGrom
d. Noah Syndergaard

22. Which team did Jacob deGrom make his debut against?
a. Philadelphia Phillies   b. Texas Rangers   c. New York Yankees
d. Pittsburgh Pirates

23. In 2015, which Met collected the first four hits of his career in one game?
a. Ruben Tejada   b. Travis d'Arnaud   c. Michael Conforto
d. Matt Reynolds

24. Which Met hit .329 in 63 games after being called up in 2018?
a. Pete Alonso   b. Jeff McNeil   c. Amed Rosario   d. Tomás Nido

25. Which 2022 Met hit his first career home run to tie the Phillies in the bottom of the ninth on *Sunday Night Baseball*?
a. Khalil Lee   b. Nick Plummer   c. Patrick Mazeika
d. Luis Guillorme

ANSWERS

1. b. Tug McGraw

Tug spent most of 1965 as a reliever, but in his third career start he outpitched Dodgers legend Sandy Koufax in a 5–2 win. On August 26, he limited Los Angeles to two runs in seven and two-third innings as the Mets defeated Koufax, who had gone 13–0 against them, with a no-hitter in 1962. McGraw made his debut on April 18 against the Giants, striking out Orlando Cepeda as the first batter he faced. But McGraw was a scuffling starter early in his career before being moved to the bullpen, where he would become an All-Star and a vital part of two Mets pennant winners.

2. c. Ron Swoboda

Rocky made the 1965 club out of spring training and hit four homers in April. And the outfielder launched two homers in a May 8 win over the Braves. He hit 15 home runs by the All-Star break but would finish with only four in the second half. His 19 home runs would be a career-high and stand as the team record until it was broken by Darryl Strawberry in 1983. Known more for his bat than his glove, his diving catch in Game 4 of the 1969 World Series is regarded as one of the best in the history of the Fall Classic. Swoboda would hit 73 home runs in nine seasons with the Mets, Expos, and Yankees.

3. c. Dick Rusteck

The 24-year-old southpaw threw a four-hit shutout against the Reds on June 10, 1966, in a 5–0 win. None of the Reds, including Pete Rose and Tony Perez, made it into scoring position. Shortstop Eddie Bressoud led the Mets' attack with a pair of homers, as Cincy ace Jim Maloney was handed the loss. It was the first and last victory of Rusteck's injury-shortened career. The Notre Dame graduate finished 1–2 in eight appearances, including three starts. He pitched in the Phillies' and Twins' minor league systems, the Mexican League, and independent ball through the 1977 season.

4. a. Tom Seaver

Fittingly it was The Franchise who was the first Met to be named Rookie of the Year. Though the 1967 Mets lost 101 games, Seaver was a bright spot, going 16–13 with a 2.76 ERA. The 16 wins was a franchise record at the time. He made his debut April 13 against the Pirates and earned his first win a week later against the Cubs. He completed 18 of his 34 starts, including two shutouts. Seaver fanned 170 batters in 251 innings. Tom Terrific was 12–12 before winning his next four starts, giving up only seven runs in those games.

5. a. Jerry Koosman

Kooz was runner-up to Johnny Bench in the 1968 NL Rookie of the Year voting, with his seven shutouts indicative of his uncommon freshman aptitude. The lefty debuted in 1967 but pitched to a 6.04 ERA in a nine-game audition. In the "Year of the Pitcher," Koosman went 19–12 with a 2.08 ERA and completed 17 of his 34 starts. In his first home start, he shut out the Giants even after San Francisco loaded the bases with nobody out in the first inning. Kooz also showed his stuff on the national stage, striking out Carl Yastrzemski to end that season's All-Star Game and secure the National League's 1–0 win.

6. b. Gary Gentry

The rookie right-hander was the third starter behind Seaver and Koosman in 1969. Gentry, who went 13–12 on the season, outpitched Jim Palmer in Game 3 of the World Series to put the Mets ahead two games to one. Gentry tossed six and two-third shutout innings with some help from two incredible catches from Tommie Agee in center field. And Gentry, who had one RBI all season, delivered a two-run double in the second inning of the 5–0 win. Gentry would finish 41–42 in four seasons as a Met. He also pitched in 26 games with the Braves. After a return to the Mets, his career ended due to injuries.

7. c. Ken Singleton

The New York City native who grew up in Mount Vernon and went to college on Long Island was selected third overall by the Mets in the 1967 draft and made his debut in June 1970. He collected his first career hit in Montreal off former Mets prospect Steve Renko on June 26. Later in the game, he hit his first career homer off Bill Stoneman. Singleton hit 18 home runs in two seasons as a Met before being traded to the Expos in the blockbuster deal that brought Rusty Staub to New York. He would go on to be a three-time All-Star in a 15-year career with the Expos and Orioles. In 1979, the ex-Met hit 35 homers and was runner-up in AL MVP balloting for the pennant-winning Orioles.

8. a. Jon Matlack
The southpaw went 15–10 with a 2.32 ERA and completed eight of his 32 starts, including four shutouts, to become the Mets' second Rookie of the Year. Teammate John Milner was third in the voting. Matlack, who started the season in the bullpen, was quickly moved to the rotation and was 6–0 with a 1.95 ERA at the end of May. On May 30, he blanked the Phillies, defeating eventual Cy Young winner Steve Carlton. Matlack would go on to become a three-time All-Star with the Mets and a key part of the 1973 NL champions. He was 82–81 as a Met, posting a 3.03 ERA. Lousy run support often cost him wins.

9. d. Benny Ayala
The left fielder homered in his first major league at-bat on August 27, 1974, at Shea Stadium. The blast off Houston's Tom Griffin gave the Mets a 1–0 lead in a game they would go on to win, 5–2. He would hit only three homers as a Met in parts of two seasons and 38 in his 10-season career. Ayala was part of the Orioles' 1979 AL pennant champs and the 1983 squad that won the World Series. Ayala did homer in consecutive at-bats of a 1979 game against Jon Matlack, then of Texas, and then repeated the feat the following week off Jerry Koosman, by this point a Twin.

10. a. Mookie Wilson
Mookie made his debut as a September call-up in 1980 and Joe Torre had no problem with letting the speedy outfielder run, as the

speedster stole seven bases in 14 attempts. On October 4, he stole two bases in a 5–2 win against the Cardinals. In 1982, Wilson would set a club record with 58 stolen bases and the fleet-footed South Carolinian would steal 54 the following year. He would also prove adept at scoring from second on ground balls that didn't make it out of the infield. Mookie would steal 281 bases as a Met and another 46 at the end of his career with the Blue Jays.

11. d. Tim Leary

The right-hander billed as the next Tom Seaver strained his elbow after facing seven batters at Wrigley Field in his debut on April 12, 1981. Leary was the second overall pick in the 1979 draft and the Mets put him on the big club after a strong showing in the minors in 1980 and a promising spring for an organization whose pitching-prospect cupboard wasn't otherwise bulging. But arm injuries, starting with the cold day in Chicago, limited his time with the Mets, and he would finish 4–4 in 23 appearances between 1981 and 1984. Despite the disappointment attendant to his Flushing tenure, he would pitch 13 seasons in the majors, with his best year a 17–11, 2.89 ERA campaign for the 1988 World Series champion Dodgers. As one of Tommy Lasorda's all-hands-on-deck relievers, Leary recorded one particularly enormous out at Shea Stadium in Game 4 of the NLCS that October (a.k.a. the Mike Scioscia Game), retiring Gregg Jefferies amidst a would-be tying rally in the 12th inning.

12. c. Mike Fitzgerald

Making his debut at Veterans Stadium, the catcher homered off Phillies starter Tony Ghelfi in his first big-league at-bat on September 13, 1983. He later added an RBI groundout off Tug McGraw and caught Walt Terrell's complete game victory. Fitzgerald would be the primary catcher for the 90-win 1984 Mets but was sent to Montreal in the 4-for-1 deal that brought Gary Carter to New York. Fitzgerald played seven seasons with the Expos before ending his career with the Angels in 1992. The primarily defensive catcher hit 48 home runs in his career.

13. d. Dave Magadan

Filling in for an under-the-weather Keith Hernandez, Magadan delivered three hits, including a pair of RBI singles off Dennis Eckersley in the Mets' 4–2 September 17 win over the Cubs. Hernandez would enter the game late, wanting to be on the field when the Mets clinched the division. Magadan actually debuted 10 days earlier, with a fifth-inning pinch-hit single against the Padres, and would go on to spend seven seasons with the Mets. In 1990, he hit .328, garnering some MVP votes. He batted .288 in a 16-season career with the Mets, Marlins, Mariners, Astros, A's, Cubs, and Padres.

14. b. Paul Byrd

Six more teams and 256 starts awaited Paul Byrd when the righty broke in as part of Dallas Green's bullpen. Acquired from Cleveland in the Jeromy Burnitz trade, Byrd went 2–0 with a 2.05 ERA in 17 appearances in 1995. He was traded to Atlanta following the 1996 season and was named to the NL All-Star team as a Phillie in 1999. Later in his career he was a hired gun, appearing in the postseason with the Braves (his second go-round with them), Angels, Indians, and Red Sox. He also developed an old-fashioned windup in which he swung his arms back and forth to throw off hitters.

15. c. Jason Tyner

A first-round pick in 1998, the outfielder made his debut in June 2000. Despite a quick start, including two hits and two runs scored in a 12–2 win over the Yankees in his fourth game, Tyner was traded after 13 games as a Met to the Devil Rays, going with another former first-rounder (Paul Wilson) to bring back outfielder Bubba Trammell and reliever Rick White for the Mets' stretch run. Tyner, whose middle name is Renyt (Tyner backward), played with Tampa Bay, Minnesota, and Cleveland. In the 2006 ALDS against the Oakland Athletics, Tyner was the designated hitter for the Twins despite having zero career home runs. (Frank Thomas, then with 487 career homers, was the DH for Oakland.) But Tyner finally hit a homer, his only four-bagger in 1,358 at-bats, in 2007 for the Twins off Cleveland's Jake Westbrook.

16. c. Mike Glavine

First baseman Mike Glavine singled with two outs in the ninth inning of Game 162 of the 2003 season for the first and last hit of his six-game career. A standout at Northeastern University, Glavine was drafted by Cleveland and later traded to Atlanta. He was signed by the Mets two months after the team signed his brother Tom. On September 14, Mike made his debut, pinch-hitting for his brother. Following his playing days, he returned to Northeastern as an assistant coach before being promoted to head coach. In 2021, he led his alma mater to the NCAA regional.

17. b. Kaz Matsui

Much was made of the Mets signing Japanese star Kaz Matsui to form a double-play combo with José Reyes (as if dictated by the old saying about best-laid plans, Reyes was injured in spring training, and the two didn't play together until June). On the first pitch he saw in the majors, Matsui hit a homer off Atlanta's Russ Ortiz. The following season, he again homered in his first at-bat, a shot off ex-Met Paul Wilson at Cincinnati. In 2006, he became the only player to homer in his first at-bat in three straight seasons when he hit an inside-the-park homer off San Diego's Jake Peavy. Unfortunately, though Matsui mastered first at-bats of a season, he struggled with consistency at the plate and in the infield and the Mets let him go during the 2006 campaign. He helped the Rockies win the 2007 NL pennant.

18. c. Montreal Expos

The 2004 season was Wright's first in the majors and the Expos' last. The highly touted third baseman was called up during the summer and made his debut at Shea on July 21. He went hitless in four at-bats but the following afternoon collected his first hit, a double off Zach Day. It was the first of a franchise record 1,777 hits. Wright hit 14 home runs in only 69 games and batted .293, providing a glimmer of hope as the Mets fell apart in the final months of the season. He would go on to become a seven-time All-Star and team captain, playing in both the 2006 and 2015 postseasons.

19. d. Nick Evans

A fifth-round pick in the 2004 draft, Evans doubled three times in his major league debut, the first NL player (since 1901) to accomplish the feat. Evans doubled twice off Jeff Francis and once off Alberto Arias of the Rockies in the Mets' 9–2 victory at Coors Field on May 24, 2008. He collected 10 doubles in 50 games for the Mets as a rookie. Going back and forth between the majors and minors, Evans played parts of four seasons in New York and briefly for the Diamondbacks in 2014. He ended his playing career in Asia and as of 2024 was the minor league field coordinator for the Arizona Diamondbacks.

20. a. Ike Davis

Called up in April 2010, Davis hit 11 home runs before the All-Star break, tying him for second-most by a Mets rookie. He would finish with 19 homers and also set the team rookie record for total bases. Davis hit two homers in a game twice, both times against the eventual World Champion Giants. Most indelibly, the nimble first baseman caught three foul balls while tumbling over railings. After an injury-shortened 2011, Davis would hit 32 homers in 2012, but his batting average plummeted as his strikeouts increased. He later played with the Pirates, A's, and Yankees. His father, Ron, was an All-Star pitcher for the Yankees in 1981. The man who spawned a revival of the "I LIKE IKE" slogan on T-shirts at Citi Field played for Team Israel in the 2017 World Baseball Classic.

21. a. Matt Harvey

On July 26, 2012, Harvey fanned 11 Diamondbacks in five and one-third innings at Chase Field in Phoenix, breaking the previous record of eight, set on April 20, 1967, by Tom Seaver and matched later that same week by Bill Denehy. Harvey was the seventh overall pick in the 2010 draft and, by summer 2012, was looked upon as the potential savior and future for a struggling Mets franchise. The team won Harvey's debut, 3–1, with the pitcher also going 2-for-2 with a single and double. Harvey would start the 2013 All-Star Game at Citi Field and help the Mets win the 2015 pennant, but injuries and off-field issues would limit his effectiveness, leading to his trade to the Reds in 2018.

22. c. New York Yankees
DeGrom made his debut in a Subway Series matchup at Citi Field on May 15, 2014. The Mets lost 1–0, not the last time the Mets star would fail to get run support. Rafael Montero made his debut the night before and was more highly touted at the time than deGrom (the Mets also failed to score for Montero). DeGrom gave up one run in four hits over seven innings while striking out six. Starting for the Yankees was Chase Whitley, also making his major league debut. Future Mets Dellin Betances and David Robertson recorded the win and save, respectively, on deGrom's first night.

23. c. Michael Conforto
The Mets' first-round pick in 2014, the lefty-swinging outfielder collected his four hits in a 15–2 drubbing of the Dodgers on July 25, 2015. He was called up from the minors to help spark a lackluster Mets offense that was holding them back in their quest for first place. After going hitless in his debut, Conforto went 4-for-4 in his second game, with three hits off Zach Lee, making his own major league debut, and the fourth hit off Chin-hui Tsao. Conforto helped lead the Mets to the World Series in 2015—where he homered twice—and hit 132 home runs in seven seasons before signing with the Giants in 2013. Scooter (a nickname hung on him by teammate Noah Syndergaard) was a 2017 All-Star, and in 2019 he launched a career-high 33 home runs.

24. b. Jeff McNeil
After batting .368 in Triple-A, the Mets finally called up McNeil in late July to inject some offense into a painfully unproductive lineup. The aggressive McNeil, who was adept at putting the ball in play, had 20 multi-hit games in a little over two months. He finished sixth in the Rookie of the Year voting despite playing only 63 games. Showing it was no fluke, McNeil batted .318 with 23 home runs in

2019 and earned a spot on the NL All-Star team. In 2022, he again made the All-Star team and led the majors with a .326 batting average, earning himself a Silver Slugger Award.

25. b. Nick Plummer

After entering three games late as a defensive replacement, Plummer made his first start on May 29 and hit a game-tying home run in the bottom of the ninth in front of ESPN's cameras. Plummer was hitless in three at-bats with two strikeouts on the night, but Buck Showalter let him lead off the ninth and Plummer drilled Corey Knebel's first pitch into the right-field stands to tie the game. The Mets won the game an inning later. Plummer also hit a three-run homer the following night in a blowout win over the Nationals. The outfielder hit .138 with two home runs in 14 games as a 2022 Met before returning to the minors.

TRADES AND FREE AGENTS

1. Who did the Mets get in return for Jay Hook?
a. Frank Lary   b. Tom Sturdivant   c. Roy McMillan   d. Tug McGraw

2. Who did the Mets trade to acquire Ed Charles?
a. Chuck Hiller   b. Phil Linz   c. Al Luplow   d. Larry Elliot

3. Who did the Mets receive for Ron Swoboda?
a. Rusty Staub   b. Don Hahn   c. Harry Parker   d. Jim Gosger

4. Who did the Mets trade to acquire Willie Mays?
a. Ray Sadecki   b. Ron Taylor   c. Charlie Williams
d. Danny Frisella

5. Who did the Mets obtain for Jerry Koosman?
a. Jesse Orosco   b. Rick Aguilera   c. Hubie Brooks
d. John Gibbons

6. Which Met was acquired from a division rival between games of a doubleheader between the two teams?
a. Tim Foli   b. John Stearns   c. José Cardenal   d. Keith Hernandez

7. Who was the first Mets free agent signing?
a. Tom Hausman   b. Pat Zachry   c. Lenny Randle   d. Richie Hebner

8. Which three-time All-Star pitcher did the team acquire and then trade away to bring George Foster to Queens before he ever pitched for the Mets?
a. Mike Marshall   b. Jim Kern   c. Sparky Lyle   d. Bruce Kison

9. Which future major league manager went from the Mets organization to the Reds to bring Tom Seaver back?
a. Bruce Bochy   b. Clint Hurdle   c. Ron Gardenhire
d. Lloyd McClendon

10. Who did the Mets obtain for Lenny Dykstra and Roger McDowell?
a. Juan Samuel   b. Frank Viola   c. Vince Coleman   d. John Franco

11. Which relief pitcher did the Mets get for Mookie Wilson?
a. Jeff Musselman   b. Don Aase   c. Bob McClure   d. Julio Valera

12. Who returned to the Mets in a deal for Bobby Ojeda?
a. Jeromy Burnitz   b. Jeff McKnight   c. Hubie Brooks
d. Lee Mazzilli

13. Which infielder did the Mets receive for Anthony Young?
a. Fernando Viña   b. José Vizcaino   c. David Segui   d. Rico Brogna

14. Which Met was sent to Toronto for John Olerud?
a. Paul Byrd   b. Blas Minor   c. Doug Henry   d. Robert Person

15. Which Mets pitcher was traded away and then reacquired five weeks later?
a. Turk Wendell   b. Mel Rojas   c. Greg McMichael   d. Rigo Beltrán

16. Which former Cy Young winner signed with the Mets only a week and a half before Opening Day?
a. Frank Viola   b. Orel Hershiser   c. David Cone   d. Tom Glavine

17. Which future All-Star was traded to the Marlins for Al Leiter?
a. Jason Isringhausen   b. A. J. Burnett   c. Preston Wilson
d. Carl Everett

18. Who did the Mets trade Jesse Orosco for during spring training 2000?
a. Mike Bordick   b. Bubba Trammell   c. Joe McEwing
d. Todd Zeile

19. Who did the Mets acquire for Armando Benitez in a rare crosstown trade?
a. Mike Stanton   b. Felix Heredia   c. Graeme Lloyd
d. Jason Anderson

20. Who did the Mets trade to obtain Carlos Delgado?
a. Preston Wilson   b. Mike Jacobs   c. Ed Yarnall
d. Armando Benitez

21. Which reliever did the Mets trade for Orlando Hernandez?
a. Royce Ring   b. Jorge Julio   c. Henry Owens   d. Alay Soler

22. Who did the Mets get for Billy Wagner?
a. Willie Harris   b. Jesus Feliciano   c. Mike Hessman   d. Chris Carter

23. Which prospect did the Mets obtain for Carlos Beltrán?
a. Noah Syndergaard   b. Zack Wheeler   c. Matt Harvey
d. Steven Matz

24. Who did the Mets trade away to reacquire Jon Niese?
a. Antonio Bastardo   b. Jim Henderson   c. Josh Edgin
d. Logan Verrett

25. Who did the Mets receive for Matt Harvey?
a. Jay Bruce   b. Devin Mesoraco   c. José Lobatón   d. Todd Frazier

ANSWERS

1. c. Roy McMillan
Jay Hook, the pitcher who recorded the first win in Mets history, was traded to the Milwaukee Braves in early 1964 for veteran shortstop Roy McMillan. A two-time All-Star with the Reds, McMillan played with the Mets through the 1966 season, but his most important role may have been serving as a mentor to young shortstop Bud Harrelson. McMillan also started a triple play in a 23-inning loss to the Giants in 1964. He was on Yogi Berra's staff in the mid-1970s, managed the team for the final 53 games of 1975, and remained as a coach under Joe Frazier in 1976.

2. d. Larry Elliot
Outfielder Larry Elliot was the first Met to homer in four straight games, but his biggest contribution was being sent to the Kansas City Athletics for third baseman Ed Charles. At 34, Charles was one of the older Mets and hit only .238 in 1967. But his 15 home runs led the 1968 Mets and his .276 batting average was one of the best on the team. He split time with Wayne Garrett at third base in Gil Hodges's platoon for the 1969 Miracle Mets and his ninth-inning single in Game 2 started a game-winning rally to turn the World Series around.

3. b. Don Hahn
Unhappy with his contract, Swoboda said he should be played more often or traded. The Mets obliged at the end of spring training in 1971, sending him to the Expos for Don Hahn, a light-hitting outfielder who was homerless in 158 career at-bats. Hahn played four seasons with the Mets, with his most memorable moment coming in the 1973 World Series when his leaping catch took an extra-base hit away from Joe Rudi in Game 3. He also had three hits in Game 7. Swoboda would play only 39 games for the Expos before being sent back to New York, this time to the Yankees, for whom he would play for three seasons.

Ron Swoboda

4. c. Charlie Williams

The right-hander went 5–6 with a 4.78 ERA in 31 games, including nine starts, as a rookie for the 1971 Mets. But Williams, who was born in Flushing and grew up in Great Neck, is much better remembered for being sent to the Giants in the deal that brought Willie Mays back to New York, fulfilling a longtime dream of owner Joan Payson. Williams's first Mets win actually came in a five-inning relief outing against the Giants in June 1971; he even retired Mays on a fly ball in the ninth inning. Used primarily as a reliever, Williams would go 18–16 with a 3.82 ERA in seven seasons with the Giants.

5. a. Jesse Orosco

Koosman, the man on the mound when the Mets won their first World Series, was traded to the Twins for Orosco, the man who would be on the mound when the Mets won their second. The veteran Koosman was sent to Minnesota after the 1978 season for minor league pitcher Greg Field and a player to be named later who turned out to be Orosco. The young lefty had spent the 1978 season in rookie ball. Orosco would go on to pitch a record 1,252 games in the majors over 24 seasons spanning four decades. He made two All-Star teams as a Met and won three games in the 1986 NLCS.

6. c. José Cardenal

The veteran outfielder was acquired by the Mets, his eighth team in the majors, from the Phillies on August 2, 1979, as Steve Henderson was placed on the disabled list. Cardenal would play 37 games over two seasons for the Mets before finishing his career with the 1980 Royals' AL pennant-winning team. But the Mets–Phillies doubleheader split (Cardenal did not appear in either contest) is remembered not for the trade but because the death of Yankees captain Thurman Munson in an airplane crash was announced on the Shea Stadium scoreboard during the first inning of game one. Cardenal, who received MVP votes as a Cub in 1972 and 1973, retired with 1,913 hits and 329 stolen bases.

7. a. Tom Hausman

The Mets signed the Brewers pitcher to a three-year deal worth approximately $175,000 before the 1978 season. He began the year in the minors and would go 3–3 in 10 starts after being brought up to the Mets. As a starter-reliever, Hausman was 12–17 with a 3.66 ERA in five seasons in New York. His best effort was a 3–2 complete game victory over Vida Blue and the Giants on Old-Timers' Day in 1979 when the Mets commemorated the 10th anniversary of their first World Championship. He suffered a freak injury in 1981 when he tripped over a drainage cover while running in the Shea Stadium outfield. Hausman pitched briefly for the Braves and in the minors for the Pirates, Dodgers, and Padres before retiring.

8. b. Jim Kern

The ace reliever made three All-Star teams with Cleveland and Texas and in 1979 finished fourth in the MVP voting, the same year he surrendered a game-tying home run to the Mets' Lee Mazzilli in the eighth inning of the All-Star Game. But after battling injuries and ineffectiveness for the next two seasons, the Rangers traded him to the Mets for Doug Flynn. Kern would never pitch for the Mets, as a few months later he was included in the deal that brought in George Foster from the Reds. Kern pitched for five teams in his final five seasons, including a return to Cleveland. He finished his career with 88 saves. Foster would hit 99 home runs in five seasons with the Mets.

9. d. Lloyd McClendon

The future major league skipper was coming off an 18-homer season for Single-A Lynchburg when he was included in the deal with the Reds that brought The Franchise back to the Mets. He made it to the majors in 1987 and would play in the big leagues for eight seasons with the Reds, Cubs, and Pirates. McClendon hit a career-high 12 home runs for the 1989 Cubs as they edged out the Mets to win the NL East. He also homered for the Pirates in the 1992 NLCS. McClendon would eventually manage the Pirates (2001–2005), Mariners (2014–2015), and Tigers (eight games in 2020), winning 501 games.

10. a. Juan Samuel

The Mets traded the duo for two-time All-Star Juan Samuel, a star second baseman who had been moved to center field. The trade was not well received by fans who were even unhappier when Samuel batted .228 with three home runs as the Mets failed to repeat as division champs. After the season, he was shipped to the Dodgers for Mike Marshall and Alejandro Peña and made the All-Star team in 1991. Meanwhile, Dykstra would make three All-Star teams as a Phillie and help lead the team to the 1993 World Series. His career ended after 1996, shortened by spinal stenosis, the same back ailment that victimized David Wright two decades later. Samuel retired after 1998, playing for seven teams during his major league career. He did return to the Mets organization briefly, as manager of Double-A Binghamton in 2006.

11. a. Jeff Musselman

When free-agent-to-be Mookie Wilson was sent to Toronto at the 1989 trading deadline, lefty Jeff Musselman, who went 12–5 out of the pen for the 1987 Blue Jays, came to Queens in exchange. Though he could start or relieve, Davey Johnson and Bud Harrelson used Musselman exclusively out of the bullpen. The Harvard product had a 4.47 ERA in 48 games over two seasons. Meanwhile, Mookie hit .298 in 54 games and helped Toronto win the AL East. The Blue Jays would again win the division in 1991 with Mookie on their roster, by which time Musselman was no longer in the majors.

12. c. Hubie Brooks

The third baseman-turned-shortstop was one of four players sent to the Expos for Gary Carter in December 1984. Brooks was a two-time All-Star with the Expos, who converted him to a right fielder in 1988. He spent 1990 with the Dodgers, but when the Los Angeles outfield became overcrowded, Brooks became expendable and he was sent to the Mets. While the Mets used Ojeda as both a starter and reliever in 1990, the Dodgers used him only in the rotation. Brooks's Flushing return lasted one year, as he was traded to the Angels for Dave Gallagher seven years to the day after he was exchanged for Carter. Brooks also played with the Royals before retiring.

13. b. José Vizcaino

The Mets sent the pitcher who lost 27 consecutive decisions for the Cubs shortstop just days before the 1994 season began. Vizcaino was one of four shortstops in Cubs camp and the Mets had spent the winter looking to fill that gap in their infield. The team had earlier tried to land Omar Vizquel, Felix Fermin, and Mark Lewis. A proposed trade to send Young to the Angels for first baseman J. T. Snow also fell through. Vizcaino played for eight teams in 18 seasons, but his most notable moment came against the Mets when he won Game 1 of the 2000 World Series for the Yankees with a 12th-inning RBI single.

14. d. Robert Person

The right-hander was 5–5 in two seasons as a starter-reliever when he was sent to Toronto. Not only did the Blue Jays give the Mets a terrific first baseman who finished third in the 1993 MVP voting, but they also gave $5 million to pay most of his salary. Olerud was coming off a disappointing season, and Toronto management thought he might have to become a platoon player. While Person pitched to a 6.18 ERA in three seasons with the Blue Jays, Olerud helped the Mets make the 1999 playoffs and was part of what *Sports Illustrated* speculated was "The Best Infield Ever."

15. c. Greg McMichael

The righty relief pitcher was traded to the Dodgers along with Dave Mlicki in the June 1998 deal that brought Japanese sensation Hideo Nomo to the Mets. The middle reliever was considered expendable, yet when the Mets bullpen struggled over the next several weeks, the team sent southpaw Brian Bohanon to the Dodgers to bring McMichael back. In 1999, the Mets again found themselves in need of a starter and sent McMichael to Oakland along with Jason Isringhausen (recently converted to relief) for Kenny Rogers. McMichael spent eight seasons in the majors, including five with Atlanta, where he notched 40 saves in his first two seasons.

16. b. Orel Hershiser

In 1999, with their starters struggling in spring training, the Mets let Hideo Nomo go and were able to beat out the Cubs to sign The Bulldog. Hershiser, a Cy Young winner, had been a Mets nemesis in the 1988 NLCS, helped propel Cleveland to two World Series in the mid-1990s, and then spent the 1998 season with the Giants. He was in spring training with Cleveland, but once released found himself in demand. Hershiser was sought by the Cubs, along with the Mets' NL East rivals in Atlanta, Philadelphia, and Florida, but he chose to pitch in Queens. Hershiser went 13–12 in his one season with the Mets, picking up his 200th win in Montreal. He returned to the Dodgers in 2000 before retiring.

17. b. A. J. Burnett

The hard-throwing right-hander was selected in the eighth round of the 1995 draft out of Central Arkansas Christian School. He pitched in the Mets farm system for three seasons before being traded in February 1998 to the rebuilding and cost-cutting Marlins in the Al Leiter deal. Burnett would pitch 17 seasons in the majors. His accomplishments included leading the NL in shutouts (2002), leading the AL in strikeouts as a member of the Blue Jays (2008), winning a World Series game for the Yankees' 2009 championship team, and making the All-Star team in his final major league season with the Pirates in 2015. Burnett also pitched a no-hitter in May 2001 as a Marlin despite walking nine Padres in the 3–0 win.

18. c. Joe McEwing

After a 13-year absence from New York, Jesse Orosco returned to the Mets in an offseason trade with the Orioles, but during spring training he was sent to the Cardinals. The transaction prevented the possibility that a teammate of Ed Kranepool—Orosco and Kranepool played together as 1979 Mets—would be active for the home team at Shea in the 21st century. The Mets had four lefties in spring training—Orosco was joined by John Franco, Dennis Cook, and Rich Rodriguez—so the move was somewhat inevitable. McEwing spent the first month of 2000 in the minors but became a valuable utilityman for Bobby Valentine, playing six positions for a pennant-winning team. Orosco was already the oldest player in the league and played through the end of the 2003 season. McEwing played five seasons with the Mets before moving on to the Royals and Astros.

19. d. Jason Anderson

The rookie reliever with 22 games under his belt was traded to the Mets for Armando Benitez, who was sought in the Bronx as a set-up man for Mariano Rivera. The Mets got a look at Anderson when he pitched a pair of scoreless ninth innings to finish them off in June, once at Yankee Stadium and once at Shea. Anderson pitched in only six games with the Mets, posting a 5.06 ERA, while wearing the number 17. He pitched one game in 2004 with Cleveland and three more when he returned to the Yankees in 2005, later becoming head baseball coach at Eastern Illinois. Meanwhile, the Yankees' plans for Benitez proved short-lived—they traded him to Seattle three weeks after acquiring him.

20. b. Mike Jacobs

The lefty first baseman hit 11 home runs in 30 games as a rookie in 2005, including four in his first 11 at-bats. But when the Mets had an opportunity to add slugger Carlos Delgado to the heart of the lineup, they sent Jacobs to Florida. Jacobs hit 69 home runs for the Marlins in three seasons, including a career-high 32 in 2008. After Delagdo's Mets tenure ended in 2009 due to injuries, Jacobs returned as the Opening Day first baseman the next year. He played seven games for the 2010 Mets but managed to hit his 100th and final home run during his stay. Jacobs later managed in the Marlins minor league system.

21. b. Jorge Julio

The relief pitcher had a 5.06 ERA in 18 appearances before being sent to Arizona for Orlando Hernandez, as the Mets needed help for an injured rotation which saw Brian Bannister, John Maine, and Victor Zambrano sidelined. El Duque had proved himself a clutch pitcher, winning four titles and five pennants with the Yankees and White Sox, and would be reliable as a Met until an injury kept him out of the 2006 postseason. Julio had a rough start to his year with a 19.64 ERA through four appearances but pitched better in May and fanned 33 batters in 21⅓ innings before becoming an ex-Met.

22. d. Chris Carter

The out-of-contention Mets sent Wagner, the six-time All-Star closer, who battled back from injuries to pitch in 2009, to the Red Sox in August. Wagner was not expected to pitch after undergoing Tommy John surgery in 2008, but pitched two games for the Mets before shipping up to Boston. Carter, who appeared in 13 games with the Red Sox, played in 100 for the 2010 Mets, batting .263 with four home runs. It was his last season in the majors, though he would later play in Mexico and Japan. The 2010 season was also the last for Wagner, who made the All-Star team as a Brave and finished that season with a 1.43 ERA.

23. b. Zack Wheeler

With the 2011 Mets not convinced their late-July wild card standing was anything more than a mirage, they sent Carlos Beltrán to the Giants for Zack Wheeler. The young right-hander was the sixth overall pick by the Giants in the 2009 draft, and prior to the 2011 season was named by *Baseball America* as San Francisco's second-best prospect. Wheeler came up to the majors in 2013 and would go 44–38 in five seasons with the Mets, though he would miss the club's 2015 and 2016 playoff runs due to injuries. He signed with the Phillies after the 2019 season, finished as Cy Young runner-up in 2021 and 2024, and helped the team win the pennant in 2022.

24. a. Antonio Bastardo

Following Daniel Murphy's departure, the Mets traded Jon Niese to Pittsburgh for second baseman Neil Walker. In the offseason, they also signed southpaw reliever Antonio Bastardo, but he struggled, posting a 4.74 ERA in 41 appearances as a Met. Niese was also scuffling as a Pirates starter and was moved to the bullpen by Clint Hurdle. The teams swapped lefty relievers returning both pitchers to familiar surroundings, though Niese's homecoming was slightly awkward given his criticism of the Mets after they traded him months earlier. Niese would appear in six games with an 11.45 ERA, his final action in the majors.

25. b. Devin Mesoraco

The Mets sent The Dark Knight to the Reds for the former All-Star catcher early in the 2018 season. Travis d'Arnaud had season-ending surgery, Kevin Plawecki had been out a month, and both José Lobatón and Tomás Nido were batting below .165. Mesoraco helped stabilize the position, handling the pitching staff—particularly Cy Young winner Jacob deGrom—well and showing a little pop with 10 homers in 66 games (nine of the long balls coming in the seventh inning or later). Yet despite the ex-Red's Met success, 2018 turned out to be the final season of his career. In 2019, he failed to make the Opening Day roster, refused to report to his minor league assignment, and retired rather than report to Triple-A Syracuse. Mesoraco later became an assistant coach with the University of Pittsburgh's baseball program.

TWO-TERM METS

1. Which Met gave up Mark McGwire's 50th home run of 1999?
a. Willie Blair   b. Jeff Tam   c. Rigo Beltrán   d. Jason Isringhausen

2. Which first overall pick was a Met twice in the 1980s?
a. Bill Almon   b. Mike Ivie   c. Shawn Abner   d. Jeff Burroughs

3. Which Met played against the Mets in the 2006 playoffs between stints in Flushing?
a. Joe McEwing   b. Cliff Floyd   c. Marlon Anderson
d. Ramon Castro

4. Which Met was on both the 103-loss 1993 squad and 1999 playoff team?
a. Melvin Mora   b. Jesse Orosco   c. Chuck McElroy
d. Bobby Bonilla

5. Which player was an All-Star with the Brewers between two Mets stints?
a. Fernando Viña   b. Jeromy Burnitz   c. Dave Nilsson
d. Ricky Bones

6. Which Met stole 66 bases in his first tour of duty with the Mets and 39 in his second?
a. José Reyes   b. Lee Mazzilli   c. Roger Cedeño   d. Angel Pagan

7. Which outfielder played 10 games with the 2002 Mets and seven more with the 2008 team?

a. Brady Clark   b. Tony Tarasco   c. Michael Tucker   d. Matt Lawton

8. Which one of these pitchers had two stints with the Mets?

a. Ron Darling   b. David Cone   c. Sid Fernandez   d. Rick Aguilera

9. Which Met was traded for Jerry Blevins but then returned briefly in 2018?

a. Kevin Kaczmarski   b. Jack Reinheimer   c. Matt den Dekker
d. José Bautista

10. Which player began 1979 with the Mets and ended it in the World Series with the Pirates?

a. Tim Foli   b. John Milner   c. Richie Hebner   d. Andy Hassler

11. Which 2006 Met went to the Nationals before returning to Queens?

a. Aaron Heilman   b. Lastings Milledge   c. Anderson Hernandez
d. Eli Marrero

12. Which Mets outfielder was on the 1969 and 1973 teams but didn't play in either postseason?

a. George Theodore   b. Rich Chiles   c. Dave Schneck
d. Jim Gosger

13. Which well-traveled player spent 18 seasons in the National League with eight teams?

a. Todd Zeile   b. Octavio Dotel   c. Lenny Harris   d. Mike Bordick

14. Which future manager was a Met in 1985 and 1987 but not 1986?

a. Clint Hurdle   b. Larry Bowa   c. Bobby Valentine
d. Lloyd McClendon

15. Which player sent to the Expos in the Rusty Staub deal became his Met teammate in the early 1980s?

a. Ken Singleton   b. Tim Foli   c. Alex Trevino   d. Mike Jorgensen

16. Which Met was a two-time All-Star with the Cubs between Mets stints?
a. José Vizcaino   b. Dave Kingman   c. Bob Bailor
d. Joel Youngblood

17. Which mid-1990s Met returned to pitch 12 games in 1999?
a. Kenny Rogers   b. Josias Manzanillo   c. Jeff Tam   d. Bill Pulsipher

18. Which Met won a World Series in 1986 in his second go-round with the team?
a. Kelvin Chapman   b. Rusty Staub   c. Lee Mazzilli   d. Bill Almon

19. Which pitcher appeared for both the 1962 and 1973 Mets?
a. Bob Miller   b. Galen Cisco   c. Al Jackson   d. Sherman Jones

20. Which player was sold to the Angels in May 2015 and rejoined the Mets less than a month later?
a. Carlos Torres   b. Anthony Recker   c. Eric Young Jr.
d. Kirk Nieuwenhuis

21. Which Met was on the 2006 and 2016 playoff teams?
a. Oliver Perez   b. Juan Lagares   c. José Reyes
d. Curtis Granderson

22. Which 2020 and 2022 Met spent the 2021 season with the Pirates?
a. Starling Marte   b. Chasen Shreve   c. Paul Sewald
d. Billy Hamilton

23. Which 1973 Met also appeared in four games for the 1977 team?
a. Ray Sadecki   b. Buzz Capra   c. Danny Frisella
d. Skip Lockwood

24. Which Mets pitcher started for them in 2007 and again in 2018?
a. John Maine   b. Mike Pelfrey   c. Joe Smith   d. Jason Vargas

25. Which two-time Met had at least 500 hits with four different teams?
a. Todd Zeile   b. Roberto Alomar   c. Rusty Staub
d. Gary Sheffield

ANSWERS

1. b. Jeff Tam
The right-handed middle reliever gave up McGwire's 50th homer of 1999 at Shea in an 8–7 Mets win in the second game of an August 22 doubleheader. Tam appeared in 15 games with the 1998 Mets and was claimed off waivers in June 1999 by Cleveland. He pitched in one game for his new club, giving up three runs in one-third of an inning. Two months later, he was claimed off waivers by the Mets and made nine appearances. Tam later pitched three seasons for the A's, including twice in the playoffs, and once with the Blue Jays before becoming a college head coach for Eastern Florida State College and Florida Tech.

2. a. Bill Almon
The top overall pick in the 1974 draft never lived up to billing in six seasons with San Diego. He was traded to the Expos, for whom he only played 18 games before he was signed by the Mets during the 1980 season. As a utility infielder, he batted .170 in 48 games and committed seven errors. Almon played for three more teams before the Mets reacquired him from the Pirates during the 1987 season. Almon batted .241 in 49 games including a game-winning single in the bottom of the ninth on June 24 off Lee Smith to beat the Cubs, 2–1. He played 20 games for the Phillies in 1988, his last major league season.

3. c. Marlon Anderson
Anderson was a reliable pinch-hitter for the 2005 Mets but left in the offseason for a bigger role with the Nationals. In late August 2006, he was traded to the contending Dodgers and faced the Mets in the NLDS, batting .308 (4-for-13). Los Angeles released him

during the 2007 season and the Mets brought him back. Anderson batted .319 in 43 games. Injuries would limit his time in 2008 when he batted .210. He was designated for assignment after playing in four games in 2009. Following his playing days, he did TV work for Phillies broadcasts and also served as hitting coach for the Brooklyn Cyclones.

4. d. Bobby Bonilla

The outfielder-infielder who starred on losing Mets teams of the early 1990s also filled in as a part-time player on the 1999 playoff team. Bonilla was traded from the Mets to the Orioles in 1995 and later won a World Series with the Marlins in 1997. After spending 1998 with the Dodgers, he was dealt back to the Mets in part because he feuded with incoming Los Angeles manager Davey Johnson when they were together in Baltimore. Bonilla had a dreadful 1999 season, batting .160 with four home runs, and not hitting it off with Bobby Valentine, either. The Mets released him (costing them $1.19 million in deferred payments annually on July 1 from 2011 to 2035) and he played with the Braves and Cardinals before retiring after the 2001 season.

5. b. Jeromy Burnitz

The young outfielder found himself in Dallas Green's doghouse and was traded to Cleveland after the 1994 season. As a Brewer in the late 1990s and early 2000s, he produced four consecutive 30-homer seasons and started the 1999 All-Star Game. The Mets brought him back for the 2002 campaign, but Burnitz hit just .215 with 19 home runs as the Mets fell to last place. He slugged 18 home runs in 65 games for the 2003 team before being traded to the Dodgers that July. In 2004, he hit 37 home runs for the Rockies. Burnitz played for seven teams in 14 seasons, hitting 315 home runs.

6. c. Roger Cedeño

The speedy Cedeño batted .313 with 66 stolen bases in 1999 after being acquired by the Dodgers in the deal that sent Todd Hundley to Los Angeles. Following his breakout season, Cedeño was sent to Houston in the trade that netted the Mets Mike Hampton and Derek

Bell. After a season apiece with the Astros and Tigers, Cedeño signed with the Mets before the 2002 season. He struggled in his Flushing encore, failing to bat .270 either year of his second stay. The speedster was traded to the Cardinals before the start of the 2004 season. Cedeño stole 213 bases in his 11 seasons in the majors.

7. a. Brady Clark

The part-time outfielder was acquired from the Reds late in 2002 for Shawn Estes. Clark batted .417, mostly as a pinch-hitter. He played for three other teams before returning to the Mets in 2008. Clark made the Opening Day roster through a combination of others' injuries and his own productive spring (management didn't hold against Clark the Grapefruit League swing that saw him shatter his bat just bizarrely enough to send one shard flying directly toward the right arm of Carlos Delgado, then a baserunner on third; Delgado required four stitches). Clark had two hits in eight at-bats in a second Met term that was about as brief as the first. He played for five teams in his nine seasons in the majors and later joined the Dodgers organization as an outfield and baserunning coordinator.

8. b. David Cone

The former Mets All-Star had seemingly thrown his last major league pitch in 2001 with the Red Sox, having spent 2002 working for the newly launched YES Network. But in 2003 he came out of retirement to pitch for the Mets, wearing 16 as a shoutout to his former Mets and Yankees teammate Dwight Gooden (Doc wore number 11 as a Yankee). In his first stint with the Mets, Cone switched from 44 to 17 in appreciation of Keith Hernandez. Cone didn't wear 16 long—his comeback lasted five games. The 40-year-old won his first start against the Expos but struggled after that. Coincidentally that lone win gave Cone 194 in his career, tying him with Gooden. The number 16 was retired for Doc in 2024.

9. c. Matt den Dekker

A fifth-round pick in 2010, den Dekker, a fine defensive outfielder, played with the Mets in 2013 and 2014. Just before the start of the 2015 season, he was sent to Washington in an intra-division deal for southpaw reliever Jerry Blevins. After playing with the Nationals and Tigers, den Dekker received an invite to spring training with the Mets in 2018. He was called up to play eight games in July, going hitless in 18 at-bats. He then batted .268 in 29 games with the Long Island Ducks in 2019 before retiring. Den Dekker later became an assistant baseball coach at Charleston Southern University in South Carolina.

10. a. Tim Foli

The veteran infielder started the season with the Mets and finished it with eight hits in the final four games of the World Series as the Pirates prevailed over the Orioles. Foli was the first overall pick in the 1968 draft and he played with the Mets in 1970 and 1971 before being traded to the Expos in the deal that brought Rusty Staub to New York. Crazy Horse, as he was known, played for the Expos and Giants before returning to the Mets for the 1978 season, when he hit .257 in 113 games. After making an impression with the Pirates, he finished out his career with the Angels and Yankees, then coached for the Rangers, Brewers, Royals, and Reds.

11. c. Anderson Hernandez

The infielder was with the Mets from 2005 to 2007 and notably pinch-ran for Paul Lo Duca in Game 7 of the 2006 NLCS. He represented the potential pennant-winning run when Carlos Beltrán struck out looking. He also deserves to be remembered for making an incredible full-out diving catch at second base in the second game of the 2006 season to take a hit from Marlon Byrd. Hernandez, who wound up missing the bulk of the 2006 regular season due to injury, was traded to the Nationals in August 2008 but 12 months later he was shipped back to the Mets, hitting .252 in 46 games in his second stint. Hernandez also played with Cleveland and Houston before retiring.

12. d. Jim Gosger

The former Red Sox and A's outfielder was acquired from the Seattle Pilots during the 1969 season and played 10 games for the Miracle Mets that September, batting .133. He was traded after the season to the Giants but never played a game with them, as he was sold to the Expos in April 1970. He returned to the Mets organization in a minor league trade after the 1971 season and played 38 games for the 1973 NL champs, filling in for an injured Cleon Jones early in the season. He drove in seven runs during his first two weeks with the team his second time around. Gosger's final season in the majors was 1974 when he played in 26 more games for the Mets (when, unlike 1969 and 1973, the journeyman was apparently not a good luck charm).

13. c. Lenny Harris

The majors' all-time pinch-hit king spent all 18 of his seasons in the National League with the Mets, Reds, Dodgers, Marlins, Diamondbacks, Rockies, Cubs, and Brewers, with two stops apiece in New York and Cincinnati. The durable Harris batted .304 for the 1990 Dodgers and .305 with the 2002 Brewers. The lefty swinger spent the second half of the 1998 season with the Mets and hit a career-high six homers before signing with the Rockies in the offseason. The Mets reacquired him from the Diamondbacks in June 2000 for Bill Pulsipher, himself a two-term Met. The veteran later won a World Series with the 2003 Marlins. Harris retired with 1,055 hits, including 212 as a pinch-hitter.

14. a. Clint Hurdle

The outfielder who once graced the cover of *Sports Illustrated* as a Kansas City Royals "phenom" would play with the Mets in two less than impeccably timed stints in the 1980s. Hurdle signed with the Mets and would play in 43 games for the 1985 team that went 98–64 and finished second to the Cardinals. He was then selected by the Redbirds in the Rule 5 draft and spent 1986 in St. Louis instead of Flushing, while the first-place Mets won 108 games and a World Championship. He re-signed with the Mets for 1987 and played in three games for a 92–70 club destined to finish second to the Cardinals. Hurdle interviewed in 2010 to be Mets manager, but landed in Pittsburgh as Pirates skipper shortly before New York hired Terry Collins.

15. d. Mike Jorgensen

The first baseman-outfielder who attended Francis Lewis High School in Queens debuted in 1968 and was traded to the Expos just before the 1972 season. He won a Gold Glove as a first baseman in 1973 before moving on to the Oakland Athletics and Texas Rangers. The Mets reacquired him in October 1979 as the second of two players to be named later (the first being Ed Lynch) in the trade that sent Willie Montañez to the Rangers in August of that year. In 1980, Jorgensen became the first Met to play in each of the first three decades of the franchise. Jorgensen was sold to the Braves on June 15, 1983, though most of the news that day focused on the Mets' acquisition of Keith Hernandez from the Cardinals. The now two-time ex-Met would spend his final two seasons with the Cardinals and play for St. Louis in the 1985 World Series. He would later manage the Cardinals, replacing Joe Torre for the final 96 games of the 1995 season.

16. b. Dave Kingman

The man many called Kong had the best year of his career in 1979 with the Cubs, hitting a league-high 48 home runs, driving in 115 runs, and hitting a career-best .288. He made his first All-Star team since he was a Met in 1976, and in 1980 he again made the squad, though injuries limited him to 18 homers on the year. He returned to the Mets in 1981 and spent the next three seasons in Queens. He hit .204 with a league-leading 37 homers in 1982 but really struggled in 1983, batting .198 with 13 home runs, mostly sitting on the bench once Keith Hernandez took his first-base job in June. Kingman played his final three seasons with Oakland, slugging 35 homers as a designated hitter in his last year.

17. b. Josias Manzanillo

The right-handed reliever pitched with the Mets from 1993 to 1995 and again in 1999 but it's a 1997 Mariners appearance that left a mark on Manzanillo. Pitching against Cleveland, he was hit in the groin by a Manny Ramirez line drive. He proceeded to throw out Jim Thome at the plate and then stayed down, as the liner caused a ruptured testicle. Manzanillo was sidelined for a month before returning to pitch. Manzanillo made the 1999 Mets out of spring training and pitched in 12 games with a 5.79 ERA. He finished his 11-season major league career with a 13–15 record for eight teams.

18. c. Lee Mazzilli

Maz, who in 1979 became the first Met to hit a home run in the All-Star Game and was a bright spot in the dark days of the Mets before being traded to the Texas Rangers in the spring of 1982 for Ron Darling and Walt Terrell, returned in August 1986 after George Foster was released amid controversial remarks concerning the popularity of Black versus white Mets players. In his fourth home game back, Mazzilli hit a game-tying homer in the ninth against the Cardinals, and it was like the kid from Brooklyn never left Queens. The erstwhile subject of his very own poster day came up clutch twice in the 1986 World Series. His pinch-hit single in Game 6 off Calvin Schiraldi led to the tying run in the eighth, and his pinch-hit single in the sixth inning of Game 7 started a three-run rally off Bruce Hurst to knot the deciding game.

19. a. Bob Miller

The right-handed Bob Miller, not to be mistaken with his 1962 teammate Bob Miller who pitched left-handed, went 1–12 for the expansion Mets. He lost his first 12 decisions before he fired a 2–1 complete game win at Wrigley Field for the team's 40th and final victory. Miller was traded to the Dodgers after the season and learned how the other half lived, contributing to a team that would win two World Series titles. He would earn another ring with the 1971 Pirates. Miller returned to the Mets in late 1973, pitching one scoreless inning in a loss to the Expos on September 26. He went 2–2 in 1974, his 17th and final season in the big leagues.

20. d. Kirk Nieuwenhuis

A third-round draft choice in 2008, the outfielder was a Met from 2012 through early in the 2015 season when he was sold to the Angels. But after 10 games with the Angels, the Mets claimed him off waivers. The former high school football star was batting .100

overall but then enjoyed a strong month. On July 12, he became the first Met to hit three homers in a home game, accomplishing the feat in a win over Arizona. On July 25, he went 4-for-4 in a 15–2 drubbing of the Dodgers. His fourth and final homer of the year came as a pinch-hitter on September 8 in Washington, a solo shot in the eighth off Jonathan Papelbon to put the Mets ahead in a crucial 8–7 come-from-behind victory that extended their first-place lead over the Nationals to six games.

21. c. José Reyes
The popular shortstop left the Mets for the division rival Marlins after he won the batting title in 2011. But after one season in Miami he was traded to Toronto, and in 2015 he was sent to Colorado for Troy Tulowitzki. The Mets signed an unexpectedly available Reyes in June 2016, seeking a little spark for a team that otherwise didn't have a single player steal more than five bases. Reyes, who took on third-base duties in the absence of his injured friend David Wright, batted .267 with eight home runs and nine stolen bases in 60 games as the Mets earned a wild card spot. The four-time All-Star played through the 2018 season, batting just .189 in his final year.

22. b. Chasen Shreve
The southpaw reliever played for three teams before joining the Mets and pitching to a 3.96 ERA in 17 games in the shortened 2020 COVID campaign. His ERA increased by two runs in the final week of the season because of two bad outings. Shreve pitched for the Pirates in 2021 but returned to the Mets in 2022. He pitched well for the first month, sporting a 1.54 ERA through 10 appearances. But he struggled thereafter, giving up at least a run in eight of his next 15 outings, and his ERA ballooned to 6.49. Shreve was released in July. He spent 2023 with the Tigers and Reds.

23. a. Ray Sadecki
The veteran lefty went 5–4 as a starter-reliever for the 1973 team and was the winning pitcher against the Pirates in the "Ball on the Wall" game, pitching the last four innings in a critical 13-inning victory on September 20. He was traded to St. Louis in the deal

for Joe Torre after the 1974 season. Sadecki had started his career in 1960 with the Cardinals and won 20 games for the 1964 World Series champs. And he got to play with Torre on the Mets when he returned for four games at the start of the 1977 season, shortly before Torre took over as manager. Sadecki won 135 games for six teams in 18 seasons.

24. d. Jason Vargas

The 24-year-old southpaw made two starts for the 2007 Mets, going 0–1 with a 12.19 ERA, and after stints with the Mariners, Angels, and Royals, he returned to the Mets in 2018 following a season in which he won a league-high 18 games and was an All-Star for the Royals. In 2018, Vargas pitched more like the 2007 version of himself, going 7–9 with a 5.77 ERA. Through the first week of August, he was 2–8 with an 8.75 ERA. He was 6–5 with a 4.01 ERA in 2019 when he was traded to the Phillies following New York's acquisition of Marcus Stroman. He retired with a 99–99 record.

25. c. Rusty Staub

The consistent Le Grand Orange collected at least 500 hits with four teams, the only player to ever do so. Staub had 792 with Houston, 709 with the Mets, 582 with the Tigers, and 531 with the Expos. He had 102 hits in his lone season with Texas. Staub played nine seasons for the Mets from 1972 to 1975, then from 1981 to 1985, serving almost exclusively as a pinch-hitter in the last three years. The legendary redhead finished with 2,716 hits and reached base more than 4,000 times. At the time of his death, 43 players eligible for the Hall of Fame had accomplished the latter feat, with 37 of them elected, four others clouded by steroid issues, and one—Pete Rose—who is confined to baseball's ineligible list.

Rusty Staub

METS AND YANKEES

1. Which pitcher played for the Mets and Yankees in 1999?
a. Octavio Dotel   b. Allen Watson   c. Rigo Beltrán   d. Dan Murray

2. Which one of these players called Shea Stadium home as both a Met and Yankee?
a. Sandy Alomar Sr.   b. Ron Swoboda   c. Billy Cowan   d. Jack Aker

3. Which Met and Yankee was also the Yankees first-base coach in the 2000 World Series?
a. Chris Chambliss   b. Tony Fernandez   c. Lee Mazzilli
d. Willie Randolph

4. Which pitcher who once threw 10⅔ shutout innings in a relief appearance for the Yankees also appeared in 11 games with the Mets?
a. Dick Tidrow   b. Mike Stanton   c. Chasen Shreve
d. Orlando Hernandez

5. Which pitcher appeared in three of his 600 career games as a Met and another 35 as a Yankee?
a. John Candelaria   b. Ray Burris   c. Allen Watson
d. Kyle Farnsworth

6. Which pitcher made his debut at Shea Stadium as a Yankee and later pitched in the World Series as a Met?
a. Glendon Rusch   b. Tyler Clippard   c. Addison Reed
d. Carlos Torres

7. Which 1986 Met made two starts for the 1994 Yankees to end his career?
a. Ron Darling   b. Sid Fernandez   c. Rick Aguilera   d. Bobby Ojeda

8. Which former Met made two starts for the 1996 Yankees?
a. Greg Harris   b. Frank Tanana   c. Wally Whitehurst   d. Tim Leary

9. Who played for the Mets and Yankees in 1977?
a. Dock Ellis   b. Dave Kingman   c. Ray Burris   d. Bill Sudakis

10. Who was the first player to play for the Mets and Yankees?
a. Gene Woodling   b. Duke Carmel   c. Marv Throneberry
d. Don Zimmer

11. Which former Met celebrated the 1988 NL East title in the Shea clubhouse despite being an active Yankee?
a. Lee Mazzilli   b. Jesse Orosco   c. Rafael Santana   d. Stan Jefferson

12. Who was the first player to appear in games for the Mets and Yankees in the same season?
a. Bob Friend   b. Hal Reniff   c. Phil Linz   d. Tucker Ashford

13. Which 1986 Met played 17 games over two seasons with the Yankees?
a. Ed Hearn   b. Kevin Mitchell   c. Bruce Berenyi   d. Kevin Elster

14. Which 30-homer Met played eight games with the Yankees?
a. Ike Davis   b. Mike Cameron   c. Lucas Duda   d. Bobby Bonilla

15. Which one of these pitchers won a World Series pitching for the Twins and also pitched for both the Mets and Yankees?
a. Dan Schatzeder   b. Rick Aguilera   c. Scott Erickson
d. Frank Viola

16. Which three-time All-Star spent parts of three seasons with the Mets and 10 games with the Yankees?
a. Joe Torre   b. Jay Bruce   c. Luis Castillo   d. Billy Wagner

17. Which Met and Yankee was part of the 1995 Cleveland team that won the AL pennant?
a. Dennis Cook   d. Eric Plunk   c. Jason Grimsley   d. Alvaro Espinoza

18. Which former Met and Yankee later became a New York City police officer?
a. Terrence Long   b. Xavier Nady   c. Stan Jefferson   d. Roy Staiger

19. Which Met and Yankee once pitched both left-handed and right-handed in a game?
a. Rich Hill   b. Aaron Laffey   c. Sean Henn   d. Greg Harris

20. Which Met and Yankee was related to *The Honeymooners* actress Joyce Randolph?
a. Al Leiter   b. Tim Redding   c. Royce Ring   d. Bill Short

21. Which St. John's product pitched for the Mets and Yankees?
a. Larry Bearnarth   b. John Franco   c. Stephen Tarpley
d. C. J. Nitkowski

22. Which four-time Yankees All-Star appeared in 16 games for the Mets?
a. Dellin Betances   b. Ralph Terry   c. Ron Davis   d. Bob Grim

23. Which former Met and Yankee gave up the walk-off home run in Game 1 of the 2023 World Series?
a. Justin Wilson   b. Miguel Castro   c. Chasen Shreve
d. Joely Rodriguez

24. Which former Met was released by the Yankees after a game in which he allowed a passed ball, allowed a runner to steal home, and struck out to end a loss to the Mets?
a. Kelly Stinnett   b. Brent Mayne   c. Alberto Castillo   d. Rick Wilkins

25. Which Toms River, New Jersey, product played at the hot corner for both teams?
a. Todd Frazier   b. Ray Knight   c. Robin Ventura   d. Todd Zeile

ANSWERS

1. b. Allen Watson

The Queens product began the 1999 season with the Mets and finished it winning a World Series with the Yankees. The Jamaica, Queens-born Watson attended Christ The King High School and pitched for the Cardinals, Giants, and Angels before signing with the Mets, where he pitched in 14 games, including four starts, before being traded to the Mariners. He was released after three games and signed by the Yankees, who pitched him in 21 regular season games and three games of the ALCS against the Red Sox. Watson would pitch 17 games with the 2000 Yankees, the last year of his career.

2. a. Sandy Alomar Sr.

The longtime infielder played 15 games with the 1967 Mets before being traded to the White Sox. Alomar, who made the 1970 All-Star team as an Angel, would return to Queens as a Yankee while Yankee Stadium was being renovated. Alomar was a Yankee from 1974 to 1976. His son Roberto played with the Mets in 2002 and 2003. The elder Sandy returned as a coach under Willie Randolph and Jerry Manuel. Sandy Alomar Jr. ended his 20-year playing career with the 2007 Mets and then coached within the organization in 2008 and 2009. Alomar Jr. served as acting manager for Cleveland in 2012 and 2020 with Terry Francona away to attend to health issues.

3. c. Lee Mazzilli

The popular Met played several seasons in Queens for Torre and then joined his coaching staff in the Bronx in 2000. He managed in the minors for three seasons before joining Torre's staff. Both first-base coaches in the 2000 World Series were 1986 Mets, with Mookie Wilson coaching under Bobby Valentine. Mazzilli was a surprise hire several years later when the Orioles tabbed him as manager over Eddie Murray, Sam Perlozzo, and Terry Francona. Mazzilli was fired during his second season, going 129–140 as skipper. He returned to the Yankees for one season as Torre's bench coach in 2006, after which he joined SNY as a studio analyst, a seat he filled until Shea Stadium closed in 2008. In 2021, Maz filled in for Howie Rose on a few late-season Met radio broadcasts and the next summer played a key role in helping Jay Horwitz organize the first Mets Old-Timers Day in 28 years.

4. a. Dick Tidrow
The right-handed reliever who won two World Series titles with the Yankees made the 1984 Mets out of spring training and even came out of the bullpen on Opening Day in Cincinnati. He was scoreless in that appearance but the good times didn't last. In his final two outings in May, he gave up six runs on 12 hits in five innings, marking the end of Tidrow's career. The most impressive performance of his career was in a 19-inning Yankees win over the Twins in 1976, during which he tossed 10⅔ shutout innings. He was also on the 1983 White Sox AL West title team.

5. a. John Candelaria
The Brooklyn-born southpaw came to the Mets in late 1987 to make three starts down the stretch for a rotation ravaged by injuries, going 2–0 with a 5.84 ERA. The Candy Man was then signed by the Yankees, going 13–7 in 1988, highlighted by a pair of two-hit shutouts. He was traded to the Expos during the 1989 season. Coincidentally, he pitched for both New York teams, both Los Angeles teams (Angels and Dodgers), and both Canadian teams (Expos and Blue Jays). He pitched for eight teams in his 19 seasons, finishing his career with 177 wins.

6. b. Tyler Clippard
"The Yankee Clippard" made his major league debut at Shea, giving up one run in six innings in a win over the Mets on May 20, 2007. He would become a two-time All-Star with the Nationals before joining the Mets as a set-up man during the team's 2015 playoff run. In his first 17 innings with the Mets, he posted a microscopic 0.52 ERA. He also earned a pair of holds in the NLCS against the Cubs. He returned to the Yankees in 2016 via a trade with Arizona. The well-traveled Clippard won 56 games and saved 74 more in his 16 seasons in the majors.

7. d. Bobby Ojeda

The Yankees signed the lefty as a minor league free agent and he made two starts for Buck Showalter. In his first outing at Tiger Stadium, he gave up four runs and failed to make it out of the first inning. His final start in the majors came on April 22 against the A's, who started Ron Darling. In a matchup of 1986 Mets, Ojeda failed to make it out of the third and Darling failed to make it out of the fourth in an 8–6 Yankees win. Ojeda won 115 decisions in 15 seasons in the majors. Following his retirement, he became popular with Mets fans again as a broadcaster on SNY for the team's pre- and postgame shows.

8. c. Wally Whitehurst

The right-hander was 20–37 with the Mets pitching mostly out of the bullpen from 1989 to 1992. In 1996, the Yankees found themselves desperate for starting pitching and Whitehurst made a pair of starts for the eventual World Series champs. In his first start, he allowed two runs in seven innings at Yankee Stadium in a win over Oakland. It was his first start since he was a Padre in 1994. But in his next start against the Angels, he recorded just three outs and gave up a Garret Anderson grand slam. It was his final appearance in the majors.

9. b. Dave Kingman

Kong made his way around the majors in 1977, playing for one team in each division. He was traded from the Mets to the Padres at the June 15 deadline. On September 6, he was claimed on waivers by the Angels. Kingman was traded to the Yankees nine days later and hit four homers in eight games, including one in his first at-bat at Tiger Stadium. He was ineligible to play in the postseason with the AL East champions because he joined them after the August 31 roster-setting deadline. Kingman would retire after hitting 442 home runs for seven teams, including two stops with the Mets.

Dave Kingman

10. c. Marv Throneberry

Marvelous Marv was part of the 1958 Yankees title team and reunited with Casey Stengel when the Mets acquired him in May 1962 in a trade with the Orioles. It also made Marv Eugene Throneberry—initials M.E.T.—the first ex-Yankee to play for the Mets. Throneberry fit in and perhaps personified the lovable-loser Mets. In one famous story, he tripled against the Cubs but was called out for not stepping on first . . . or second. Throneberry also committed three errors in one game against Houston, cementing his defensive reputation. But he also hit 16 home runs, second-most on the team. He later found fame as Miller Lite spokesman in TV ads in the 1970s, poking fun at himself and admitting to the camera, "I still don't know why they asked me to do this commercial."

11. c. Rafael Santana

The steady shortstop the Mets plucked from the Cardinals in 1984 won a World Series in Queens in 1986 before being traded across town a year later once Kevin Elster loomed as his in-house replacement. Santana had been a Yankees minor leaguer in the late 1970s and early 1980s, though he didn't reach the majors until after they let him go to St. Louis. Ralphie, as his teammates called him, played 148 games for the 1988 Yankees, but clearly a part of him was still a Met. When the Mets clinched the division on September 22, Santana spent his Thursday night—the Yankees were idle—in the clubhouse celebrating with many of the players he scaled the highest of heights with two Octobers earlier. He moved on to the shores of Lake Erie for the 1990 season and played a final seven games for Cleveland (alongside Keith Hernandez) before retiring at the age of 32. Santana later became a coach in the minor leagues.

12. a. Bob Friend

The four-time All-Star pitcher with the Pirates spent the first 15 seasons of his career in Pittsburgh before joining the Yankees in 1966. He pitched in 12 games before being sold to the Mets. The Mets were wise to keep him away from other teams considering he went 14–2 against them. He went 5–8 with a 4.40 ERA in 22 games, including a shutout against the defending champion Dodgers. It was the final year for Friend, who retired with a 197–230 record but a more than respectable 3.58 ERA in more than 3,600 innings pitched, including 314⅓ in 1956.

13. d. Kevin Elster

The shortstop was a Met from 1986 to 1992, but shoulder surgery ended his 1992 campaign early and he wouldn't make it back to the majors until 1994 with the Yankees. He would bat .054 (2-for-37) in 17 games over two seasons before being let go. But he bounced back with the Rangers, hitting 24 home runs with 99 RBIs in 1996. He also hit .333 in the playoffs against the Yankees. Elster played with the Pirates and Rangers before sitting out the 1999 season. His former Met skipper Davey Johnson talked him out of retirement and convinced him to play for the Dodgers in 2000. Giants fans would forever remember their archrival's shortstop for christening their new downtown ballpark that year with three home runs that took the edge off their home opener.

14. a. Ike Davis
The slugging first baseman launched 32 home runs in 2012 but struck out in nearly one-third of his at-bats in 2013 and batted .205. After spending time with the Pirates and A's, he played eight games for the Yankees in 2016. His father, Ron, had started his career as a Yankees pitcher in 1978, went 14–2 in 1979, and made the All-Star team in 1981. Ike was in the Dodgers system in 2017 and converted to pitcher in the minors before retiring in 2018. He hit 81 homers in his major league career and represented Israel in the 2017 World Baseball Classic.

15. c. Scott Erickson
The right-hander who was runner-up for the AL Cy Young Award in 1991 as a Twin pitched in a combined 11 games with the Mets and Yankees. He went 0–1 in two starts with the 2004 Mets, including a start against the Expos on July 26 in which he failed to make it out of the third inning in a 19–10 loss. In 2006, he joined the Yankees for the final nine games of his career, pitching to a 7.94 ERA out of the bullpen. Erickson went 142–136 in 15 seasons. In 1998 as an Oriole he led the league with 11 complete games and 251⅓ innings pitched.

16. b. Jay Bruce
The Mets acquired the three-time All-Star for the 2016 playoff push but the outfielder struggled, batting .219 with eight home runs. The next season he hit 29 home runs in 103 games but was traded to contending Cleveland as the Mets sold off at the deadline. Bruce was signed by the Mets before the 2018 season, hitting .223 in 94 games but was traded to Seattle in the offseason as part of the Edwin Diaz deal. He returned to New York, briefly, as a Yankee, playing 10 games in 2021. He hit the 319th and final home run of his career in a win against the Orioles.

17. d. Alvaro Espinoza

Espinoza was the Yankees' regular shortstop from 1989 to 1991, averaging 148 games a season before moving on to Cleveland. Notably, Espinoza was on their 1995 World Series team and started at third base in Game 4 instead of Jim Thome as manager Mike Hargrove looked to match up against Braves southpaw Steve Avery. He was traded to the Mets in 1996 as part of the Jeff Kent–Carlos Baerga deal. Espinoza batted .306 in 48 games for the Mets and had three three-hit games between August 5 and 14. He was released by the Mets late in spring training in 1997 as the team looked to get younger. Espinoza later managed in the Dodgers farm system.

18. c. Stan Jefferson

A first-round pick in the 1983 draft, Jefferson played 14 games with the 1986 Mets in September and even scored a run in the division-clincher against the Cubs. He was included in the Kevin Mitchell-Kevin McReynolds deal with the Padres following the season, and went on to hit a career-high eight homers in 1987. Jefferson returned to New York for 10 games with the 1989 Yankees, playing for six teams in all before joining the New York City Police Department in 1997. He was on duty during the terror attacks on September 11, 2001, and worked at Ground Zero. Jefferson retired from the NYPD in 2004.

19. d. Greg Harris

The ambidextrous pitcher played for both New York teams in strike-shortened seasons—he debuted with the 1981 Mets and appeared in three games for the 1994 Yankees. He made 14 starts and even picked up a save to close out a 13-inning win at Wrigley in his rookie year before being sent to the Reds in the George Foster deal. Harris later pitched in the postseason with the 1984 Padres and 1990 Red Sox. In the second-to-last game of his career with the 1995 Expos, Harris, a natural righty, switched back and forth between left- and right-handed pitching, tossing a scoreless ninth inning against the Reds.

20. b. Tim Redding

The former Padre and Astro made one start for the 2005 Yankees at Fenway Park and failed to make it out of the second inning in a 17–1 drubbing on July 15. Redding returned for a bigger bite of the Big Apple in 2009, bouncing from the rotation to the bullpen and back to the rotation, finishing 3–6 in 30 games. Fitting for a member of a team that had some of its games aired over Channel 11 in New York, the righty was also the grandnephew of *The Honeymooners* actress Joyce Randolph, who played Trixie Norton. By the time the remote clicked "off" on his big-league career, Redding finished up at 37–57, winning a career-high 10 games with the 2003 Astros and matching the total with the 2008 Nationals. He later became a minor league pitching coach following his playing days.

21. d. C. J. Nitkowski

The southpaw reliever pitched in five games for the 2001 Mets and 19 for the 2004 Yankees. The St. John's product was the ninth overall pick by the Reds in the 1994 draft. Nitkowski pitched for three teams before joining the Mets, for whom he made five scoreless appearances making him the first hurler to post an ERA of 0.00 in a Mets career encompassing that many outings. After pitching for the Rangers and Braves, he had a 7.62 ERA late in the 2004 season for the Yankees. His last season in the majors came in 2005 with Washington, but he later played in Japan, South Korea, and in the Mets minor league system. Nitkowski later became a broadcaster with the Rangers and Braves.

22. a. Dellin Betances

The Grand Street Campus High School alum was a superb setup man with the Yankees, making the All-Star Game each year from 2014 to 2017. Injuries limited him to one game in 2019 and he signed with the Mets after the season. He posted a 7.71 ERA in 15 appearances in the COVID-shortened 2020 season. Eleven of those outings were sparkling—no runs—but a few *really* bad ones spiked his ERA toward the stratosphere (a statistical hazard of relief pitching). He pitched only one inning, his last for the Mets, in 2021 because of an injured shoulder. Betances struggled in the Dodgers system in 2022 before retiring.

23. b. Miguel Castro
The former Mets and Yankees reliever gave up a walk-off homer to Adolis Garcia in the opener of the 2023 World Series in Texas. Castro pitched for three teams before joining the Mets in 2020, where he went 4–6 in 79 appearances over two seasons. In 2021, he posted a career-best 3.45 ERA. Just before the 2022 season he was traded to the Yankees for lefty reliever Joely Rodriguez. Castro went 5–0 in 34 games and signed with Arizona in the offseason. He pitched in a league-high 75 games for the NL champion Diamondbacks. Castro made eight other appearances in the postseason.

24. c. Alberto Castillo
Castillo was a part-time Mets catcher for four seasons, best known for his walk-off 14th-inning single on Opening Day 1998. He returned to New York as a Yankee in 2002, batting .135 in 15 games before getting released. He was hitless in his first 14 pinstriped at-bats. When he singled against the Twins, organist Eddie Layton played the "Hallelujah" chorus. During the Mets' 11–2 win at Yankee Stadium on June 29, Castillo allowed a passed ball that led to a run, failed to tag Roger Cedeño on a steal of home, and also struck out to end the game. He did return for one game in September as a pinch-hitter.

25. a. Todd Frazier
The third baseman was a two-time All-Star with the Reds and hit 40 home runs for the 2016 White Sox. The Yankees acquired him for the 2017 playoff run and he hit 11 homers in 66 games (including a dinger in Queens when the Rays borrowed Citi Field to host the Bronx Bombers the September night Hurricane Irma precluded the teams playing as scheduled in Tampa Bay) and also went deep in the ALCS. In the offseason, he signed a two-year deal with the Mets and hit 39 home runs from 2018 to 2019. He moved on to the Rangers in 2020 but returned to the Mets late in the season and hit two homers in 14 games. Frazier joined the Pirates in 2021 and finished his career with 218 home runs in 11 seasons.

TEAM RECORD HOLDERS

1. Who is the Mets' all-time hits leader?
a. Ed Kranepool   b. Keith Hernandez   c. David Wright
d. José Reyes

2. Who played the most games for the Mets?
a. Bud Harrelson   b. David Wright   c. Cleon Jones
d. Ed Kranepool

3. Which Mets batter holds the record for most strikeouts in a season?
a. Pete Alonso   b. Dave Kingman   c. Michael Conforto
d. Tommie Agee

4. Which Mets starting pitcher has the lowest single-season ERA?
a. Jacob deGrom   b. Dwight Gooden   c. David Cone   d. Jerry Koosman

5. Which pitcher holds the Mets' record with 25 wins in a season?
a. Tom Seaver   b. Jerry Koosman   c. Dwight Gooden
d. R. A. Dickey

6. Which pitcher lost the most games as a Met?
a. Tom Seaver   b. Jerry Koosman   c. Bobby Jones   d. Jon Matlack

7. Which closer saved 51 games in a season for the Mets?

a. Billy Wagner   b. Francisco Rodriguez   c. Edwin Diaz
d. Jeurys Familia

8. Tom Seaver started 36 games in a season three times. Whose Mets record did he tie?

a. Al Jackson   b. Roger Craig   c. Jack Fisher   d. Tracy Stallard

9. Which Mets pitcher gave up a team record 35 home runs in one season?

a. Roger Craig   b. Jay Hook   c. Pete Harnisch   d. Steven Matz

10. Who was the last Met to lead the league in winning percentage?

a. David Cone   b. Dwight Gooden   c. Sid Fernandez   d. Al Leiter

11. Which pitcher appeared in the most games for the Mets?

a. Pedro Feliciano   b. Jesse Orosco   c. Jeurys Familia
d. John Franco

12. Who was the first Met to lead the league in fewest walks per nine innings in a season?

a. Tom Seaver   b. Rick Reed   c. Bret Saberhagen   d. Bartolo Colón

13. Which pitcher surrendered the most home runs as a Met?

a. Sid Fernandez   b. Tom Seaver   c. Bobby Jones
d. Steve Trachsel

14. Who is the Mets' career leader in ERA?

a. Jacob deGrom   b. Dwight Gooden   c. Tom Seaver
d. David Cone

15. Roger Craig gave up a team-record 261 hits in 1962. Who gave up the second most in a season?

a. Craig Swan   b. Al Jackson   c. Frank Viola   d. Rick Reed

16. Frank Thomas hit 34 home runs in 1962. Who was the next Met to produce a 30-homer season?

a. Donn Clendenon   b. Cleon Jones   c. Dave Kingman
d. Darryl Strawberry

17. Which Met led the league in winning percentage during their 1988 NL East title season?

a. Dwight Gooden   b. David Cone   c. Frank Viola   d. Rick Aguilera

18. Which Mets pitcher blasted two home runs in a 2016 game to tie Walt Terrell's club record?

a. Noah Syndergaard   b. Bartolo Colón   c. Jacob deGrom
d. Steven Matz

19. Which Mets pitcher led the NL in fewest hits allowed per nine innings three times?

a. Jerry Koosman   b. Sid Fernandez   c. Matt Harvey
d. Jacob deGrom

20. Which Met led the NL in fewest walks per nine innings in 2015 and 2016?

a. Bartolo Colón   b. Noah Syndergaard   c. Jacob deGrom
d. Matt Harvey

21. Who was the single-season leader in strikeouts for the Mets prior to Tom Seaver?

a. Carl Willey   b. Galen Cisco   c. Roger Craig   d. Al Jackson

22. Which Met has the highest single-season batting average?

a. Jeff McNeil   b. Cleon Jones   c. John Olerud   d. José Reyes

23. Which Met was caught stealing 21 times in a season, a record later tied by José Reyes?

a. Tommie Agee   b. Lenny Randle   c. Vince Coleman
d. Brett Butler

24. Who is the Mets' all-time leader in slugging percentage?
a. Dave Kingman   b. Pete Alonso   c. Mike Piazza
d. Carlos Delgado

25. Which Mets pitcher hit the most home runs?
a. Tom Seaver   b. Dwight Gooden   c. Ron Darling
d. Noah Syndergaard

ANSWERS

1. c. David Wright
The Captain had 1,777 hits, the club record by 243 over José Reyes. Ed Kranepool long held the record with 1,418. Wright passed him with hit number 1,419, an infield single against the Pirates on September 26, 2012. The Virginian was drafted by the Mets in 2001 and made it to the majors a little after the 2004 All-Star break, collecting his first hit on July 22 against Montreal's Zach Day. Wright had at least 164 hits each year from 2005 to 2010, but injuries would limit him drastically in the second half of his career. He played a combined 75 games in 2015 and 2016 before spinal stenosis put him on the shelf for good, save for two farewell games in September 2018.

2. d. Ed Kranepool
Steady Eddie played in 1,853 games in an 18-season career that coincided with the first 18 seasons of Mets baseball. He appeared in a career-high 153 games in 1965, his lone All-Star season. The amazing thing about Kranepool's record is how often he was on the bench. He collected enough plate appearances to qualify for the batting title in only 1965, 1966, and 1967. Later in his career, he became a highly efficient pinch-hitter. In 1974, he batted .486 (17-for-35) in a pinch-hitting role, while in his career he registered 90 pinch-hits with six homers. In his final major league at-bat, he came through with—what else?—a pinch-hit single in St. Louis off Bob Forsch on the final day of the 1979 season.

3. a. Pete Alonso

One downside to Alonso's great rookie season in which he hit 53 homers was his team record 183 strikeouts. David Wright held the previous record with 161 strikeouts in 2010. Alonso had 66 strikeouts through the first two months of 2019. In July, he struck out 26 times in only 79 at-bats. Alonso also fanned 38 times in the final month of the season. The first baseman cut down on his strikeouts with 127 in 2021 and 128 in 2022, though the number jumped to 151 in 2023. Pre-Polar Bear, Michael Conforto almost broke Wright's record, striking out 159 times in 2018.

Pete Alonso

4. b. Dwight Gooden

At the age of 20, Dr. K had a 1.53 ERA over 276⅔ innings with 168 strikeouts. The phenom also completed 16 of his 35 starts in 1985 with eight shutouts to finish 24–4 and win the Cy Young Award. His ERA is the second-lowest in the Live Ball Era behind only Bob Gibson's 1.12 mark from 1968. In Gooden's final six starts, he went 4-0 and pitched nine shutout innings in each of the no decisions.

Gooden finished fourth in MVP voting though teammates jokingly blamed him and his four losses for the Mets finishing three games behind the Cardinals.

5. a. Tom Seaver
The Franchise won 25 of the Mets' 100 games in 1969, helping them overtake the Cubs for the NL East title. He saved his best for last. In the final month of the season, he went 6-0 in six starts with a 0.83 ERA. After a loss to the Reds in August dropped him to 15-7, Seaver went 10-0 in his final 11 starts, including three shutouts. He notched win number 25 on September 27 in a 1-0 win at Philadelphia, with Bobby Pfeil delivering an RBI single in the eighth. Seaver would win 20 games in a season five times in his career.

6. b. Jerry Koosman
The lefty who won 140 games as a Met was often a victim of poor run support and found himself on the short end of 137 decisions. The offense was bad enough that he went 14-15 with a 2.84 ERA in 1973. But the losses really piled up his last two years in Queens. Koosman went 8-20 in 1977 and 3-15 in 1978, despite respectable ERAs each season. He was traded to the Twins after 1978, and glad to finally have offensive support, he went 20-13 and finished sixth in Cy Young voting in 1979. Koosman finished his career with a 222-209 record and a 3.36 ERA.

7. d. Jeurys Familia
Familia saved 51 of the 2016 Mets' 87 wins, going 3-4 with a 2.55 ERA. His 51 saves led the league and Familia even received some MVP votes. He had 10 saves apiece in June and July. In a 5-2 win against the Marlins at Citi Field on August 31, he pitched a 1-2-3 ninth for his 44th save, breaking the team mark originally set by Armando Benitez in 2001 and tied by Familia himself in 2015. In the Wild Card Game against the Giants, Familia, who gave up one homer all year, surrendered a three-run blast in the ninth inning to Conor Gillaspie in New York's 3-0 loss. (To be fair, it was a non-save situation.)

8. c. Jack Fisher

Tom Seaver made three dozen starts in 1970, 1973, and 1975, but it was Jack Fisher who first did it in 1965. Though he went 8–24 and led the league in earned runs allowed, he gave Casey Stengel and Wes Westrum 253⅔ innings, completing 10 of his starts while also making seven relief appearances. He pitched 13 innings on the final day of the season in a loss to the Phillies and finished 2–16 after a 6–8 start. Fisher's eight wins tied for the most on a Mets squad that only had two pitchers make at least 20 starts.

9. a. Roger Craig

The right-hander gave up 35 home runs in 1962, setting a Mets record that still hasn't been surpassed. He gave up nine home runs in July and 11 more in August. Craig surrendered three long balls in a start five times, including in consecutive starts at the end of August against the Dodgers and Phillies. On the road, he was 2–15 with a 5.16 ERA and 22 homers allowed. Hinting that gophers can bite different pitchers on different teams differently, Phillies starter Art Mahaffey led the league with 36 homers allowed but went 19–14, made the All-Star team, and received MVP votes. Craig allowed 28 more home runs in 1963, his final season with the Mets.

10. c. Sid Fernandez

The southpaw went 14–5 in 1989 for a .737 winning percentage, which tied him with Giants righty Scott Garrelts, who posted the same record for the NL West champions. El Sid actually began the year in the bullpen because of some bad weather and scheduled off-days, with Davey Johnson using a four-man rotation. When the native Hawaiian reentered the rotation, he won his first three starts. And he bookended the season by winning his final three starts, including a three-hit shutout of the Phillies at Shea in which he also stroked an RBI double. Fernandez was awarded with a three-year, $6 million contract after the season.

11. d. John Franco

The Brooklyn-born reliever appeared in 695 games with the Mets between 1990 and 2004. Tom Seaver held the previous record at

401, which Franco surpassed in a one-batter outing against the Marlins on June 19, 1998, at Shea. The third captain in Mets history appeared in at least 30 games every year he was a Met, except in 2002, when he missed the entire season. Franco came into 61 games in 1998 and 62 more in 2000. The gritty southpaw, who also pitched for the Reds and Astros, appeared in 1,119 games, third most all-time for a pitcher. Only Jesse Orosco and Mike Stanton, two other Mets lefties, played in more.

12. c. Bret Saberhagen
The two-time Cy Young winner had a minuscule rate of 0.660 bases on balls per nine innings in the strike-shortened 1994 season. Saberhagen finished the year with 14 wins and 13 walks, coming in third in Cy Young voting behind Greg Maddux and Ken Hill. Five of the former Royal ace's 13 walks were issued in the first month of the season. He walked only one batter over 35 innings in May. Saberhagen's best month was July, when he went 4–0 with a 1.53 ERA and walked three batters in 50⅓ innings. Saberhagen would pitch in the majors until 2001, retiring with a 167–117 record and a 3.34 ERA.

13. b. Tom Seaver
The Mets icon is also the franchise leader in home runs allowed, giving up 212 (matching Shea's area code when he answered the call there). Tom Terrific gave up at least 20 homers in a season four times, including a high of 24 in 1969. He led the Mets in home runs allowed six times, including 1969 when he tied with Gary Gentry. The first homer he allowed was to Cincinnati's Lee May and the last he gave up as a Met was to Cardinals catcher Darrell Porter. In his career, Seaver allowed 380 home runs, which as of 2024, is in the top 20 of all time. Rick Monday hit 11 off Seaver, the most by any batter.

14. a. Jacob deGrom
The two-time Cy Young winner posted a 2.52 ERA in nine seasons with the Mets, bettering Tom Seaver's 2.57 mark (albeit in less than half as many innings). In 2018, his first Cy Young season,

deGrom posted a 1.70 ERA. Three years later, he had a 1.08 ERA through 15 starts before injuries ended his season. DeGrom made 209 starts in nine seasons with the Mets but only won 82 games, an illustration of terrible run support he received. While deGrom and Seaver being at the top of the list is of little surprise, fans may not realize Jesse Orosco (2.73) and R. A. Dickey (2.95) are third and fourth on the list.

15. c. Frank Viola

Viola had a tale of two seasons in 1991. Coming off a 20-win 1990 in which he finished third in NL Cy Young voting, the lefty jumped out to a 10-5 start and made the All-Star team. But in the second half, he went 3-10 with a 5.53 ERA, giving up the most runs and home runs on the staff. He surrendered eight or more hits in a game 19 times. Viola would leave the Mets after the season, signing with the Red Sox as a free agent. He would win 25 games in Boston from 1992 to 1994 before pitching briefly for the Reds and Blue Jays.

16. c. Dave Kingman

Kingman's 36-homer outburst in 1975 was the first 30-homer season for the franchise since Frank Thomas did it in the Mets' first season. In fact, no Met between Thomas and Kingman had hit more than the 26 Tommie Agee socked in 1969. Kingman had 11 homers through June and then exploded in July with 13 dingers while batting .322 and driving in 31 runs. On July 20, he homered twice to power a comeback win over the Astros and on July 31 he again went deep twice in a victory over the Pirates. Kingman hit number 30 on September 5 off Cardinals pitcher Eric Rasmussen. He set the team record in style, with his 35th home run beating the Cubs in the bottom of the ninth on September 18.

17. b. David Cone

The 25-year-old first-time All-Star went 20-3 to lead the league with an .870 winning percentage and finished third in the Cy Young voting behind Orel Hershiser and Danny Jackson. He was actually in the bullpen for the first month of the season before an injury to Rick Aguilera landed him in the rotation. Cone went 5-0 in May with a 0.72 ERA, and 6–0 in the final month of the season. As a starter, he was 18–3 with a 2.10 ERA. Though shelled in Game 2 of the NLCS after his hubristic ghostwritten column in the *Daily News* served to fire up the Dodgers, Coney pitched a scoreless ninth in Game 3 and went the distance in Game 6 to even the series.

18. a. Noah Syndergaard
On May 11, 2016, Thor hit two home runs at Dodger Stadium to help himself register a 4–3 win in which he drove in all four runs. He went deep to lead off the third against Kenta Maeda and hit a three-run homer off his mound opponent in the fifth. Walt Terrell was the first Mets hurler with a multi-homer game, accomplishing the feat on August 6, 1983, at Wrigley Field against Ferguson Jenkins. Terrell drove in all four runs in that 4–1 win over the Cubs. Coincidentally, Syndergaard's two-homer game came on Terrell's 58th birthday. Syndergaard would homer six times as a Met.

19. b. Sid Fernandez
The southpaw led the league in fewest hits per nine innings in 1985, 1988, and 1990. In fact, his 6.85 hits per nine innings for his career stands third all-time behind Nolan Ryan and Sandy Koufax. He ranks in the top five in Mets history in wins, innings pitched, and starts made. In addition to leading the league in hits per nine innings in 1985, he also led the league in strikeouts per nine innings that season. On May 15, 1987, he tossed five no-hit innings against the Giants before being removed with an injury. Fernandez finished his career going 114–96 with five teams.

20. a. Bartolo Colón
The veteran righty was an expert at pounding the strike zone late in his career, even if he gave up the most hits in the league in 2015. Between 2015 and 2016, he walked a mere 56 batters in more than 385 innings of work, and that included seven intentional walks. Early in the 2015 season, Colón went 48⅔ innings without issuing a walk, breaking the club record of 47⅔ set by Bret Saberhagen in 1994. As a member of the A's in 2012, Colón once threw 38

consecutive strikes in a game against the Angels. The 2005 AL Cy Young winner retired with 247 wins.

21. d. Al Jackson

The southpaw fanned 142 batters in 1963, the team record until Tom Seaver struck out 170 in 1967. It was a career high for Jackson, who was a full-time starter for five of his 10 seasons in the big leagues. He went 13–17 with a 3.93 ERA for the offensively challenged 1963 squad that finished 51–111. He was at his best in the final month of the season, going 5–1 with a 2.28 ERA. Finishing with a flourish, he struck out a season-high eight batters in a win at Houston on September 27, when the Colt .45s used an all-rookie lineup that included Joe Morgan, Rusty Staub, Jimmy Wynn, and Jerry Grote.

22. c. John Olerud

Olerud batted .354 in 1998, far surpassing Cleon Jones's mark of .340 from 1969. It wasn't even Olerud's best, as the sweet-swinging lefty first baseman led the AL with the .363 average he posted for the 1993 Blue Jays who won the World Series. His brilliant year at the plate, highlighted by a four-month charge at .400, earned Olerud third place in AL MVP voting. Olerud batted third for most of 1998, though Jays manager Cito Gaston slotted him in at cleanup quite a bit as well. His numbers were impressive all around: .346 versus righties and .375 versus lefties; .335 at home and .373 on the road; .326 in the first half and .381 after the break. Olerud batted .413 in the final month of the season.

23. b. Lenny Randle

In 1977, the Mets leadoff hitter inadvertently set a club record by getting caught stealing 21 times, a total later matched by José Reyes but never passed. And Randle set the mark—along with one for bases actually stolen by a Met (33)—despite not playing until April 30. He was in spring training with the Rangers but his second-base job was given to rookie Bump Wills. Manager Frank Lucchesi, unhappy with his veteran's unhappiness, was quoted as calling Randle a "punk." Randle responded by hitting his manager, giving Lucchesi a concussion and a broken jaw. The infielder was suspended for 30 days and traded to the Mets. Randle would adapt nicely to New York, batting .304 in 1977 before struggling in 1978, when he dropped to a .233 average and 14 bags swiped.

24. c. Mike Piazza
The leading home run-hitting catcher of all time had a .542 slugging percentage as a Met. In 1998, he hit 23 homers and doubled 33 times despite not joining the team until late May. Mighty Mike tied

Mike Piazza

his career highs in 1999 with 40 home runs and 124 RBIs, both initially set in 1997 as a member of the Los Angeles Dodgers. Piazza also delivered three 30-homer seasons from 2000 to 2002. His .545 career slugging percentage is the highest in major league history for catchers with at least 1,500 at-bats. He retired with 427 home runs, 396 as a catcher, and entered the Hall of Fame in 2016. Piazza ranks fourth in total bases among catchers with 3,404.

25. b. Dwight Gooden

The Mets ace was not only a great pitcher but a respectable hitter, batting .200 seven times as a Met (he also hit 1.000 in two at-bats as a pinch-hitter) and winning the 1992 Silver Slugger. His seven home runs are the franchise record for a pitcher. Gooden's first homer came in late September 1985 off Pittsburgh's Rick Rhoden, stroked the same afternoon he recorded his 22nd win of the season. Doc homered once in 1988, 1990, 1991, and 1992, and went deep twice in 1993, off John Smoltz at Shea and knuckleballer Charlie Hough in Florida. Even the designated hitter rule couldn't completely sap the pitcher of his "other" power. In 1999, Gooden hit a home run for Cleveland in an interleague game at Cincinnati.

METSCELLANEOUS

1. Name the southpaw who was the first-ever first-round pick by the Mets.
a. Jon Matlack   b. Jerry Koosman   c. Tug McGraw   d. Les Rohr

2. Who hit the first pinch-hit grand slam in Mets history in 1966?
a. Jerry Buchek   b. Dick Stuart   c. Hawk Taylor   d. Billy Murphy

3. Which Mets pitcher gave up Roberto Clemente's 3,000th hit in 1972?
a. Tom Seaver   b. Jon Matlack   c. Jim McAndrew   d. Tug McGraw

4. Which 1975 Met grounded into four double plays in one game?
a. Mike Phillips   b. Joe Torre   c. Del Unser   d. Felix Millan

5. Which Mets pitcher tossed a complete-game shutout and hit a home run in a late-season 1981 win?
a. Greg Harris   b. Dave Roberts   c. Dyar Miller   d. Pete Falcone

6. Which Little League teammate of Keith Hernandez reunited with him on the Mets in 1988?
a. John Mitchell   b. Lou Thornton   c. Bob McClure   d. Jeff Innis

7. Who played for the Mets in the 1970s, 1980s, and 1990s?
a. Lee Mazzilli   b. Mookie Wilson   c. Wally Backman
d. Alex Treviño

8. Who is the only Mets position player with a career batting average of 1.000?

a. Armando Benitez   b. Jorge Toca   c. Dave Liddell   d. Randy Milligan

9. Which longtime football announcer called a few Mets games for WWOR Channel 9 in 1991?

a. Marv Albert   b. Don Criqui   c. Dick Stockton   d. Tim Ryan

10. The Mets traded Frank Tanana and his 240 career victories for this pitcher who would earn his first and only major league victory in late September 1993.

a. Kenny Greer   b. Jeff Kaiser   c. Mauro Gozzo   d. Mickey Weston

11. Which future Met made the last out of the 1986 NLCS?

a. Dickie Thon   b. Kevin Bass   c. Craig Reynolds   d. José Cruz

12. Which Mets skipper managed parts of four seasons but never 162 games in a single season?

a. Yogi Berra   b. Joe Frazier   c. Dallas Green   d. Luis Rojas

13. Which former major league catcher announced Mets games for more than 20 years?

a. Joe Garagiola   b. Fran Healy   c. Buck Martinez   d. Tim McCarver

14. Which Met earned a save by striking out four Braves in the ninth inning of a 1996 game?

a. Cory Lidle   b. Barry Manuel   c. Toby Borland   d. Derek Wallace

15. Which Met had an unsuccessful comeback attempt in spring training 1997 but threw out the first pitch for the home opener?

a. Howard Johnson   b. Ron Darling   c. Bobby Ojeda   d. Kevin McReynolds

16. Which speedster was the Mets' first-round pick in 1998?

a. Jason Tyner   b. Roger Cedeño   c. Lastings Milledge
d. Jeff Duncan

17. Which pitcher won his major league debut in the first game the Mets wore black jerseys?
a. Willie Blair   b. Brian Bohanon   c. Masato Yoshii
d. Octavio Dotel

18. Who is the Mets' all-time leader in on-base percentage?
a. Jeff McNeil   b. Dave Magadan   c. John Olerud
d. Keith Hernandez

19. Which former Met made the last out of the 2000 NLCS?
a. Rick Wilkins   b. Shawon Dunston   c. Fernando Viña
d. Craig Paquette

20. True or False: Mike Jacobs was the first Brooklyn Cyclone to be called up by the Mets.

21. Which Mets first-round pick later pitched a perfect game?
a. Paul Wilson   b. Tim Leary   c. Philip Humber   d. Scott Kazmir

22. Which Met—a former Montreal player—hit the final home run against the Expos?
a. Todd Zeile   b. Cliff Floyd   c. Endy Chavez   d. Ryan McGuire

23. In 2010, which Met earned his first career save in a 20-inning win against the Cardinals?
a. Mike Pelfrey   b. Johan Santana   c. Hisanori Takahashi
d. Jon Niese

24. Which Met pitched eight innings of relief in a 20-inning loss to the Marlins in 2013?
a. R. A. Dickey   b. John Lannan   c. Shaun Marcum
d. Chris Capuano

25. Which Met homered at Yankee Stadium and was later traded to the Yankees in the same season?
a. Kelly Stinnett   b. Chris Young   c. Robin Ventura   d. Todd Zeile

ANSWERS

1. d. Les Rohr

The lefty pitcher was the second overall pick in the very first major league amateur draft in 1965. He made his debut on September 19, 1967, with a 6–3 win against the Dodgers. Eleven days later he beat the Dodgers again, outpitching Don Drysdale with eight shutout innings in a 5–0 win. He pitched in three games across the next two years, including a loss when he gave up an unearned run in the 24th inning of a 1–0 defeat at the Astrodome. He made one appearance, against the Pirates, for the 1969 Mets. Spinal fusion surgery in the early 1970s ended Rohr's career at age 24.

2. c. Hawk Taylor

The catcher and first baseman hit the first Mets pinch-hit grand slam against the Pirates on August 17, 1966, at Shea Stadium. Inserted for Ed Kranepool in the fourth inning with the Mets down 7–2, Taylor went deep against Pirates flamethrower Bob Veale. The Mets came back to win 8–7. It was the only grand slam Taylor hit in his 11-year career. Taylor slugged three of his 16 home runs in 1966. He previously had a two-homer game off the bench on June 20, 1964, after Chris Cannizzaro was injured in the second inning. Taylor also produced a two-homer game in 1965.

3. b. Jon Matlack

Roberto Clemente's 3,000th and final hit came on September 30, 1972, at Pittsburgh, a double into the Three Rivers Stadium gap off Pennsylvania product Jon Matlack. Clemente was removed from the game and wouldn't bat in the final days of the season, as the Pirates rested him for the NLCS. The Pirates won the game, 5–0, with future Met Dock Ellis going six innings for the win. It was the first hit Clemente had in seven plate appearances against Matlack, who was on his way to the NL Rookie of the Year award. The legendary right fielder had been 0-for-6 with a walk and two strikeouts off the Mets southpaw before the historic double. Clemente died tragically in a plane crash on New Year's Eve 1972 on his way to deliver supplies to Nicaragua, which had suffered an earthquake a week earlier.

4. b. Joe Torre

On July 21, 1975, Felix Millan singled four times against Ken Forsch, and four times the Houston pitcher followed by getting Joe Torre to ground into a double play as the Astros won, 6–2. It was the first four-hit game Millan had all season, and he would have two more later that month. Torre's four double plays tied a record set by the Tigers' Goose Goslin in 1934 and the White Sox's Mike Kreevich in 1939. The future Hall of Fame manager did set the NL mark (whether he sought it or not), surpassing 20 players who hit into three double plays in a nine-inning game, most recently the Mets' own Ted Martinez a year earlier.

5. d. Pete Falcone

On September 29, 1981, Falcone pitched a four-hit shutout at Veterans Stadium and also homered off the Phillies' Mark Davis in the Mets' 7–0 victory. The lefty added a two-run single off Warren Brusstar to help his cause. Falcone was a Brooklyn product, having attended Lafayette High School and Kingsborough Community College. He pitched for the Giants and Cardinals before being traded to the Mets. He went 26–37 in four seasons as a starter and reliever with New York. The homer was the only one of his career. He also had five RBIs in 1981, a career-high despite it being a strike-shortened season.

6. c. Bob McClure

Keith Hernandez's childhood friend from California also crossed paths with him in the majors. In Game 7 of the 1982 World Series, played on Hernandez's 29th birthday, Mex tied the game with a two-run single off McClure in what would become a 6–3 Cardinals win over the Brewers. The Mets picked up McClure in July 1988 and he appeared in 14 games for them with a 4.09 ERA, although altogether had 12 scoreless outings. A reliable reliever for most of his career (though he was a starter for the 1982 Brewers), McClure pitched for seven teams in his 19-year career, finishing with the expansion Marlins in 1993.

7. d. Alex Treviño

The Mexican-born catcher played with the Mets from 1978 to 1981 before being sent to the Reds in the deal that brought George Foster to Shea. He played with five teams before the catching-strapped Mets signed him in August 1990. But he only had 10 at-bats in a month in his return and was put on waivers once the team acquired Charlie O'Brien. Treviño holds the Mets record for most at-bats without a home run, with 733, but he did hit two of his 23 career home runs against the Mets in 131 at-bats. He later became a broadcaster with the Astros.

8. c. Dave Liddell

On June 3, 1990, Dave Liddell pinch-hit for Mackey Sasser and singled on the first pitch he saw from Phillies starter Pat Combs. The hit in the 8–3 loss would be the only at-bat of Liddell's career. Liddell was called up to the majors due to the death of backup catcher Orlando Mercado's father. He also caught the bottom of the eighth inning and had one putout giving him a lifetime fielding percentage of 1.000. He spent nine seasons in the minors with the Cubs, Mets, Brewers, and Orioles, but that Sunday afternoon at Veterans Stadium was his only appearance in the big leagues.

9. b. Don Criqui

With Tim McCarver missing select games to call the *Game of the Week* with Jack Buck for CBS, WWOR brought in the veteran NBC broadcaster to fill the seat next to Ralph Kiner. Criqui is best known for his football announcing, calling games for nearly 50 years on CBS and NBC. He was the voice of 14 Orange Bowl games, including four that decided the national championship. He famously called the Eagles' "Miracle at the Meadowlands" win against the Giants in 1978 and also announced football games for Notre Dame, his alma mater, from 2006 to 2018. Criqui grew familiar to New York radio listeners on WNBC Radio's *Imus in the Morning* program.

10. a. Kenny Greer

With the Mets out of the race and the Yankees trying to win the AL East, Frank Tanana was sent to the Bronx for Kenny Greer. Greer pitched in one game as a Met and had to wait for it—his appearance came in the 17th inning of a scoreless game against the Cardinals on September 29. He pitched a 1-2-3 inning, striking out the last two batters he faced. The Mets won when Jeff Kent doubled in Eddie Murray in the bottom of the inning. It was Greer's only appearance as a Met. Greer would also pitch in eight games for the 1995 Giants, going 0–2 with a 5.25 ERA.

11. b. Kevin Bass

The switch-hitting outfielder was an All-Star in 1986, batting .311 with 20 homers and finishing seventh in MVP voting. Mets fans remember him striking out against Jesse Orosco's slider in the 16th inning of the 1986 NLCS to send the Mets to the World Series. Bass joined the Mets in August 1992 after being acquired in a trade with the Giants, hitting .270 with two homers in 46 games with the Mets. Coincidentally, in his third game as a Met, he went 0-for-7 in a 16-inning loss to the Pirates. He finished his 14-season career with 118 home runs and 151 stolen bases.

12. c. Dallas Green

The stern skipper rarely managed a 162-game season. A former Mets pitcher (four games in 1966), Green became the team's manager during the 1993 season, saw the 1994 and 1995 seasons shortened because of a players' strike, and was fired during the 1996 season. Not managing a 162-game slate was nothing new for him. He managed the Yankees in 1989 but was fired by George Steinbrenner before the season ended. In 1979, he was named Phillies manager with the season in progress, and the 1981 season was interrupted by a players' strike. The only time in his eight seasons as a manager he managed 162 games was 1980, when his Phillies won the World Series.

13. b. Fran Healy

Healy spent nine seasons in the majors as a catcher with the Royals, Giants, and Yankees, most notably as Thurman Munson's backup on the 1977 Yankees championship team. After announcing Yankees games, Healy shifted across town to call Mets games from 1984 to 2005 on SportsChannel, WOR, and MSG. He also hosted *Halls of Fame* and *The Game 365* on the MSG Network, interviewing players and coaches. He's one of three men, along with Tom Seaver and Tim McCarver, to call games for the Mets and Yankees. He was not signed by SNY when the new network began broadcasting Mets games in 2006. If you're wondering, Tim McCarver (choice "d") spent 16 seasons in the Shea Stadium broadcast booth from 1983 to 1998.

14. d. Derek Wallace

The rookie right-hander recorded his second career save in style against the Braves on September 13, 1996. With a 6–4 lead, he struck out Terry Pendleton but a passed ball allowed him to reach. Chipper Jones struck out looking. After a Fred McGriff double, Wallace struck out Ryan Klesko and Mike Mordecai to end it. Wallace pitched in 19 games for the 1996 Mets, going 2–3 with a 4.01 ERA and three saves while John Franco was sidelined. Wallace was touted as the possible heir apparent to Franco, but injuries hindered his advancement. He would pitch in eight games for the 1999 Royals.

15. a. Howard Johnson

HoJo played with the Rockies and Cubs after his Mets days but attempted a return to the Mets in 1997. The 36-year-old was in camp as a non-roster invitee. He showed a little power with a homer off the Dodgers' Ramon Martinez but struggled for most of spring training, batting .129. Rather than seek another shot elsewhere, he chose to retire as a Met. Johnson did return to Shea to throw out the first pitch before the home opener on April 13, and don a Mets uniform 10 years later, first as first-base coach, then as hitting coach.

16. a. Jason Tyner

The Texas A&M outfielder was second-team All-American and was selected by the Mets with the 21st overall pick. He was first in school history in hits and stolen bases despite playing only three seasons.

Tyner was called up to the majors in June 2000 and batted .195 in 13 games before being traded to the Devil Rays with Paul Wilson for Bubba Trammell and Rick White. The Mets believed Tyner would hit but were unsure about his defense. Tyner would play parts of eight seasons in the majors, notably socking his first and only home run after 1,220 at-bats in 390 games.

17. c. Masato Yoshii
Both Yoshii and the black jerseys debuted on April 5, 1998. While opinions on the jerseys were mixed, the 32-year-old rookie righty was well-received once he pitched seven shutout innings and struck out seven in the 7–0 win over the Pirates. The Mets scored three in the first and Edgardo Alfonzo's two-run homer in the eighth capped the scoring for the newly outfitted men in black. Yoshii would go 18–16 in two seasons with the Mets, including 12 wins for the 1999 playoff team. The Mets would wear the black jerseys as an alternate from 1998 to 2012 and then bring them back for Friday night home games beginning in 2021.

18. c. John Olerud
The sure-handed first baseman, who won the 1993 American League batting crown as a member of the Toronto Blue Jays, had a .425 on-base percentage in his three seasons with the Mets. His best season in Queens was 1998 when he batted .354 with a .447 OBP and finished 12th in MVP voting. Olerud had a whopping .526 OBP in the final month of the season. His hot September seemed to carry over into the next year as he posted a .495 OBP during the first month of the 1999 season. Olerud drew 125 walks in 1999 and finished with a .427 OBP. He retired in 2005 after 17 seasons in the majors with a .395 OBP.

19. a. Rick Wilkins
The journeyman lefty-swinging catcher flied out in a pinch-hitting role against Mike Hampton to end the 2000 NLCS. Wilkins played five games for the 1998 Mets, with Tim Spehr and Todd Pratt on the disabled list in the days before the team acquired Mike Piazza to

fully fill the void Todd Hundley's elbow injury had created. Instantly superfluous, Wilkins was designated for assignment once the superstar slugger arrived from Florida. The backstop played only four regular-season games in 2000 for the Cardinals (all in July), but a back injury to Carlos Hernandez forced Tony La Russa to carry three catchers. Wilkins played with eight teams in his 11-year career. His best season came for the Cubs in 1993, when he hit .303 with 30 home runs.

20. False

Mike Jacobs delivered the walk-off sacrifice fly in the Cyclones' first game in 2001, but it was second baseman Danny Garcia who was the first player to move up from the Cyclones to the Mets. Garcia batted .321 in 15 games for Single-A Brooklyn in 2001 and quickly worked his way up. Assigned number 12, last worn by Roberto Alomar two months earlier, Garcia made his major league debut on September 2, 2003, singling in his first at-bat off ex-Met Mike Hampton, now a Brave. He singled again off Hampton later in the game. Garcia played parts of two seasons with the Mets, batting .227 with five home runs.

21. c. Philip Humber

The right-hander was the third overall pick in the 2004 draft (one spot after Justin Verlander) but made only five appearances with the Mets before being traded to the Twins in the Johan Santana deal on the eve of spring training in 2008. Humber would finish his eight-season career going 16–23 with a 5.31 ERA for five teams. But pitching for the White Sox on April 21, 2012, he set down 27 Mariners in a row, striking out nine and making history on 96 pitches. With two out in the ninth, Brendan Ryan offered at a 3–2 pitch and argued with the umpire while catcher A. J. Pierzynski chased down the pitch—it had gotten away—and threw to first to complete the perfecto. Mets fans feeling cursed in the realm of no-hitters at that point were less than six weeks away from learning that the guy they got for Humber four years earlier actually represented their salvation.

22. a. Todd Zeile

The well-traveled Zeile hit a three-run homer off Montreal's Claudio Vargas in the Mets' 8–1 win at Shea on October 3, 2004. Zeile also got the start at catcher, the position he played when he first broke in with the Cardinals in 1989 but had mostly given up in his later years. He played with 11 teams in his 16 seasons, including two stints with the Mets. Zeile retired with 253 homers and 2,004 hits, including a 31-homer season for the Dodgers. The game also marked the final one for the Expos before they moved to Washington and became the Nationals. The first Expos game was also at Shea, an 11–10 win on April 8, 1969.

23. a. Mike Pelfrey

Big Pelf struck out Ryan Ludwick to end the six-hour and 53-minute marathon, a 2–1 win over the Cardinals. The Saturday afternoon game was scoreless through 18 innings until the Mets scored against utilityman Joe Mather in the 19th on Jeff Francoeur's sac fly, but Yadier Molina's RBI single off Francisco Rodriguez with two outs in the bottom of the inning tied it. The Mets again scored off Mather in the 20th on another sac fly, this one off the bat of José Reyes, and Pelfrey stranded two runners to close it out. It was the longest scoreless game in the majors since the Dodgers and Expos were 0–0 through 21 innings in a 1989 game at Montreal before Rick Dempsey homered for Los Angeles.

24. c. Shaun Marcum

What began as a Matt Harvey–José Fernandez afternoon duel on June 8, 2013, turned into a six-hour, 25-minute journey into the night with Marcum throwing 105 pitches in an eight-inning relief appearance. The Marlins finally broke through in the 20th when Adeiny Hechhavarria singled in the go-ahead run to make it 2–1. Kevin Slowey got the win for the Marlins, scattering eight hits in seven shutout innings. The Mets left 22 runners on base and were 0-for-19 with runners in scoring position. The Marlins improved to 7–3 against the Mets while 10–41 against everyone else. The loss dropped Marcum, who had been signed as a free agent before the

2013 season, to 0–8, and he was released a month later with a 1–10 record and a 5.29 ERA.

25. b. Chris Young

The Mets signed the former All-Star outfielder to a one-year deal after the 2013 season, but his average hovered around .200, aka the Mendoza line. Young did hit eight homers in 88 games, including a two-run shot off Preston Claiborne at Yankee Stadium to break an eighth-inning tie and give the Mets a 9–7 win on May 12, 2014. The Chris Young who was inevitably confused with the "other" Chris Young (the pitcher who'd been a Met a couple of seasons earlier) was released that August and signed by the Yankees. He hit .282 with three homers in September, including a walk-off three-run blow to beat Tampa Bay. Young also stole home in a win against the Orioles. Despite his playoff-push contributions in 2014, the Yankees failed to make the postseason with him on board. Young played 13 seasons in the majors for six teams, hitting 191 home runs and stealing 142 bases.

ACKNOWLEDGMENTS

This book is dedicated to the memory of Ross Adell, the coauthor of the original *Amazing Mets Trivia*. Ross was not only an incredible baseball researcher (without the benefit of the internet; Ross was somehow able to function without a computer), he was always happy to share his (mostly handwritten) research with anyone interested. He was a regular at New York area and national SABR conventions, where he won trivia competitions, and the organization remembers him to this day with an annual "Ross Adell First-Time Attendee Coffee Talk" in his honor at their annual convention. According to SABR, "He enjoyed making new friends and introducing them to kindred baseball spirits. That's what the SABR convention is all about. For those of you attending your first convention, we know it can be a bit daunting. But we want you to feel welcome and Ross would, too." Ross, who lived in Flushing not too far from Shea Stadium, knew Mets history as well, if not better, than just about anyone and also provided the team with historical nuggets that were used in their annual media guides. He passed away at the age of 50 in 2006, and he is truly missed.

From Ken: I would like to thank David for stepping up and coauthoring the book with me. His encyclopedic Mets knowledge made him a natural for this project. While we can talk for hours on a wide variety of subjects including various sports, classic TV shows, movies, and music, the discussion always comes back to the Mets.

Extra special thanks to Greg Prince, the co-writer of the best Mets blog in existence, *Faith and Fear in Flushing*, for reading through and improving the manuscript in so many ways. It was always a kick getting to edit his books, including *Faith and Fear in Flushing*, *Amazin' Again*, and *Piazza*. This time, it was Greg's turn to do that thing he does, and his sharp eye for detail as well as spot-on suggestions, including adding many fun facts and various other tidbits from his deep well of Mets knowledge to the manuscript, enhanced this volume immeasurably. He is a wonder.

Thanks also to Rick Rinehart, Gene Brissie, Alden Perkins, Jason Rossi, and the winning team at Lyons Press, including the late Niels Aaboe, a good friend who brought this project on board and left us too soon.

I couldn't have done this without the support of my family starting with Liz, who has endured nearly five decades of my Mets fandom, from the lows of sitting through a horrific 14-inning loss in freezing weather at their 1979 home opener next to me without a complaint to the highs of us witnessing from the upper deck in left field Mookie Wilson hitting a groundball through Bill Buckner's legs seven years later, and all the ups and downs since. We have two fantastic Mets-crazy adult children: Spencer, who wore number 10 in honor of Rey Ordoñez throughout his youth sports career (and wore Mike Piazza's 31 as a college pitcher), who was originally my co-author on this project until law school got in the way; and Lena, who also wore number 10, except for her Kirk Nieuwenhuis junior year of varsity softball, when she had to wear 9 before switching back to 10 as a senior. In 2024, Lena fulfilled her dream of working for the Mets and is now a member of their front office. Thanks for the tickets!

I would also like to remember my late parents, Milton (who grew up a Yankees fan) and Audrey (a New York Giants fan), who passed their love of baseball on to me while transferring their allegiances to the Mets. I am thankful for all your love and support through the years, and you'll be forever in my heart.

From David: I want to thank Ken for bringing me in on this project. To Globe Pequot for publishing this well-researched guide for Mets fans. To my parents, Ray and Heidi, for always supporting me. And to the Mets for always entertaining me, win or lose.

SOURCES

BOOKS

Bock, Duncan. *The Complete Year-by-Year N.Y. Mets Fan's Almanac.* New York: Three Rivers Press, 1992.

Bucek, Jeanine, Ed. *The Baseball Encyclopedia*, 10th ed. New York: Macmillan General Reference, 1996.

D'Agostino, Dennis. *This Day in New York Mets History*. New York: Stein & Day, 1982.

Reichler, Joseph L. *The Baseball Trade Register*. New York: Macmillan, 1984.

Russell, David. *Fabulous to Futile in Flushing.* South Orange, NJ: Summer Game Books, 2020.

Sugar, Bert Randolph, Ed. rev. Ken Samelson. *The Baseball Maniac's Almanac*, 6th ed. New York: Sports Publishing, 2023.

PUBLICATIONS

New York Daily News
New York Mets Media Guides, 2022–24
New York Post
New York Times
Newsday
Sports Illustrated

WEBSITES

https://www.baseballalmanac.com
https://www.baseball-reference.com
https://milkeespress.com/lostninth.html
https://www.mlb.com
https://www.mlb.com/mets
https://www.retrosheet.org/
https://sabr.org
https://stathead.com/baseball/
https://www.ultimatemets.com/
https://vault.si.com
https://www.youtube.com

ABOUT THE AUTHORS

Ken Samelson has authored or edited scores of baseball books including *The Baseball Encyclopedia*, *Amazing Mets Trivia* (with Ross Adell), and *Incredible Baseball Stories*. A two-time member of SABR (Society for American Baseball Research) championship trivia teams, he has also served as associate producer for *Mets Extra* on WFAN Radio and wrote a monthly quiz for *New York Mets Inside Pitch*. Born in the Bronx, he currently lives in Mamaroneck, New York.

David Russell is an associate digital editor at the *New York Post*. A St. John's graduate with a degree in journalism, he has written for several Queens weekly papers as well as NYSportsDay.com. He coauthored *Tom Gamboa: My Life in Baseball* and *Rod Gaspar: Miracle Met*, and also wrote *Fabulous to Futile in Flushing: A Year-by-Year History of the Mets*. He lives in Forest Hills, New York.